9/11 and the Literature of Terror

9/11 and the Literature of Terror

Martin Randall

Edinburgh University Press

© Martin Randall, 2011

Edinburgh University Press Ltd
22 George Square, Edinburgh

www.euppublishing.com

Typeset in 10.5/13 pt Sabon
by Servis Filmsetting Ltd, Stockport, Cheshire, and
printed and bound in Great Britain by
CPI Antony Rowe, Chippenham and Eastbourne

A CIP record for this book is available from the British Library

ISBN 978 0 7486 3852 9 (hardback)

Contents

Acknowledgements

Many sincere thanks to Edinburgh University Press, in particular Mairead McElligott and Jackie Jones who showed enormous patience whilst this book was being produced.

Thanks also to all colleagues at the University of Gloucestershire, especially Manzu Islam, Nigel McLoughlin, Charlotte Beyer, John Hughes, David Webster, Tyler Keevil and Kate North.

Sincere thanks to Peter Childs for his intellectual guidance and enduring friendship. And to James Thorp for being an inspiring humorous fellow cynic. To Jennie who got me started.

Thanks also to the undergraduate and postgraduate students with whom I have had so many incisive and lively debates about 9/11 over the years.

Special mention must go to Michael Johnstone – a true comrade.

In memory of Professor Peter Widdowson, who would have patiently pointed out all the mistakes I was making.

This book is dedicated to Penny – for listening and for staying interested.

A bomb outrage to have any influence on public opinion now must go beyond the intention of vengeance or terrorism. It must be purely destructive. It must be that, and only that, beyond the faintest suspicion of any other object. You anarchists should make it clear that you are perfectly determined to make a clean sweep of the whole social creation. But how to get that appallingly absurd notion into the heads of the middle classes so that there should be no mistake? That's the question. By directing your blows at something outside the ordinary passions of humanity is the answer . . .

But what is one to say to an act of destructive ferocity so absurd as to be incomprehensible, almost unthinkable; in fact, mad? Madness alone is truly terrifying, inasmuch as you cannot placate it either by threats, persuasion, or bribes . . .

The attack must have all the shocking senselessness of gratuitous blasphemy . . .

Joseph Conrad, The Secret Agent (1907)

Introduction: Eyewitnesses, Conspiracies and Baudrillard

The ten-year anniversary of the terrorist attacks in the USA on September 11 is fast approaching and the inevitable and necessary analysis of their impact has begun (if, indeed, it ever went away). The historical significance of 9/11 appears relatively assured in that it provides us with a convenient starting date for the twenty-first century in that so many of the decade's most important events have been triggered by the attacks. The Bush Administration's 'War on Terror' – with the controversial invasions of Iraq and Afghanistan – is only the most pronounced of a number of consequences that have emerged following the devastation in New York, Washington and Pennsylvania. These include the massive investment in security and surveillance, the rise of anti-Islamic sentiment and a more general mood of paranoia, fear and political instability. If the election victory of Barack Obama, at the very least symbolically, signalled the end of Bush's aggressive foreign policies, 9/11's impact can still be felt in many areas of society these ten years on. Indeed, it is on the symbolic level in particular that the attacks continue to, as it were, 'haunt' the present.

Subsequent terrorist atrocities in Bali, Madrid, London and Mumbai and the countless other suicide bombings in Israel, Palestine, Chechnya, Pakistan and Sri Lanka (not forgetting the various thwarted attacks), far from dimming the memory of 9/11 have, if anything, consistently drawn collective memory back to September 2001. This has much to do, of course, with the sheer scale of the visual spectacle that 9/11 represented. The sudden shock of hijacked planes flying into the Twin Towers and the Pentagon and the staggering collapse of the Towers (beamed live around the globe) mean that 9/11 will, for the foreseeable future, remain a defining historical moment. But, as this study reflects, responses to 9/11, many and varied that they are, have radically changed as the distance grows from the immediate days and weeks after the attacks. In one sense this observation merely confirms a historical truism in that it takes time for individuals and communities fully to understand the importance of any given public event. Thus, as the trajectory of many of these texts under scrutiny emphasise, first responses to 9/11 (the adoption of this numerical abbreviation itself an aspect of the posthumous assimilation of the event into history) differ hugely, in tone and in form, from later versions.

First responses tended to be survivor/eyewitness reports that provided commentators with empirical evidence to begin to formulate what was happening at the time and then in the bewildering aftermath. It is interesting to note that a number of fiction writers were asked to offer their, assumed, more objective contemplations on the meaning of what had only recently occurred. As will be shown, these accounts, mixing journalism with memoir and written with a self-consciously 'historical' register, far from being objective, were actually contributing to, if not, to some degree, helping to shape, the hegemonic discourses of tragedy and memorialising. Given the massive loss of life and the still largely unquantifiable psychological and emotional impact of the attacks, this urge towards respectful mourning is perhaps understandable. But as, so to speak, the 'dust settled' (both figuratively and in reality), a more complex narrative began to emerge and a 'Literature of Terror' gradually started to develop a politics and poetics of representation.

In the first few years after 9/11,[1] the majority of books published were constructed around survivor/eyewitness accounts, the most resonant being Dwyer and Flynn's *102 Minutes: The Untold Story of the Fight to Survive inside the Twin Towers* (2005), a work of journalism that relies heavily upon individual testimony. This commitment to focusing on the accounts of those actually involved reflects the contemporary media's reliance on immediate reactions to news stories but it also helps to inform the reader/viewer of experiences they mostly watched on TV or the Internet. This profound disparity between the lived experiences of those 'on the ground' and the vast audience watching is a dominant theme in the 'Literature of Terror' and has been one of the most discussed discourses post 9/11. As will be seen, there are examples of early literary responses – in short, generally commemorative fiction, in hastily written plays and poems, slowly appearing in graphic novels and commix – as the iconography of, in particular, the burning WTC Towers, began to be assimilated into culture.

Perhaps by its nature, it takes some time for 9/11 to appear in literary fiction – Beigbeder's *Windows on the World*, for example, is published in 2004. And gradually more writers turn to the attacks, including novelists such as Amis, McEwan and DeLillo who had initially responded in journalistic essays. Perhaps one of the most significant texts to be published at this time is the *9/11 Commission Report* that was presented to the American public in 2004 after a two-year investigation. The report was immensely popular and went on to become a surprising bestseller. Unlike most other government documents the *9/11 Commission* was heralded by many critics as not only a historically important text but also one that was unexpectedly well written. Thus, there was almost as much debate about the report's aesthetics as there was about its politics. This phenomenon has great significance in the representation of 9/11 and highlights a number of issues with which this study will engage. Indeed, the literary success of the *9/11 Commission Report* provides a useful starting point for many of the themes that dominate the problematic 'Literature of Terror'.

Craig A. Warren writes:

> By standing beyond the generic conventions of both popular literature and bureaucratic prose, the *Report* at once invited and challenged classification. It demanded that readers train their interpretative powers not only on the accessible language of the commissioners, but also on the wounds behind that language. In American literary history, few bestsellers have required so much of the reader, or illustrated so clearly the public's hunger for literature as a means of shaping national identity.[2]

The 'hunger for literature as a means of shaping national identity' that Warren describes might have been fulfilled by a work of fiction. Indeed, it might have been expected that an American author would have already written the, so to speak, 'Great American Novel' about the events of 9/11. It is the contention of this study that not only has a certain kind of realist fiction generally failed to identify and describe the 'wounds' left after the attacks but that furthermore other more hybrid forms have helped to reveal the profound difficulties of representing such a visually resonant, globally accessible and historically significant event. As Warren's comments suggest, one of the primary reasons for the *Report*'s success was that it was written in 'accessible language' but more than this that it was often described by critics in terms familiar from literary analysis rather than historical over-view. Evidently the authors had unprecedented access to the relevant documents and hence it was received by a public eager to read the 'official' version of the attacks, the plot behind the attacks and security systems before, during and after 9/11. But it was also the *Report*'s 'novelistic qualities', valued by critics and readers alike,[3] that characterised the Commission's findings.

The mixture of authoritative documentation and accessible, even exciting, prose provided the background to the attacks and by doing so helped to historically contextualise 9/11. It is important also to remark that by the time of the publication of the *Report* there had been a remarkable rise in conspiracy theories both in print and, most strikingly, on the Internet. It is perhaps no surprise that this phenomenon has arisen given the global impact of the attacks and their obvious significance in the ensuing 'War on Terror'. Indeed, the controversies surrounding the invasions of Afghanistan and Iraq, along with the deeply divided response to President Bush and his neo-Conservative administration, have been a fundamental aspect of these competing conspiracies. Paranoia and suspicion have fuelled such interpretations along with any number of perceived lacunae and inaccuracies in reports of the details of 9/11. Many of these conspiracies have been debunked but doubts remain to this day surrounding the collapse of the WTC Towers,[4] the attack on the Pentagon, what happened to Flight 93 (speculations of which informed Paul Greengrass' *United 93*) and, of course, the identities of the hijackers and who they had been working for. This is not the space to investigate these counter-claims to the Official Report but their existence and longevity suggest further issues for the artist representing 9/11. We will return to this subject later in the Introduction.

In one sense these are all attempts to 'understand' the meaning of 9/11, to assimilate it into the realm of representation. Indeed, if one returns to the American TV news channels on the day itself one sees this phenomenon played out 'as it happens'.[5] Hindsight gives the footage a palpable frisson as the minutes elapse and 8.46 approaches (the time of Flight 11's crash into the North Tower), signified by an on-screen clock. It then takes a number of minutes before footage appears of the burning tower. TV reporters are, naturally enough, audibly shocked by these first aerial shots of an event, initially, they find extremely hard to describe. Early reports confirm that a plane *was* responsible but profound uncertainty remains and the journalists are careful not to speculate about whether the crash was deliberate. These minutes, as eyewitness accounts merely add to the confusion, are again imbued with an even stronger sense of ominous foreboding as one is keenly aware of the imminent 'arrival' of Flight 175. Martin Amis describes this epochal moment for the TV audience as 'the worldflash of a coming future'.[6]

Flight 175's sudden, terrifying, entirely unforeseen smashing into the South Tower represents a traumatising rupture in the conventional temporality of TV news coverage of major events. Here, television cameras capture, as it were, history occurring in the actual moment of broadcast rather than retrospectively, 'after the event'. *This* is the event itself, a spectacular act of excessively destructive terrorism filmed live, beamed around the world. Paul Virilio describes this as a 'global super-production'[7] in which terrorists, with comparatively meagre resources, were able to create an astonishingly potent visual symbol that would go on to be endlessly repeated. Indeed, it is only a few brief moments before the TV news is replaying the footage of Flight 175, again and again, until finally, predictably, in slow motion the audience is forced to relive the 'special effect' repeatedly as the towers are enveloped by smoke and flames. It is immediately understood that the world – mediated as it is through television – is now watching, as it occurs, History.

This 'live' spectacle of History – a terrorist attack on the US – then unfolds in real time on TV. Reports emerge of other hijacked planes, of the emergency services and their efforts to manage the situation, of eyewitness accounts and stories from street level. What then follows is a further series of shocking events – Flight 77 crashes into the Pentagon, the South Tower collapses, United 93 crashes in Pennsylvania, the North Tower collapses too. All these unimaginable catastrophes occur within 102 minutes and it is instructive to return to the TV footage because it reveals a central trope of representation that so many of the artists and writers who have created work dealing with 9/11 have struggled with – namely the tensions between what is 'seen' and 'not seen'. All the way through this study the 'Literature of Terror' – novels, short stories, poems, plays (and films) – with varying degrees of self-consciousness, is structured around the previously described 'spectacle' and what was not directly included, for different reasons, in the 'spectacle'. Put one way, this can be understood as a kind of crisis, if this is not too hyperbolic a claim, for language. A number of questions quickly arose: How can a writer put into words what had already been watched by millions? What could language add to those images that they don't already articulate? Indeed, *why* write at all given the staggering enormity of the visual symbolism? Eyewitness and survivor accounts emerged in the subsequent hours, days and weeks and their visceral authenticity again seemed to make any kind of fictional representation redundant.

In *The Second Plane*, Amis deals with this problematic directly. In the immediate aftermath he suggests that 'all the writers on earth were considering . . . a change in occupation'.[8] He goes on to argue that the early responses from writers, implicitly including himself, were merely 'playing for time' and that there was now a new onus on writers 'to snap out of their solipsistic daydreams: to attend, as best they could, to the facts of life'.[9] In other words, for Amis, fiction itself was, as it were, 'under attack' from the 9/11 terrorists' 'atrocious ingenuity'.[10] Amis defends fiction against such assumptions:

For politics – once defined as 'what's going on' – suddenly filled the sky. True, novelists don't normally write about what's going on; they write about what's not going on. Yet the worlds so created aspire to pattern and shape and moral point. A novel is a rational undertaking; it is reason at play, perhaps, but it is still reason.[11]

This is a familiarly conventional view of the novel and one that Amis uses, in a perhaps unavoidably self-valorising way, to critique the pervasive 'anti-reason' of religion, in particular Islam. After describing his agnosticism and his relationship with religion in childhood, Amis establishes a clear binary between Belief and Literature. Amis understands this 'war' as being between the individual voices of writers and, using a quote by Northrop Frye, 'the voice of the lonely crowd'. This is, then, the 'chorus' of literature set against the 'monologue' of religious faith.[12]

Reductive though this binary evidently is it reveals a discourse of literature that highlights an especially pressing problem for writers dealing with 9/11. As has been noted, the events that unfolded on September 11 have no real precedent and thus incorporating them into conventional realist fictional structures represents a challenge to writers, a challenge Amis accepts. After dismissing the Leavisite school of Literary Criticism and the phenomenon of Political Correctness (as forms of semi-religious 'cultification'),[13] Amis offers his defence of literature post-9/11:

After September 11, then, writers faced quantitative change, but not qualitative change. In the following days and weeks, the voices coming from their rooms were very quiet; still, they were individual voices, and playfully rational, all espousing the ideology of *no* ideology. They stood in central opposition to the voice of the lonely crowd.[14]

Certainly some of Amis' pronouncements on Islam have been far from 'playfully rational'[15] and it is hard to imagine what a non-ideological literature might look like but what is important here is to look at the kind of literature that Amis is espousing. He attacks what he perceives as 'anti-intellectualism' in society, one that demands a certain kind of novel with believable, sympathetic characters, a coherent plot, some kind of resolution – what Amis refers to as a 'literature of ingratiation'.[16] So, Amis argues for a literature of 'opposition' against radical Islam (and by extension all religions) but in doing so, by over-emphatically setting up a simplistic binary, he inadvertently reveals a deeper problem in representing 9/11.

Indeed, albeit perhaps inadvertently, Amis' combative stance mirrors, with the kind of irony one imagines he might even appreciate, the Bush administration's political response to the attacks. This, as it were, 'us and them' opposition informed much of the early writing on the attacks and it also, of course, rapidly became part of the official foreign policy of the US (along with other countries, not least the UK). These false oppositions – literature (reason)/faith (un-reason); West (Christianity/democracy)/East (Islam/theocracy) – determine that the events of 9/11 can be dangerously simplified. This has had obvious implications for the world in terms of invasions, war, further terrorist attacks and a huge rise in security and surveillance. But it also dictated how writers initially, mostly American, discussed the impact of the attacks. Inevitably it was the real voices of survivors and witnesses – perhaps in particular the gradually released tapes of people phoning family and friends from the hijacked planes and from inside the Twin Towers – that provided the public information on what had not been seen in the TV footage. To some degree, then, the *Committee Report*'s publication represented both a real and symbolic collation of data and background detail with the added attraction of being written in an accessible, even exciting, narrative. Some of the qualities of fiction had been utilised in order better to make sense of the terrorist spectacle, the plot leading up to it and the, largely unsatisfactory, defence groups' responses.

The 'opposition' that Amis characterises as intrinsic to literature was mainly articulated in terms of memorialising the dead, offering bewilderment at the sheer scale of the destruction (not least in perhaps the most common trope of these initial reactions – that the spectacle recalled Hollywood thrillers) and a rueful acknowledgement that, in ways it was too soon to explicate, the world had changed irrevocably.

So, what is the 'quantitative change' that Amis argues writers faced in the aftermath of the attacks? It seems clear that 9/11 was an epochal event that has had a profound effect on global politics and it seems equally clear that many writers would feel compelled to write about it. Despite Amis' assertion that writers don't write 'about what's going on' it comes as no surprise that a 'Literature of Terror' has emerged to discuss the issues that the event has given rise to. But, as this study will argue, the kind of literature that Amis celebrates as a 'rational' response to religious fundamentalism has largely failed in adding to the sum of knowledge surrounding 9/11. Amis characterises the early responses as being relatively muted – perhaps cowed by the political and symbolic enormity of the attacks – but as the years have gone on this sense of tentativeness around the subject has continued. Very few writers have explicitly described, or rather redescribed the events other than in the early works of journalism and in essays (*Windows on the World* and Simon Armitage's *Out of the Blue* (2008) are notable exceptions).

So when one says that a work of literature is *about* 9/11 – i.e. the TV spectacle of the attacks and the immediate aftermath, the 'event' itself –

it is rarely a work that actively describes what occurred on the day. As will be seen, many of the texts under scrutiny in this study are concerned with the impact that the events have on their characters, indeed one might consider 'The Aftermath' as a useful title for a proposed work of fiction given the posthumous nature of the majority of the representations. DeLillo's *Falling Man* – perhaps the most discussed text in this study (though certainly not the most significant) – begins immediately with its central protagonist escaping from the WTC and subsequently looks at how the attacks 'haunt' the days, weeks and months afterwards. The two plays included here – *The Guys* and *The Mercy Seat* – also are concerned with issues surrounding healing psychological scars and ethical problems of memory and compassion. And, perhaps surprisingly, another text included in the study is the memoir (and subsequent film version) of Philippe Petit's *To Reach the Clouds* (also known as *Man on Wire*) that does not make any mention of the attacks and yet, in strikingly rich and allusive ways, still is able to 'speak' of them.

As will hopefully become clear, these texts each reveal the profound difficulties that writers have had in representing the events of 9/11. Aside from *Windows on the World* and the poem/film *Out of the Blue* (two decidedly ambitious, yet flawed texts), the 'spectacle' itself remains mostly absent from explicit description. In one sense it is possible to understand this 'looking away' as a tacit acknowledgement by these writers that the events transcend literary representation, their visual symbolism, immediacy and unprecedented historical significance (or rather their global reach on TV) rendering fictional reinterpretation unnecessary. As has been alluded to earlier, many of these texts actively engage with just such a problematic – most self-reflexively in *Windows on the World* – whilst other texts (i.e. Messud's *The Emperor's Children* and Hamid's *The Reluctant Fundamentalist*) use the event as background for their narratives. But it may also be explained by recognising not only the primacy of the visual image in the attacks (and also what was, crucially, not filmed) but further by understanding how the testimonial voice of survivors and witnesses has provided so much of the emotional and existential information that has developed in the post-9/11 years.

Cinema, too, has grappled with similar issues of how to represent the attacks and has also, like literature, struggled fully to come to grips with how best to accommodate them into film narrative. Paul Greengrass' *United 93* utilises a documentary aesthetic in order to dramatise events on the hijacked flight that eventually crashed in Shanksville, Pennsylvania. The film achieves an impressively high level of verisimilitude as it cuts between the bewildered air-traffic controllers, the armed forces and, most contentiously, the experiences of passengers and hijackers alike on the plane. Despite being based on details taken from the testimony of many who were involved (and telephone conversations many of the passengers and crew had had with those on the ground), Greengrass has to speculate, particularly towards the end of the film, on what might have happened given what we already know. Undoubtedly *United 93* does not shy away from immersing the audience in the rising atmosphere of panic and incomprehension. But the film also accepts the commonly held perception that the passengers were able to break into the cockpit and force the plane down.

Whilst not suggesting that this in fact is not what did occur on the real hijacked plane it is nevertheless important to note that *United 93* adheres to a number of dominant discourses surrounding 9/11: first, the passengers were, on the whole, 'heroic' in realising what the hijackers intended and forcing the plane to crash before it reached its (speculated) target; second, that the various official organisations were unprepared, often disorganised and their systems were slow in responding; and third, that the terrorists were, essentially, unknowable. Of course these three statements may indeed be true and believed by many but they also feed into particular political and cultural discourses that have dominated and arguably stymied artistic representations of 9/11. This phenomenon can be seen even more clearly in Oliver Stone's *World Trade Center*, based on a true story but weighted down with sentimentality and a surprisingly conservative political agenda. Stone's protagonists are New York firemen and as will be seen in Nelson's *The Guys*, because of the cultural championing of their profession both on the day and more powerfully in the days and weeks afterwards, their 'heroic' status demands rather sanitised, and hence bland, portraits.

Susan Faludi's hugely significant *The Terror Dream* revealed the conservative backlash against feminism following the attacks. Much of the imagery and iconography that has arisen in the intervening years has been dominated by images of self-sacrificing, patriotic, largely working-class men. Faludi explores this hegemony and exposes the ideological tropes that determined how 9/11 was accommodated back into the American collective psyche. This is part of what she refers to as the 'magnification of manly men' (*TD*: p. 14) and was propagated by the media and the Bush administration. Artists have been understandably reluctant to transgress the dominant modes of response to the attacks – tragedy, memorialising, 'sacralising'. As will be seen, comments by Karl Heinz Stockhausen and Damien Hirst suggesting that there is an artistic element in the spectacle of the attacks have been hugely controversial. And yet, despite their provocative nature such responses have potential to be more fully developed and in *Man on Wire*, perhaps, they are most fruitful in opening out possibilities for the representation of 9/11.

And it is this less respectful response to the attacks that is revealed in what might be thought of as a kind of alternative 'Literature of Terror' – namely the massive proliferation of counter conspiracy theories that has developed, in particular on the Internet. Indeed, one could argue that rather than a collective 'hunger for literature' there has in fact been quite plainly a 'hunger for conspiracy'. The main areas of 9/11 that dominate conspiracy theories are: first, the alleged controlled demolition of the towers, including the collapse of WTC Seven that occurred later on September 11; second, the alleged inconsistencies surrounding the attack on the Pentagon fuelled largely by the inconclusive CCTV frames released by the FBI; and three, the alleged lacunae in events surrounding the hijack and crash-landing of Flight 93 – in particular the lack of photographic evidence of the plane's fuselage in the impact area. There are many others involving the identities of the hijackers, alleged cover-ups surrounding the American government's involvement and officials' behaviour in the immediate aftermath. The vast majority of these theories have developed thanks to the growth of Internet forums, blogs and non-mainstream sites but there is also a literature of conspiracy that includes work by David Ray Griffin, Jim Marrs, Ian Henshall and Roland Morgan.

This is evidently a huge subject and one that remains outside the parameters of the present study. But in light of such discussion of issues surrounding 9/11 representation it is useful to spend a small amount of time in looking at how such conspiracies shed more light on the intrinsic problems of 'fictionalising' the attacks. While in no way endorsing any of these conspiracies it is nevertheless revealing that so many people have turned to them as a way of understanding the enormity of the event. Many of these alternative scenarios seem fuelled by a general mistrust of the Bush administration and more broadly of politics and politicians. Added to such scepticism of the 'official version' of history is a concomitant cynicism towards the mainstream media and a rapidly growing belief in the Internet as a vital and flourishing alternative news outlet that is unmediated and unregulated and therefore, at least to a percentage of people, inherently more 'true'. Also, of course, these conspiracies join other 'urban myths' that, sometimes playfully, sometimes with genuine sceptical analysis, challenge the 'official version' of events such as JFK's assassination, the Apollo Moon landing and Princess Diana's death. Many, of course, can be dismissed as ludicrous, paranoid and hopelessly biased. Others, though, reflect a postmodern uncertainty concerning 'grand narratives' and a sense of individual and social unease with contemporary politics.

And, of course, a conspiracy theory is essentially a kind of fiction. Just as *The Commission Report* was being published and read and discussed, these conspiracy theories began to gather a startling degree of legitimacy for a growing number of people. While it is obviously difficult fully to ascertain the degree of influence any text might have, it seems certain that Michael Moore's *Fahrenheit 9/11* (2004) has made a hugely significant contribution to the rise of paranoia surrounding 9/11. Moore's allegations against Bush – from stolen elections to links with the Saudi royal family, from an unconvincing response to the attacks to abuses in Iraq and Afghanistan – made the film very popular but many of these assertions have been hugely controversial. Released to coincide with the 2004 American elections, *Fahrenheit 9/11*'s stylish but often factually suspicious use of montage in retrospect seems much more of a product of liberal disenchantment with Bush's politics than any genuine belief that the terrorist attacks were not the responsibility of Islamist groups.

The following year, Dylan Avery released *Loose Change* exclusively on-line and it is undoubtedly this film more than any other that has contributed to what has been referred to as the '9/11 Truth Movement'. The documentary has gone through a number of different versions, excising certain footage here, adding new 'facts' there. It has been seen by many millions of people and has exerted an unquantifiable influence over how 9/11 is written and spoken about. The film alleges a conspiracy by the Neo-Con government that involves right-wing plans for the new century (using the attacks to kick-start an aggressive campaign of capitalist expansionism), corrupt financial motivations (involving insurance, stocks and shares and gold), controlled demolitions of the towers and faked phone calls. Despite a relatively small budget the film is extremely well made, utilising found footage, interviews, persuasive music and animation to argue its often implausible thesis that 9/11 was essentially an 'inside job'. Indeed, it is revealing to mention that Avery's initial plan was to write a fictional screenplay about a 9/11 conspiracy but after research he felt compelled to make a documentary about what he had discovered.[17]

As has been already discussed, many fiction writers, though compelled to write about the attacks also felt a strong sense of ethical and aesthetic difficulty in representing such massive trauma. Indeed, what could possibly be added to the reality of the events that hadn't already been revealed in the TV footage, the testimony of survivors and witnesses and the data that began to emerge about the hijackers' (and their pay-masters') motivations? Amis argued for a literature of reason that would act as an intellectual and cultural bulwark against Islamist fundamentalism but as previously discussed, this, mostly, has not appeared. And *Loose Change*, along with the other concomitant conspiracy sites and blogs, provides an answer to this phenomenon. George Monbiot writes: 'People believe *Loose Change* because it proposes a closed world: comprehensible, controllable, small. Despite the great evil which runs it, it is more companionable than the chaos which really governs our lives, a world without destination or purpose.'[18] Thus the myriad conspiracies that *Loose Change* alludes to suggest that Amis' assertion of a 'quantitative change' after 9/11 is perhaps of a slightly different character from the one he assumes.

The rapid growth of the cultural significance of the Internet and the concomitant flourishing of conspiracy theories suggest that the conventional pre-eminence of the novel has been usurped. Hence it may well be a mistake to identify 'the voice of the lonely crowd' as essentially religious (and by extension potentially tyrannous and terroristic). Instead the 'lonely crowd' is more accurately the millions of people who are now able to share their often ill-researched, often hastily composed, opinions on any and every possible subject. And as the Internet has grown in the years following 9/11 so has grown a vast network of inter-connecting, self-generating counter-factual interpretations. Such global reach has allowed these interpretations to dominate many peoples' perceptions concerning the attacks. And this has meant that this alternative 'fiction', popular and readily accessible, has had much more influence over the representation of 9/11 than literary fiction has been able to create.

These conspiracies also reveal a profound uncertainty surrounding the visual image. Some of the more outlandish theories have been inspired by such uncertainty, verging on paranoia, resulting in some cases in doubt concerning footage of the planes crashing into the towers. It is relatively easy to dismiss such claims - and there are few better texts than David Aaronovitch's *Voodoo Histories: How Conspiracy Shapes Modern History* (2009) that readily do so – but if one is able to suspend one's justified scepticism for a moment, these fears surrounding the efficacy of the visual image clarify why 9/11 has had such enormous impact upon the contemporary psyche. As has been mentioned earlier, the sudden 'intrusion' of the terrorist attacks into the normal 'flow' of TV news – of the medium itself in effect – instigated a 'rupture' in the relationship between reality and the image. A global audience was held transfixed by images that recalled disaster movies and yet clearly transcended them by the sheer shock of their unimaginable reality. To help unpick this dilemma it is useful briefly to engage with Jean Baudrillard whose essay *The Spirit of Terrorism* (2002), a work of philosophy, clarifies the tensions between the real and further elucidates the central problems faced by fiction writers.

September 11 seemed to be, as it were, a 'perfect' subject for Baudrillard to comment on. Indeed, it would have been highly unusual if the philosopher had remained silent on the events. The controversial aspects of *The Spirit of Terrorism*, as with so many of Baudrillard's pronouncements on the nature of contemporary society, led to accusations of tastelessness in the media. In an interview with *Der Spiegel*, Baudrillard, asked if he believed he was obliged to retract some of his published opinions on the events of 9/11, replied: 'I have glorified nothing, accused nobody, justified nothing. One should not confuse the messenger with his message. I have endeavoured to analyze the process through which the unbounded expansion of globalization creates the conditions for its own destruction.'[19] He goes on:

> Even if it were a matter of addressing the catastrophe in-itself, it would still have symbolic meaning. Its fascination can only be explained in this way. Here something happened that far exceeded the will of the actors. There is a general allergy to an ultimate order, to an ultimate power, and the Twin Towers of the World Trade Center embodied this in the fullest sense . . . with its totalizing claim, the system created the conditions for this horrible retaliation. The immanent mania of globalization generates madness, just as an unstable society produces delinquents and psychopaths. In truth, these are only symptoms of the sickness. Terrorism is everywhere, like a virus.[20]

In relation to 'less respectful' responses to 9/11 – ranging from Beigbeder's semi-autobiographical metafiction to the wildest of conspiracy theories – Baudrillard's essay was considered provocative because of its intimations of an uncanny collusion between the terrorists and the audience, played out at the level of the symbolic. 'Without this deep-seated complicity,' Baudrillard writes, 'the event would not have had the resonance it has, and in their symbolic strategy the terrorists doubtless know they can count on this unavowable complicity' (*ST*: p. 6).

Baudrillard's sense of 'complicity' is found in what he calls the 'unforgettable incandescence of the images' (*ST*: p. 4) that were so, as it were, compelling, that they reminded the audience of 'that (unwittingly) terroristic imagination which dwells in all of us' (*ST*: p. 5). Baudrillard argues that 'we' have been dreaming of just such a violent spectacular, a collective desire of murderous intent eager to see such a dominant power – perfectly symbolised in the WTC Towers – destroyed. This phenomenon, he suggests, is shared even by those who benefit from America's economic might because humanity shares an 'allergy to any definitive order, to any definitive power' (*ST*: p. 6). Here, it is possible to discern a theme that perhaps provoked some to call into question Baudrillard's ideas surrounding 9/11: that he is, however explicitly or implicitly he articulates it, paying a certain amount of 'respect' to the terrorists' imaginative and destructive powers. As has been noted, such a position, within the context of an overwhelmingly memorialising culture, can be interpreted as being tasteless and of questionable judgement. But as has also been noted, such a cultural consensus can potentially, and damagingly, prohibit serious enquiry. And this dilemma defines how the 'Literature of Terror' has struggled over the years to come to terms with the representation of 9/11.

Baudrillard clarifies how he interprets terrorism as an inevitable result of American hegemony:

> When global power monopolises the situation to this extent, when there is such a formidable condensation of all functions in the technocratic machinery, and when no alternative form of thinking is allowed, what other way is there but a *terroristic situational transfer*? It was the system itself which created the objective conditions for this brutal retaliation. By seizing all the cards for itself, it forced the Other to change the rules. (*ST*: pp. 8–9)

Thus, for Baudrillard, 9/11 is an event that is the result of globalisation, or rather perhaps, the globalisation of American economic, cultural and military power. Given the ubiquity of this power and its complete dominance over the world, Baudrillard argues, a spectacular terrorist attack is inevitable. This, he suggests, is 'terror against terror' (*ST*: p. 9), the hijackers compared to 'double agent[s]' (*ST*: p. 9) of the system that produced them. Baudrillard does not deny that the terrorists were 'immoral' (*ST*: p. 12) but he also accuses the globalised economy of being similarly immoral. '[S]pectacular set pieces' (*ST*: p. 12), he writes, including 'the Gulf War or the war in Afghanistan' (*ST*: p. 12) are the unavoidable eruptions endemic within any 'hegemonic domination' (*ST*: p. 12). One can see, perhaps, how Bush's rhetoric of 'shock and awe' tactics in the invasion of Iraq fits in with this interpretation – the president and his administration aware of the importance of visual symbolism in world politics.

But Baudrillard goes on to argue that 9/11 'defies not just morality, but *any form of interpretation*' (*ST*: p. 13; my italics). This statement feeds back to the earlier idea that the sheer size and scale of the attacks and their enormous visual symbolism posed specific problems for writers attempting to accommodate the subject into conventional fictional narratives. Indeed, contrary to Amis' assertion of a literature that would stand in opposition to what he sees as irrational, religious violence, the realist novel has struggled profoundly to represent the events. As

Baudrillard's self-consciously lyrical essay proves, it has been in other, more mixed forms, that 9/11 has been more successfully spoken about: in discursive non-fiction, film/poems, graphic novels, operas and fine art. This is not to suggest that the novel *cannot*, in its very essence, as it were, 'cope' with the attacks. It is merely to suggest that the visual, symbolic power and sudden, traumatising violence of 9/11 poses great problems for the fiction writer. And it is these problems that make the 'Literature of Terror' a necessarily flawed yet fascinating genre to explore.

Baudrillard's mercurial essay underlines many of these problems and it is with DeLillo's *Falling Man* that such ideas are examined within fiction. September 11, Baudrillard writes, brought to the world 'a death which was symbolic and sacrificial – that is to say, the absolute, irrevocable event' (*ST*: p. 17). If one is able to forgive the slightly apocalyptic tone to Baudrillard's rhetoric it is useful to see the events through this prism. By the time of *The Reluctant Fundamentalist* (2007) it is possible to see how 9/11 can be more radically represented. Changez, the novel's narrator and central protagonist, is surprised that he feels 'remarkably pleased' (*ST*: p. 72) when he witnesses the attacks on TV. September 11 represents not only an epochal moment for Changez individually within the novel's narrative, it is also more broadly a hugely important event in the lives of those deemed 'other' in American society. Baudrillard also refers to 'the prodigious jubilation' (*ST*: p. 4) many experienced as they watched events unfold on TV. For Changez, born in Pakistan and working in the US, the attacks mean that he immediately feels 'under suspicion' and uncannily 'guilty' (*RF*: p. 74). For Baudrillard it is because 'we' have been secretly yearning for just such a symbolic act and the fascination with which 'we' watched events unfold indicates our collusion with the terrorist imagination.

And this is because, Baudrillard suggests, 9/11 was such a symbolic 'success' (*ST*: p. 4):

> This impact of the images, and their fascination, are necessarily what we retain, since images are, whether we like it or not, our primal scene. And, at the same time as they have radicalized the world situation, the events in New York can also be said to have radicalized the relation of the image to reality. Whereas we were dealing before with an uninterrupted profusion of banal images and a seamless flow of sham events, the terrorist act in New York has resuscitated both images and events. (*ST*: pp. 26–7)

Perhaps unexpectedly, such comments suggest that the problems that writers have faced in representing 9/11, whilst serious and often seemingly insurmountable, are in fact the very issues that will generate new ways of 'speaking' about the event. And it is with Baudrillard's speculative, discursive responses that one is able to find possible areas for fiction to begin to explore. Indeed, the texts scrutinised in this study all search for ways to understand the attacks and if some ultimately fail in such endeavours it is nonetheless intriguing to analyse how they each 'look at' the attacks and conversely 'look away' from them whilst also establishing new possibilities for artistic interpretation. If 9/11 is a 'problem' for writers then it remains a problem that is constantly being reinvigorated and reinvented by successive artistic representations. Baudrillard's view that conventional notions of reality and fiction have become so blurred that it is almost impossible to separate the two can be interpreted as a ethical and aesthetic challenge for writers as there is more distance from the events themselves. And it is perhaps at this juncture that it is possible to conclude this Introduction with some final thoughts on the subject of representing 9/11 in fiction.

Robert Spencer and Anastasia Valassopoulos, in their Introduction to 'Literary Responses to the War on Terror' in *Journal of Postcolonial Writing* (2010) allude to a number of these issues. They write that the mainstream media's response to 9/11 and the subsequent 'War on Terror' is largely 'simplistic and invidious' (*JP*: p. 330). Like Amis they see literature as 'somehow intrinsically opposed to the thought-stopping fury of fundamentalism' (*JP*: p. 330) but they make an important distinction in saying that this fundamentalism is not reserved solely for extreme religious dogma. Instead, they interpret fundamentalism with a more 'expansive definition' (*JP*: p. 331), one also articulated in Hamid's *Reluctant Fundamentalist*, that includes other ideologies not least the neo-liberalism that characterised the Bush administration. For Spencer and Valassopoulos fundamentalism 'entails a dogmatic attitude to the inviolability of a particular attitude or practice' (*JP*: p. 331). Such a position inevitably 'prohibits criticism and innovation' (*JP*: p. 331) and thus creates taboos and boundaries that threaten to shut down ideas and representations that are deemed to have, in some way, transgressed what can and cannot be said about a particular event.

As has been seen, many of the more dominant discourses surrounding 9/11 have spoken about the events in memorialising and even sacralising ways. These discourses have had an enormous impact on the 'Literature of Terror' and the texts under scrutiny in this study each deal with the inherent tensions and problems of them and each text struggles with how best to speak of 9/11 and its aftermath. As Spencer and Valassopoulos argue, it is also precisely because of the hybrid nature of so much of fiction that it is best situated to grapple with the complexity of responses to the attacks. If indeed much of this literature has been 'muted', tentative, sometimes evasive, perhaps even daunted, uneasy, anxious, sometimes sentimental, even trite, it also expresses tenderness, empathy, anger, sadness, confusion and fear. At its best – in DeLillo's haunted, traumatised aftermath, in Beigbeder's self-critical metafiction, in Hamid's subtle analysis of an outsider's point-of-view, in LaBute's caustic look at compassion and selfishness, in *Man on Wire*'s melancholic atmosphere of absence – the 'Literature of Terror' reflects on 9/11 with an appreciation of the intrinsic difficulties in representing an event so globally significant and so visually stunning.

As will be seen in the opening chapter on 'Initial Responses' to 9/11, early essays and fiction are characterised by a perhaps understandable sense of shared incomprehension, shock and, at times, hurt that, as the years go by, becomes much less powerful. If the recent controversies surrounding the proposal of an Islamic centre to be built near the site of 'Ground Zero' are anything to go by, it would seem in certain circles to have remained something of a 'sacred' subject. But as the 'Literature of Terror' displays, such sentimentality and self-appointed 'ownership' of the attacks remains mostly in the mainstream media, in political rhetoric and in conservative discourses that, for evident ideological reasons, seek to maintain deliberately simplified perspectives on 9/11. Ian McEwan's 'Beyond Belief', published on 12 September 2001, for example, includes this revealing peroration:

> *Our* civilisation, it suddenly seemed, *our* way of life, is easy to wreck when there are sufficient resources and cruel intent. No missile defence system can protect *us* . . . Like millions, perhaps billions around the world, *we* knew *we* were living through a time *we* would never be able to forget. *We* also knew, though it was too soon to wonder how or why, that the world would never be the same. *We* knew only that it would be worse. (*BB*: p. 1; my italics)

Such distinctions – resonant in the use of the pronouns 'our' and 'we' – are subsequently played out in McEwan's 2003 novel *Saturday*. Spencer and Valassopoulos write that the novel does not have 'sufficient critical distance from the official account of events post-2001, an account which sees a progressive West resisting a series of irrational and violent external threats' (*JP*: p. 332).

Such banal, defensive, hyperbolic oppositions stymie intellectual and artistic enquires into the attacks and their aftermath. The 'fiction' of conspiracy theories reflects what David Aaronovitch refers to as the 'shadow armies whose size and power is unknowable' (*VH*: p. 221) on the Internet (and its exponential rise in the years post-9/11). These are made up of 'semi-anonymous and occasionally self-invented individuals' (*VH*: p. 221) whose 'construction and circulation' (*VH*: p. 222) of sites 'with the smallest fraction of research and resource' (*VH*: p. 222), although ingenious, dangerously distort the truth of the historical event. They reflect anxieties surrounding government, security and the media and they also suggest an uncertainty about the 'truth' of the image that Baudrillard characterises. On the one hand there is a platitudinous, sacralising, oppositional discourse that strives to enshrine 9/11 (the adoption of this numerical shorthand is arguably one such example), keeping it, so to speak, 'protected' from more critical, subversive representations; on the other a fierce and popular community of 'sceptics' who provide an 'alternative history' of the attacks, making wild allegations and speculative suppositions.

So the 'Literature of Terror' exists somewhere in the middle of these two extreme positions. It risks both sentimentality and tastelessness in the pull between honouring the integrity of the event and also by potentially transgressing certain inchoate but nonetheless powerful boundaries of representation. Spencer and Valassopoulos usefully sum up the nature of this 9/11 literature:

> (T)he articulation of multiple voices, the interrogation of received wisdom, the imaginative engagement with unprecedented points of view ... They encourage critical, analytical responses to situations that are usually caricatured by corporate media to manufacture consent, belligerence and paranoia. (*JP*: p. 330)

This study will examine how successfully the texts under scrutiny have interrogated 'received wisdom' and how 'unprecedented points of view' have been incorporated into their narratives. If indeed each text has its own set of unresolved problems and tensions, this study will argue that such problems and tensions are endemic in the subject of 9/11. McEwan wrote in 'Beyond Belief' that '(t)he pictures obliterated the commentary' (BB: p. 1). It is the central thesis of this study that the images of 9/11 did not 'obliterate' language with its stunning visual symbolism but the terrorist attacks do pose significant and hugely complex challenges for writers of fiction.

Chapter 1

'Beyond Belief': McEwan, DeLillo and 110 Stories

On 12 September 2001, Ian McEwan published 'Beyond Belief' in *The Guardian*. What is interesting about this, beyond the mere fact of the article's haste and proximity to the events of the day before, is that McEwan, a novelist, felt compelled to write about scenes that, as he readily admits, 'only television could bring.'[1] McEwan was only one of many novelists who, in the days and weeks that followed, attempted to write about 9/11 whilst, invariably, recognising the difficulties of such a task. The events became a 'spectacle' with remarkable speed and, as McEwan describes, unfolded before a global audience (as, it would appear, was fully intended). Because of the startling drama of such images, the 'shock and awe' of them, was the 'word', as it were, needed at all?

McEwan opens his article with what has become a familiar observation that the attacks on the Twin Towers were reminiscent of scenes from countless Hollywood films. He writes that 'American reality always outstrips the imagination' and that writers 'from Tolstoy and Wells to Don DeLillo' could never have fictionalised such a 'nightmare'. McEwan writes:

> We had seen this before, with giant budgets and special effects, but so badly rehearsed. The colossal explosions, the fierce black and red clouds, the crowds running through the streets, the contradictory, confusing information, had only the feeblest resemblance to the tinny dramas of *Skyscraper*, *Backdraft* or *Independence Day*. Nothing could have prepared us.[2]

The sense that fiction, whether literary or cinematic, cannot satisfactorily represent such trauma is exacerbated by the fact that events unfolded on television. Indeed, by the time United Airlines Flight 175 slammed into the South Tower, the live audience was massive. As McEwan suggests later in the article, it took some time for news channels to, as it were, 'make sense' of events and effectively 'fix' these startling images into some kind of a coherent narrative. The repetition of the images through-out the day coalesced into something like a narrative of events but, as McEwan points out, what was striking about these early images was that people were aware of 'watching death on an unbelievable scale, but we saw no one die'. 'The nightmare,' McEwan continues, 'was in this gulf of imagining. The horror was in the distance.'[3]

Before returning to novelists' initial responses to the events of 9/11 it is instructive to turn to McEwan's 2005 novel *Saturday* in which the author's writing in 'Beyond Belief' is refashioned into a fictional milieu. The text opens with neurosurgeon Henry Perowne waking early on 15 February 2003 (the day of the massive anti-war demonstrations in London and across the world). He hears a 'low rumbling sound' outside and goes to his bedroom window to investigate.[4] Perowne sees a 'fire in the sky' that is 'two thousand feet up, in the final approaches to Heathrow'.[5] The plane's 'nearside wing' is on fire and its 'landing lights are flashing' but Perowne hears that 'the engine note gives it all away':

> Above the usual deep and airy roar, is a straining, choking, banshee sound growing in volume – both a scream and a sustained shout, an impure, dirty noise that suggests unsustainable mechanical effort beyond the capacity of hardened steel, spiralling upwards to an end point, irresponsibly rising and rising like the accompaniment to a terrible fairground ride. Something is about to give.[6]

McEwan's use of sound 'fills in', so to speak, the 'silence' that he describes when watching the first images of the WTC under attack in 'Beyond Belief'. The 'straining, choking' sounds mix with 'a scream and a sustained shout', phrases that evoke the subsequent 'soundtrack' that began to emerge in the post-9/11 culture, most particularly in the Naudet brothers' documentary, *9/11* (2002).

Through Perowne, McEwan writes on from his essay, contemplating the radically changed perceptions of air-flight since 9/11. He writes that outside the plane 'beyond a wall of thin steel and cheerful creaking plastic, it's minus sixty degrees and forty thousand feet to the ground'. 'Air traffic,' McEwan argues, 'is a stock market, a trick of mirrored perceptions, a fragile alliance of pooled belief; so long as nerves hold steady and no bombs or wreckers are on board, everybody prospers.'[7] The sight of the stricken plane causes Perowne to contemplate what it is to be on a hijacked flight with all the accompanying 'last words', 'terror' and 'levelling smell of shit'. This then turns to the events of 9/11:

> It's already almost eighteen months since half the planet watched, and watched again the unseen captives driven through the sky to the slaughter,

at which time there gathered round the innocent silhouette of any jet plane a novel association. Everyone agrees, airliners look different in the sky these days, predatory or doomed.[8]

McEwan's prose, engaging as it does directly with contemporary historical events, suggests an essayistic or journalistic register. Perowne's contemplation of the changed political landscape since September 11 explicitly recalls McEwan's 'Beyond Belief' essay and as such it suggests something of the ways in which fictional prose representing 9/11 often turns to historical document and journalism. This relationship between fiction and history, whilst a familiar one from much literary criticism, is a defining theme of the present study. But given the temporal proximity of 9/11, the 'spectacular' nature of its violence and the subsequent political, cultural and ethical ramifications generated in the subsequent five years, such a theme is, the present study will argue, weighted with a sense of urgency and perhaps understandable caution.

Perowne continues to watch the plane. Again he filters his perception of what is happening back to events of 9/11:

This is the other familiar element – the horror of what we can't see. Catastrophe observed from a safe distance. Watching death on a large scale, but seeing no one die. No blood, no screams, no human figures at all, and into this emptiness, the obliging imagination set free. The fight to the death in the cockpit, a posse of brave passengers assembling before a last-hope charge against the fanatics. To escape the heat of that fire which part of the plane might you run to?[9]

It is tempting to interpret McEwan's evocation of the 'obliging imagination' to also signify the role of the novelist in reaction to such shocking imagery. McEwan would be, in this respect, fulfilling his, as it were, 'duty' to try to understand the events and also to extend empathy to those who suffered, to 'fill in' what so much of the footage and perhaps subsequent visual images failed to achieve (aside from survivor and witness testimony). Although *Saturday* cannot be strictly thought of as a '9/11 novel' in the same way that, say, Beigbeder's *Windows on the World* is, it does reflect back upon the events and, crucially, allegorises the post-9/11 world. But as has been discussed in the Introduction, McEwan also articulates such observations through a very partisan perspective. The passengers are merely 'brave' and the hijackers are merely 'fanatics'. Such simplistic binaries are common in the early responses to 9/11 – redolent as they are of much mainstream opinion at the time. Indeed, one can see how writers such as McEwan actively contributed to such views.

As has been seen, McEwan's two responses, one journalistic, one fictional, are closely intertwined. Both use 'literary' language to describe the visual 'spectacle' of 9/11 while acknowledging the 'impossibility' (and necessity) of doing so. Both suggest the sense of impotency inherent in seing such a scene, evoking distressing feelings of being unprepared, of witnessing obscenity, and the experience of nightmares, of events being 'unspeakable' and 'beyond' imagination. This language suggests an experience of trauma, a consistent trope in 9/11 representations. It is also a useful beginning point towards a broader analysis of how writers have responded to September 11, suggesting as it does that whilst an ethical obligation, literary representations of the events are intensely problematic and potentially controversial. This is, of course, partly due to the cultural discourses of 'sensitivity' and even 'sanctity' when applied to work dealing with 9/11. But it is also, as McEwan's writing shows, about the aesthetic, epistemological and ontological dilemmas inherent in responding to an event that many have interpreted as ushering in the 'twenty-first century'.

It transpires that the possible hijacking or terrorist attack that Perowne fears he has witnessed is in fact a technical difficulty that resulted in an emergency landing for the plane. If 'Beyond Belief', for example, has a tone of shock, hurt and horror it is perhaps understandable given how swiftly McEwan must have composed it. As the study will show, more nuanced responses have developed as the decade has gone on, responses that begin to include less emotionally charged language and that utilise the events to try to understand the enormous social and cultural impact of the attacks. From the vantage point of ten years later it is perhaps rather easy to criticise writers for making what seem now like somewhat ill-judged comments. One the one hand McEwan's faintly overwrought prose perhaps reminds one of the experience of watching events unfold live on TV – the attacks are 'horrifying' and a 'nightmare'; the audience is 'numbed' as they passively, but compulsively, watch the 'misery' play out; the world suddenly feels 'fragile and vulnerable' and 'frail' (BB: p. 1). McEwan feels intense empathy for those inside the towers and on the streets of Manhattan and yet he also feels a great urge for visual information and at one point he briefly imagines the 'cruelty of the human hearts that could unleash this' and wonders if they too are watching. This thought fills McEwan, somewhat oddly, with 'shame'.

While it seems surprising that McEwan should be so troubled by a thought that surely many have entertained, his sensitivity is expressive of the immediacy with which he is writing. Indeed, he dismisses the need for an 'expert' to 'pronounce on the politics or the symbolism', preferring instead 'information, new developments – not opinion, analysis or

noble statements; not yet'. Indeed, McEwan tracks the way in which the
TV channels gradually became 'smoother', they 'steady themselves' and
by doing so they move beyond 'sentiment'. He wonders if this is reflective of 'a kind of acceptance' or even 'avoidance'. Again he castigates
himself for continuing to watch – 'I was sickening of the surfeit and horrified at myself for wanting it.' Finally he deploys a novelistic register:

> Now it was punishment to watch, and see replayed from new angles, the
> imploding towers, 102 storeys enfolding into their own dust. Or see the con-
> flagration at the 'exit hole' of the second tower. Or see two women cowering
> in terror behind a car. (BB: p. 2)

It is perhaps only with hindsight that one is able to critique more closely
some of the implications of McEwan's essay. But it is somewhat unclear
as to precisely what McEwan is articulating and it is undoubtedly his
proximity to 9/11 that explains his unclear thinking (and emotional
investment). And as has been seen, McEwan's impassioned reaction
leads him to articulate some rather crude 'us and them' oppositions.

His essay raises a number of questions. For example, why would
someone feel ashamed by simply speculating that the people who
planned and funded the attacks were also watching the events on TV?
Why does McEwan initially dismiss 'the politics or the symbolism'?
Why does he condemn the growing 'professionalism' of the TV coverage
as it gradually eschews 'sentiment'? And why does he so explicitly speak
of 'we' and 'us' and 'our civilisation'? Arguably, the answers to these
questions help to show that the tone and underlying ideology of 'Beyond
Belief', whilst unquestionably redolent of the trauma of 9/11 also reflects
discourses, subsequently described in *Saturday*, that dominated early
representations and established certain boundaries that close down
alternative responses. McEwan writes of the 'febrile, mutual depend-
ency' that the attacks have revealed but sees this only as an eruption of
unimaginable irrationality in 'our civilisation', the pronoun implicating
the reader into an ideological cul-de-sac. The essay's title, moreover,
with its connotations of events being beyond anyone's imagination but
also suggesting an allusion to the terrorists' faith, is a further indication
of McEwan's point of view.

Ten years on, it seems self-evident to assume that the people who
plotted and funded the attacks also watched the events on TV. It seems
equally self-evident that they were, at the very least unconsciously,
aware that an attack on as well-known (and densely populated) a place
as Manhattan, not to mention as iconographically powerful a place as
the WTC Towers, would generate massive global interest. Likewise,
McEwan's rather testy denial of politics and symbolism is imbued with

a pervasive sense of the author's heightened sensitivity when writing about the events. Indeed, this sensitivity borders on the kind of sacralising that occurred in the mainstream culture and media in the immediate aftermath of 9/11. Such 'sacred' and 'taboo' discourses are precisely the ones that define how writers represent, or even feel able to represent, the attacks. As will be seen in Nelson's *The Guys*, another hastily written response, invariably sentimental and, though well intentioned, rather mawkish narratives can be aesthetically problematic. Nelson, as is the case with DeLillo and writers included in the anthology *110 Stories*, is a native of New York and perhaps it seems forgivable that on occasions his and their writing strays into the personal and the local. But McEwan, of course, is watching merely as a member of the vast TV audience and because of this his alternately angry, mournful, despairing, empathising tone seems incongruous.

Or maybe this is simply because of the hindsight that is a result of temporal distance from 9/11 and such distance provides one with a critical detachment that allows more nuanced, less emotionally charged, observations. And McEwan perhaps intuits this development in the growing professionalism of the TV journalists whose task it is to make sense of what is happening. McEwan sees this as 'surpassing sentiment' and as such all but condemns the news coverage as being somehow 'inhuman' as it reports on the attacks. But, of course, news coverage is not necessarily the place to which one would turn for expressing 'sentiment' and so it seems a puzzling conclusion. McEwan does lacerate himself for his fascination with these images and his anger towards TV footage is perhaps a further act of displacement. It is even tempting to suggest that the TV coverage, because of the rapidly changing nature of the mainstream media, is merely enacting, in an incredibly short space of time, what has happened as writers have gradually 'come to terms' with 9/11. In other words, McEwan is simply too close to events fully to make sense of them. The 'Literature of Terror' becomes more nuanced and more intellectually analytical as the decade goes on. And, of course, because of this perhaps obvious phenomenon one should not condemn McEwan for his emotional response.

It is, though, in the final question's enquiry into 'Beyond Belief's evocation of a clash of 'civilisations' that one can discern a central problem for writers dealing with 9/11 and also the subsequent 'War on Terror'. As has been noted, it is not only that writers, like a majority of people, imbibe particular ways of thinking from the society around them, they also contribute to these discourses in their work. McEwan's strikingly early response to 9/11 actively establishes a very clear connection between 'the world's mightiest empire' and 'our civilisation', suggesting that these are one and the same thing. 'We' have been reduced to 'ruins' by those unnamed others who have 'sufficient resources and cruel intent'. This rhetoric explicitly reflects that of so many of the political statements released in the weeks and months that followed 9/11 and that directly inspired US foreign policy with the invasions of Afghanistan and Iraq. As will be seen with DeLillo and Amis, such a comparatively crude political distinction, whilst admittedly expressed straight after the attacks, has been instrumental not only in the crucial area of social and cultural relationships but also in determining 'how' 9/11 is spoken about. McEwan's sense of 'our way of life' now being under severe threat, by the time of Hamid's *The Reluctant Fundamentalist* being published becomes an highly critical examination that is more ambiguous in its analysis.

Indeed, McEwan was far from being the only novelist enlisted to write about the terrorist attacks in the immediate aftermath of September 11. Don DeLillo wrote 'In the Ruins of the Future' which was published two months after the events. DeLillo's work has dealt with terrorism before (most explicitly in *Mao II*) and in his essay he recalls his own fiction as he describes the significance of the WTC as symbolising the 'high gloss of our modernity' and the world as 'living in a place of danger and rage'.[10] He goes on, in highly novelistic fashion, to imagine the life of a suicide bomber (recalling most strongly the way in which DeLillo described Lee Harvey Oswald in *Libra*). This terrorist is imagined 'planted in a Florida town, pushing his supermarket trolley, nodding to his neighbour'. DeLillo continues:

> Plots reduce the world. He builds a plot around his anger and our indifference. He lives a certain kind of apartness, hard and tight. This is not the self-watcher, the soft white dangling boy who shoots someone to keep from disappearing into himself. The terrorist shares a secret and a self. At a certain point he and his brothers may begin to feel less motivated by politics and personal hatred than by brotherhood itself. They share the codes and protocols of their mission here and something deeper, a vision of judgement and devastation.[11]

In contrast to McEwan's sense of horrified awe and efforts to understand the plight of the hijacked passengers, DeLillo turns to the terrorist mind. He also writes quite distinctly in oppositional, partisan language, evoking 'we' and 'they', 'our' and 'he/their'. This is perhaps less surprising when one considers that DeLillo is American and a native of New York. The tone underlines the strong sense of anger and grief many Americans felt after the attacks whilst also revealing the author's own sense of patriotic identification.

Indeed, given DeLillo's self-evidently more 'personal' response to the events, it is telling how he reconfigures the reasons for the attacks and their impact upon 'ordinary' people, or, as DeLillo writes, the 'defence-less human'. The essay moves between many differing registers: from journalistic to novelistic, from critical analysis to autobiography, from political polemic to personal reflection. DeLillo utilises the tropes of coincidence and chance that inform much 9/11 writing. These are the 'doctors' appointments that saved lives' and the 'one person saved by a flash of forewarning'. He describes the 'desolate epic tragedy' of two female friends, one on Flight 11, the other on Flight 175 and one of the women's brothers, who worked in the WTC and survived. This sense of the arbitrary is a central theme in literary responses to 9/11. In Hugh Nissenson's *The Days of Awe* (2005), for example, two friends, Sut and Guy, who have fallen out over Guy's relationship with Sut's fiancée Judy, work in the WTC. Sut survives simply because he has been drink-ing heavily since Judy's departure and hence did not get to work in time. In Neil LaBute's *The Mercy Seat* (2003), Ben Harcourt, who should have been working in the WTC, escapes death because he is having an affair with his boss, Abby Prescott. Ben, who is married, sees that he can now use this luck to run away with Abby and turn his back on his mar-riage and old life. These, and other examples that the present study will analyse, suggest something of DeLillo's evocation of a 'symmetry' that is both 'bleak and touching'.

This atmosphere of serendipity, bleak irony and interconnectedness is one that pervades 9/11 writing. DeLillo uses a literary discourse as he describes these moments of chance as being part of all the 'stories' that proliferate out of the attacks. These are the 'marginal stories in the sifted ruins of the day' that go on to inform the essay. DeLillo shifts to a novelistic narrative style – writing in the third person he describes the experiences of 'Karen' and 'Marc' in the aftermath of the planes hitting the towers. DeLillo reveals that 'Marc' is in fact the author's nephew. This 'filling in' of ordinary details of survival owes a debt to the huge number of testimonies – the 'stories' – that have accumulated in the wake of 9/11. The sheer number of these voices reflects the size of the 'audience' who were watching the attacks, either in New York or on tel-evision. Like many other traumatic events in recent years – the Rwandan genocide, the Balkan wars, the tsunami in 2004 and the bombings in Madrid and London – there is a cultural and political emphasis on the 'existential witness' of major conflicts and disasters. Likewise McEwan's essay mixed objective analysis with personal, as it were 'I-was-there', reflection. This intertwining of the intimate and the social is a major theme in writing about 9/11 – the trope of an individual's sudden, unexpected and accidental 'entry' into the flow of history and politics informs the majority of 9/11 fiction.

Later in DeLillo's essay, the author starts to contemplate the forces behind the attacks. Echoing his binary opposition of 'us' and 'them', DeLillo writes of technology being 'our fate, our truth' and of the 'astonishment' and 'miracle' of American 'systems and networks'.[12] These systems are under attack from 'the old slow furies of cut-throat religion'. DeLillo characterises the hijackers and the men behind them as having 'fashioned a morality of destruction' who are people who have the 'presumptive right', because of 'violence and death to speak directly to God'.[13] As has been noted, given DeLillo's physical and emotional proximity to the attacks it is perhaps not surprising that the novelist interprets the events in such stark opposition (and perhaps, unwittingly, reflects the language used by the Bush administration). And DeLillo's essay, like McEwan's, certainly benefits from the rawness of the author's response to the events. If at times DeLillo sinks slightly into sentimentality – he wonders, for example, whether the sight of a woman and her child could 'soften the man (the terrorist) to her humanity and vulnerability (RF: p. 2) – and, at other times, Baudrillardian hyperbole – 'the world narrative belongs to terrorists' (RF: p. 1) – it is perhaps understandable, even forgivable. But, like 'Beyond Belief', DeLillo also establishes certain ideological discourses that, ten years later, reveal how 9/11 representation has developed.

DeLillo himself is very much part of this process given his subsequent novel *Falling Man*, a text that extends many of the tropes and images from 'In the Ruins of the Future'. If McEwan utilised the pronouns 'we' and 'us' to indicate a form of Western solidarity, DeLillo's position is defiantly American. He writes that it is 'the power of American culture to penetrate every wall, home, life and mind' (RF: p. 1) that 'drew' the terrorists' 'fury' (RF: p. 1). DeLillo's patriotism is striking: he speaks of 'our tradition of free expression' and of a justice system founded on the 'provisions for the rights of the accused'. Americans are 'rich, privileged and strong' and its technological systems are a 'miracle' (RF: p. 6) whilst 'their' culture is suffused with 'hatred' (RF: p. 2), 'a morality of destruc-tion' (RF: p. 6) and 'suicidal fervour' (RF: p. 9). DeLillo briefly concedes that there may well be reasons for such resentment that they were 'not so damnable as to bring this day down on our heads' (RF: p. 2). As with McEwan, the opposition is clear: American techno-modernity opposed by medievalist theocratic violence. DeLillo refers to the 'blessings of our technology' (RF: p. 6) and mocks those who wish to return to a time 'before the waves of western influence' (RF: p. 6) became so all pervasive.

DeLillo alludes to the anti-globalisation protests 'in Genoa, Prague, Seattle and other cities' and tacitly agrees with their efforts to 'decelerate the global momentum' of capitalism that has meant that there are many people whose 'chance of self-determination (is) probably diminishing' (RF: p. 1). But such protests, DeLillo suggests, are generally intended as a 'moderating influence' (RF: p. 1) rather than the actions of those who are 'willing to die' (RF: p. 2) for their 'vision of judgement and devastation' (RF: p. 2). There seems to be an almost wilful disregard for the facts in these pronouncements, written, as they are, from a highly personal, subjective point of view. The anti-globalisation protests that DeLillo refers to were notoriously chaotic and violent events, in particular at the G8 in Genoa. DeLillo's essay is striking in the way it mixes highly personal, localised reflection with broader cultural and political statements. As with McEwan, and as will be seen with other early responses to the attacks, DeLillo writes from a perspective that is evidently hurt and troubled by the terrorist atrocities. And again it seems initially understandable that the general tone and mood of such responses should reflect what many were indeed feeling and thinking in the immediate aftermath.

Certainly DeLillo's *Falling Man*, published in 2007, provides the reader with a more subtle and nuanced view of the events and in many ways it is instructive to see how the author's views have developed over the years. But 'In the Ruins of the Future' is also sentimental, disingenuous and perhaps surprisingly partisan in its ideological positioning of a defensively sanitised view of American capitalist democracy, and a deliberately simplistic understanding of the terrorist motivations. If McEwan's and DeLillo's essays are, in part, laments for the loss of life and the destruction caused by men who know 'what we mean in the world' (RF: p. 2), they also articulate, rather uneasily, an aggressively oppositional perception of how the world has changed. One consequence of this approach is a deepening of resentment towards the outside 'other': DeLillo, as he will subsequently show in *Falling Man*, can only really understand the terrorists through a particularly narrow set of descriptions emphasising the hijackers' misanthropy, irrational fury and violently fundamentalist belief systems. But perhaps even more insidious is that by demonising the 'enemy' DeLillo also, in at times quite startling ways, valorises and sanctifies American society.

For DeLillo, the towers were more than merely an 'emblem' of the awesome power of American capitalism, they were also a 'justification ... for technology's irresistible will to realise in solid form whatever becomes theoretically allowable' (RF: p. 7). Here, 'technology' is used as an over-arching term to denote American capitalism and by using it in this way it all but becomes a euphemism that, in approximately the same way as simplifying Jihadist terrorism, merely serves to bolster the essay's pervasive sense of grievance. This leads DeLillo to even sentimentalise the towers themselves: 'The tactful sheathing of the towers was intended to reduce the direct threat of such straight-edge enormity, a giantism that eased over the years into something a little more familiar and comfortable, even dependable in a way' (RF: p. 7). These comments are, of course, to be understood as expressions of a local New Yorker whose 'home' has been invaded and attacked by outside forces that are motivated by religious anger but also by jealousy of what America stands for in the world. For DeLillo, what America symbolises globally is almost universally positive.

He writes that 'they see something innately destructive in the nature of technology' (RF: p. 7) but refuses to acknowledge that there might indeed be something potentially dangerous about the rise of American hegemony. DeLillo implies that American supremacy is a force for good, its technological advances all but entirely benign. These advances meant that Americans, for DeLillo, lived 'in the future': 'We are comfortable with the future, intimate with it' (RF: p. 8). The terrorists, on the other hand, yearn to halt America's relentless progress and to take the world back to the 'past'. And DeLillo is certain in his sense that 9/11 was indeed an epochal event that has seemingly changed everything. He implies that before the attacks there was some kind of existential certainty inherent in Americans that has been severely destabilised – but crucially, patriotically, not destroyed – in the aftermath of the attacks. Whilst this is a dubious claim to make anecdotally it seems even more surprising coming from a writer celebrated for his literary dissections of American history. Surely there was unease, paranoia, fear and inequality *before* 9/11? Is DeLillo implying that America was somehow 'secure' socially, culturally and politically and that 9/11 alone has ruptured that security?

Oddly, DeLillo, who has already described the charged significance of ordinary objects in the immediate aftermath of the attacks, turns to symbols of affluence to underline his argument that the world is irrevocably changed:

> The new Palm Pilot at a fingertip's reach, the stretch limousine parked outside the hotel, the midtown skyscraper under construction, carrying the name of an investment bank – all haunted in a way by what has happened, less assured in their authority, in the prerogatives they offer. (RF: p. 8)

Such 'prerogatives', of course, are only available to an exclusive and select group of people but DeLillo seems content for them to symbolise the triumph of technology (denoting American success) that have, momentarily, lost their sheen of invincibility. Later in the essay DeLillo offers a paean to the plurality of New York, its 'panethnic swarm of shoppers' that help to contribute to the 'old jostle and stir' (RF: p. 9) of the city. And so it is clear that DeLillo is making an explicitly patriotic point that, despite the 'inequalities of the system itself' (RF: p. 9), 'modern democracy', or rather more specifically American capitalism, has become the dominant mode of governance since the end of the Cold War. This democracy, seen entirely as something to be celebrated and protected is for DeLillo now under direct attack from 'countless thousands massing in anger and vowing revenge' (RF: p. 9).

Naturally, given the essay's partisan approach, DeLillo does not investigate further why people would feel resentment towards America and its wealth, power and diversity. Indeed, 'In the Ruins of the Future' ends with further praise for New York, what the author refers to as the 'daily sweeping taken-for-granted greatness' (RF: p. 10) of the city and its inhabitants. DeLillo, rather manipulatively, finally focuses on a woman kneeling on a prayer rug as he walks the post-9/11 streets. He asserts that she has correctly ascertained the direction pointing towards Mecca thanks to the 'Manhattan grid' (RF: p. 10) and because of this image of religious piety DeLillo himself rejoices in the city's acceptance of difference. In a rather surprising climax, the essay lurches from the lone woman praying as a metaphor of the ethnic and religious diversity of the city to a consideration of the millions who make the annual pilgrimage to Mecca. DeLillo acknowledges the thousands of dead whose bodies, at that stage, were still largely missing but goes on to imagine an afterlife for the dead, what he calls a 'union of souls' (RF: p. 10). Again, perhaps, it is possible to forgive the author's rather sentimental eulogy as being a natural expression of empathy and grief for his native city. But his jarring jump cut to describing the masses of people congregating in Mecca suggests a rather perplexing conclusion.

DeLillo writes:

> During the hadj, the annual pilgrimage to Mecca, the faithful must eliminate every sign of status, income and nationality, the men wearing identical strips of seamless white cloth, the women with covered heads, all recalling in prayer their fellowship with the dead.
> Allah akbar. God is great. (RF: p. 10)

Here the author appears to be attempting to bridge the divide that he has identified between America and its potential enemies by claiming a kinship with Islamic people involved in a ritual to honour the dead. One assumes that the asceticism adopted by the pilgrims is likened to the newly, but not irrevocably, chastened American public who have been traumatised by the terrorist attacks. In contrast to the essay's earlier sense of anger, shock and confusion, DeLillo attempts to reclaim 'god' from the hijackers' violent fervour and create an imagined global bond between Islam and the 'modern democracy' he advocates. But, as has been seen in DeLillo's sanitised adoption of 'technology' to indicate the capitalist splendour of American society, his efforts similarly to simplify and depoliticise Islam reveal something of an ideological dead-end. As the decade has gone on it is comparatively easy to see how such a position inadvertently foreshadows the Bush administration's foreign policies regarding Afghanistan and Iraq.

A further example of early literary responses to 9/11 can be found in *110 Stories: New York Writes after September 11* (New York: New York University Press, 2002), edited by Ulrich Baer. This is a valuable and diverse collection of short stories, poems, critical essays and memoirs that complements and contrasts in fascinating ways with the essays by McEwan and DeLillo (and Amis). The '110 stories' – the number signifying the floors of one of the Trade Towers – come from an eclectic mix of writers and artists living in New York. Hence, understandably, and given the (acknowledged) comparative haste of its publication, many of the pieces are highly autobiographical and provincial. Indeed, the tensions inherent between the local and the global, familiar from much 9/11 fiction, inform many of the texts in Baer's collection. Because of the sheer number of pieces, this chapter will review a sample from the anthology in order to offer critical thoughts on the many and various ways of representing the events. Before doing this it is instructive to read Baer's Introduction in order to understand better something of the collection's over-arching ambitions.

Baer's Introduction suggests many areas of discussion that will be addressed throughout the present study. Early on he describes the 'need for narrative' after the attacks and this argument, which runs right through the Introduction, is a theme that emerges in the post-9/11 world (a phrase that Baer challenges). The 110 stories, Baer argues, 'explore the possibilities of language in the face of gaping loss, and register that words might be all that's left for the task of finding meaning in – and beyond – the silent, howling void' (*110*: p. 1). These discourses that Baer evokes are familiar from much post-trauma criticism and theory (and also recall the 'silence' described in McEwan's essay 'Beyond Belief'). This urge to 'put into words' the personal and collective suffering endured on 9/11, to 'narratavise' the seemingly inchoate events and then in some way be able to 'speak' of the day's trauma and therefore, however incompletely, 'heal' some of the massive loss, is redolent of

Holocaust literature. Indeed, one of the driving issues in representations of the Holocaust is namely the often tense relationship between 'speaking' and 'silence' that the trauma embodies.

This anxiety surrounding the ability of language adequately to represent extreme violence can be seen as defining representations of 9/11. As Baer's evocative language suggests, the 'silent, howling void' left after the terrorist attacks requires the ordering, sequential and empathetic qualities inherent in narrative in order for such a trauma at least to begin to be understood. In many different ways the authors in the anthology each grapple with this subject, some explicitly, wishing to 'speak' whilst cognisant of the 'silence' the overwhelming shock of the event created. It has been seen that the first authors who wrote essays immediately after the attacks also engaged with this discourse, questioning whether fiction had, in some way, been 'superseded' by the visual spectacle of the attacks. Whilst many of the authors under discussion acknowledge this potential rupture in the assumed centrality of the written word adequately to describe reality, they also assert the importance of initially making tentative attempts to speak about the spectacular events. And as has been seen with DeLillo's 'native's' view of 9/11, the location of the writer in relation to the attacks is fundamental in understanding their engagement with them.

Baer's language also suggests something of the 'void' left by the collapse of the towers (again, perhaps more specifically for a native of the city). The disappearance of the towers from the iconic, mythologised skyline of Manhattan, the 'loss' of the instantly recognisable architecture, is a trope that many of the 9/11 writers refer to. But this 'void' is also the, as it were, imaginative, figurative and even existential 'void' felt by many in the event's aftermath. Indeed, as has been inferred from these early essays and stories, there is a prevailing fear that previously accepted genres or styles are not suitable or even capable of representing the day. Thus, the 'speaking' of trauma is seen as a vital act of 'reconstructing' a narrative or, in this case, a collection of disparate narratives. With cautious optimism, Baer sees a restorative and cathartic purpose in writing about the attacks. Again, as in much post-traumatic discourse, the paradox of needing to speak while acknowledging the inherent difficulties of doing so remains a fundamental point. It is arguable that as writers are more distanced from the initial trauma that such issues will lessen although this may not indeed be the case given the current political climate.

Baer goes on to write of the need to 'remember the destruction of the towers without numbing the reader and without relegating the deed to the realm of the incomprehensible' (*110*: p. 2). The 'numbness' Baer refers to underlines theories surrounding trauma in which the patient only comes at the source of his/her suffering belatedly. This temporality is naturally vital in understanding individual cases – the patient learns to 'speak' of their trauma, putting it, ideally, into a sequence of events (or narrative) which, again ideally, contributes to their recovery. On a wider, less clinical, scale, Baer suggests a post-traumatic New York, initially numbed by the violence and spectacle of the attacks and then, belatedly, struggling to narratavise and, by implication, 'cure' the hitherto chaotic sense of wounding felt by many thousands of people. But as will be seen throughout this study, writers have struggled to accommodate 9/11 into narratives, in particular conventional realist narratives. As a number of pieces in the collection suggest, more hybrid forms begin to appear more appropriate in capturing the impact of the terrorist attacks.

Again, one is reminded that Baer writes from a strikingly provincial point of view. Thus, in comparison with many writers (in particular Beigbeder who actively engages with the sense of distance between himself and the TV images he watches), Baer, and the collective authors, write from a position of proximity and, perhaps understandably, a sense of personal affront and communal pain (see the Introduction of DeLillo's essay). Baer writes as much from an autobiographical and local perspective as he does from a cultural critic's point of view. Not only then does he champion this provincial solidarity but he privileges 'fiction' as an especially adept way to 'rebuild' after the attacks. He suggests 'these writers provide scale to what dwarfed the imagination before its destruction, and now stumps us in its absence' (*110*: 2). In other words, New York writers ('us') are peculiarly situated to begin working towards coherent narrative representations of what threatened to overwhelm the city (and, by implication, the world). Such sentiments are echoed in the development of Nelson's *The Guys*, a play that relied upon the local community and that self-consciously dramatised the necessary healing of a wounded city.

Baer repeatedly returns to this trope of narratavising trauma. He describes the 'city's unshakeable tendency to write itself out' (*110*: p. 2) and how the event 'calls upon us to put into words the feeling of being at a loss, of not having an adequate expression for what happened' (*110*: p. 3). But Baer states that there is little or no 'solace' in these literary acts, instead fiction 'cauterizes the wound with uncomfortable questions and unflinching reflection' (*110*: p. 3). These examples in the anthology are 'the first stirrings of a story' (*110*: p. 3) rather than, if it could be conceivably achieved, any final, fixed narrative that provides complete 'recovery'. Again, two important issues arise: firstly, the sense of New York writers contributing to a specific genre of 'New York' fiction where the city is imaginatively and aesthetically 'mapped' and in a perpetual state of flux; secondly, that the collection has been hastily put together, no more than a year after the events. In other words, proximity and the passing of time define the anthology in Baer's estimations.

Added to these concerns is Baer's engagement with the efficacy and social importance of fiction as a vital ingredient in understanding 9/11. He describes literature as the 'unconscious history-writing of the world' (*110*: p. 5) and celebrates its resistance to the 'calls for closure' (*110*: p. 5) that perhaps more mainstream, conservative voices pleaded for. Indeed, these statements inform the whole of the present study, as it is the key beginning point in the discussion of *how* writers have represented the attacks. The sense that literature contributes to history – in many various ways – is a central point of debate, as is its 'freedom' to go beyond certain perceived boundaries of taste, decency and taboo. Baer here suggests a political and historical importance 'within' literature that contributes, adds to, the post-9/11 world. Of course, one is encouraged to ask what precisely such literature contributes to. As we have seen so far, early responses to 9/11 are characterised by confusion, anger, mourning and a prevailing sense of 'working through' the enormous impact of massive violence inflicted upon America. But, as many of the pieces in Baer's collection demonstrate, there is also a burgeoning discourse that gradually develops over the years of writers struggling to accommodate both the vast loss of life and the immensity of the visual spectacular that played out on TV.

The fear that perhaps the attacks were so vast and traumatising that the 'functions of language and thought' may 'seem permanently disabled' (*110*: p. 4) is directly challenged by the anthology. But still the question remains: how to actually write about a 'psychic rupture in the world's imagination?' (*110*: p. 4). Again, comparisons with Holocaust literature are fruitful. Alvin H. Rosenfeld, for example, writes of 'the end of one era of consciousness and the beginning of another' that the Holocaust marks.[14] He goes on to argue:

> Following upon that closure [of the distance between the imagining of violence and its occurrence], the eye opens to gaze unbelievingly on scenes of life-and-death, death-and-life, which the mind cannot rationally accept or the imagination take in and adequately record. Stunned by the awesomeness and pressure of event, the imagination comes to one of its periodic endings; undoubtedly, it also stands at the threshold of new and more difficult beginnings.[15]

Rosenfeld's sentiments are echoed throughout Holocaust critical discourse and suggest some of the ways in which 9/11 has been discussed.

Moving on from Theodor Adorno's 'no poetry after Auschwitz' quotation, Rosenfeld, amongst many others, suggests a new set of 'rules' for representation and a broader sense that the global consciousness has been radically, irrevocably changed. This change will necessarily demand other kinds of art and narrative that reflect such a momentous shift.

Of course, at this stage, it is arguably premature to state that 9/11 represents as profound a 'rupture' as the Holocaust. But what can be said with some certainty is that the terrorist attacks ushered in a radically changed political climate, not least with the bombing of Afghanistan and later Iraq (two situations that continue to remain deeply problematic at the time of writing). Furthermore, as Baer implies, echoing the thoughts of Rosenfeld, the individual and collective imagination in the wake of 9/11 has been severely challenged by the tumultuous violence and also by the sense of being, in Baer's words, 'saturated with grief' (*110*: p. 7). If writers with more physical and emotional distance from the events, such as Ian McEwan, Martin Amis, Iain Banks and Frederic Beigbeder, write with less of a sense of immediate grief, they all recognise the significance of the attacks and register a tentative sense that global affairs have dramatically been altered. Baer writes of the 'unwanted traumatic knowledge' (*110*: p. 7) of 9/11 and of the 'series of images that no one wanted to contemplate' (*110*: pp. 7–8), evoking again this discourse of radical change. Initially such change, Baer argues, can be felt subtly in the uncanny shift of meaning intrinsic to the ordinary and the everyday:

A nail clipper at the airport un-spooled images of force and destruction. During the course of every in-flight meal, the imagination was triggered to replay a scenario so horrible that it had to be kept at bay with great effort. Each plastic knife made us feel, wrongly, improperly, brashly, that our imagination had failed us before September 11; who would have thought that butter knives could be ominous? (*110*: p. 8)

As has been seen, the trope of quotidian objects being transformed by their symbolic significance in relation to the attacks is a common one and, in microcosm, defines perhaps this most persistent and dominant discourse in the 'Literature of Terror'. In essence this can be articulated as a conviction that whatever 9/11 may or may not mean for the global political situation there is little doubt that it has fundamentally and irrevocably ruptured reality. In the immediate aftermath that these texts represent this is described in terms of hitherto bland and mostly unconsidered objects being immediately imbued with new symbolic meaning. Hence a new consciousness has been created in response to something so unprecedented in history. A 'plastic knife', once perhaps redolent only of functional airline food, is now a potential weapon in the hand of a terrorist hijacker. All the way through these 9/11 texts there is a continual return to this concern about the newly unstable conditions brought about by the attacks. On one level this amounts to a 'before/after' binary that is based on the assumption of 9/11's epochal and global importance. Put simply, if not crudely, this can be summarised as a belief that 'before' 9/11 the world was one thing and now 'after' 9/11 everything has changed irrevocably. There are perhaps obvious reasons why this position is potentially dangerous.

As has been seen in particular with DeLillo's early essay, such sentiments, while emotionally understandable, can lead to a rather entrenched view of local and national victim-hood. This in turn can lead to potentially intransigent political and cultural attitudes towards global 'others' that later fiction has sought to redress, perhaps especially in Hamid's *The Reluctant Fundamentalist*. Subsequent attacks – in Bali, Madrid, London, etc., whilst not on the same scale as 9/11, remind individuals and communities that terrorism remains a constant threat. But, as has been widely reported, 9/11 has also contributed to racism, cultural paranoia, illegal invasions, war crimes, civil rights abuses and global political tensions. In particular there remains the subject of Islam and its relationship with Islamist terrorism and how this problematic impacts upon individuals, communities and nations. In one sense the 'before/after' binary evident in so many of the initial responses to 9/11, inadvertently or not, is a certain kind of barely articulated American (Western) 'innocence' destroyed by an outside 'evil'. Such a position formed the central rhetoric of the Bush administration's justifications for invading Afghanistan and, more pointedly, Iraq. Such 'innocence' is, of course, a convenient myth and one that continues to prevail in many aspects of political and cultural discourses.

Baer continues his analysis of the changed meanings instigated by 9/11:

> With the exception of severe neurotics, sociopaths, and, well, artists, no one had routinely assessed the propensity of everyday objects for great violence. It would be hard to put a limit on the invasive qualities of these intrusions. And sometimes it's just the body that remembers; sunny, blue-skied weather in Manhattan was for many more difficult than rain. (*110*: p. 8)

This evocation of the 'invasive qualities of these intrusions' is a useful starting point for an exploration of some of the work included in Baer's collection. How the pieces grapple with the 'before/after' discourse is intriguing in that an atmosphere of confusion and uncertainty is maintained. The 'working through' of this uncertainty forms the central metaphor of much of the writing in *110 Stories* but there are also examples of writers already beginning to question how the events are being represented and how literature might add to such responses. Indeed, the first story in the collection, Humera Afridi's 'Circumference', suggests a decidedly ambiguous reaction to the attacks, one often silenced in the immediate aftermath.

The story is written from the perspective of an unnamed Islamic woman who has only very recently arrived in the United States. She lives in Manhattan and it emerges that her husband remains at 'home' whilst she engages in an adulterous affair. It is not stated where 'home' precisely is but one can speculate that it is a South Asian country, perhaps Pakistan or India. The story follows her journey, just days after 9/11, from her apartment to an Islamic centre around the circumference of the cordoned off zone surrounding Ground Zero. As she negotiates her way around the city she experiences the charged tensions amongst many of the people she encounters and she increasingly feels isolated and as if she is under a particular kind of racist scrutiny. Afridi describes Manhattan as having a 'sudden newness' (*110*: p. 12) about it, brought on by the 'world destroyed' (*110*: p. 10) only a mile from where the woman lives. Already an outsider by virtue of being fresh to the city the woman's lack of belonging and status is compounded by her race and religion.

This feeling of separation from those around her is deepened still further by the fact that the woman is not fully accepted by certain parts of her own faith and culture. She has a nose stud that she removes before leaving her apartment and despite the fact that she is not devout she 'gropes about for a scarf to cover her hair' (*110*: p. 11). It emerges that she is wearing jeans and boots and that she drinks wine and, as has been mentioned, she is having sex with a man outside of her marriage. In an ironic twist Afridi's protagonist puts on a surgical mask, protecting her from the dust that still permeates the city. This mask evidently alludes to the tradition of Islamic women who wear the Niqab and other similar veils and scarves. This combination of Western-style dress and a traditional 'dupatta' (*110*: p. 11) indicates the duality of her perilous position, which has been exacerbated by the attacks. To add further to this feeling of dislocation she has chosen to visit an Islamic centre on a 'national day of prayer and mourning' (*110*: p. 10) where barricades have been lifted and she is able finally to leave the designated zone created by the authorities.

Afridi compares her protagonist's inner feelings – she is haunted both by images of home ('aquamarine seas, limestone villas, sand the colour of caramel custard' (*110*: p. 10)) and by the erotic memories of her lover ('remembering the breadth of him against her' (*110*: p. 10)) – with the

broader realities of the 'acrid haze' (*110*: p. 11) consuming her neigh-
bourhood. Afridi stresses how these private and public concerns collide:
'Each time, in the days following his visit, the sensation of his presence
dissipates, but now she does not let him out of her head. To do so will
mean creating space for the horror outside, the sinking in that this life
is no longer a fiction' (*110*: p. 11). Although aroused by the secrecy
of this transgressive act Afridi is keen to show that her protagonist's
immersion in her own inner life acts as a way to keep at bay the 'horror
outside'. As has been mentioned already, it is apparent that one of the
dominant themes to emerge from the 'Literature of Terror' is that of
the tension between individual, private and intimate lives as set against
the historical backdrop of 9/11. Despite the comparative insignificance
of a woman's private life in comparison with the immensity of the terrorist attacks, Afridi finds a symbolic power in her protagonist's short
journey across a section of Manhattan.

She is immediately aware of how quickly the 'world has been sabo-
taged' (*110*: p. 11). As she walks she receives what she believes is a glare
from people who pass her by and she is reminded of a woman's words
on the afternoon of 9/11 who shouted 'These fucking Arabs! I don't
understand them' and who then turned to confront her, asking if she is
an 'Arab' or a 'Palestinian' (*110*: p. 11). Four men push past her and she
decides to take a cab to the Islamic centre but she does not specify this
is where she is going, preferring instead merely to give the address. Her
driver is, as she describes, 'brown and complicit' (*110*: p. 11). The cab
is then accosted by a man with a 'thin pasty face' who shouts through
the window, 'I'm going to fucking kill Osama. I want you to know I'm
going to get him.' He repeats the threat again directly at her before
the driver speeds away muttering 'under his breath in Punjabi' (*110*:
p. 11). Afridi thus evokes the tense racial atmosphere on the streets of
Manhattan immediately after the attacks – she is immediately 'under
suspicion' simply because of her cultural background. Afridi exposes
the racist assumptions that arose post-9/11, one of the perhaps less
addressed results of the attacks, so to speak, 'repositioning' of Muslims
in cultural, political and social terms.

While it takes some years for such points of view to emerge in longer
works of fiction it is perhaps here that one is able more fully to appreciate the ways in which McEwan, Amis and DeLillo's initial work
colluded with, however tacitly, particularly partisan discourses that
interpreted the attacks in limited ways. Although 'Circumference' is a
comparatively slight story it does however provide the reader with a
markedly different point of view. Afridi's protagonist leaves the cab
and approaches the Islamic centre outside of which she meets 'a man

in a mustard kurta-pyjama' (*110*: p. 12). He is openly hostile to her as he surveys her clothes but she ignores him and enters the centre. Here, 'there are only men' (*110*: p. 12) and she is told that she is not allowed in because she is a woman. Out on the street again she feels ashamed and alone, neither accepted in the city still reeling from the impact of the attacks nor welcome in her own culture. The story ends with a moment of existential crisis and clarity:

> You are here, she thinks, in this city, among things and people, vehicles and street vendors, but you cannot say a word . . . There is a sudden newness to the street, there is a sudden stark separation of the soul from the world that sifts around and through the body. You are here, she thinks. When you awake tomorrow, and the day after and the day after that, this is where you will be. (*110*: p. 12)

Silenced, estranged and unsettled in the post-9/11 atmosphere of a traumatised and paranoid city, Afridi's protagonist symbolises the profoundly ambiguous position of many Muslim people in America and by extension the world. But the story also concludes on a note of weary resignation that, for the time being at least, this experience of 'separation' from reality will continue.

Another piece in Baer's collection likewise looks at the attacks in an original way. Lev Grossman's 'Pitching September 11th' presents nine satirical suggestions for films dealing with the attacks and their aftermath. Each 'pitch' parodies a film or a film genre and by doing so Grossman critiques the potential ways in which the attacks might be appropriated into particular narratives. Increasingly acerbic, these imagined scenarios not only satirise Hollywood conventions but also hint at the ways in which the trauma of 9/11 might be exploited, sentimentalised and cheapened. Number one describes a *Wall Street*-like morality tale in which an unscrupulous bonds trader (played by Robert Downey, Jr), about to be exposed by a whistleblower, survives the attacks and is able to escape because it is believed that he had perished in the towers. As will be seen, this is not dissimilar to LaBute's *The Mercy Seat* that includes a character who sees the attacks as an opportunity to turn his back on his marriage and run away with his extremely sceptical lover. Grossman includes an ironic conclusion: 'Torn between ecstatic relief and crushing survivor's guilt, he changes his name and flees to Belize to start life anew as a simple fisherman' (*110*: p. 123). In similar fashion, number seven in 'Pitching September 11th' imagines a 'shot-for-shot remake' of Mike Nichols' *Working Girl* – a key Hollywood film of the 1980s – that ends with the 'plucky secretary' (*110*: p. 125) triumphing in exposing her 'scheming boss' (*110*: p. 126). Her moment of glory is short lived: 'American Airlines Flight 11 appears in the window' and the screen fades to black (*110*: p. 126).

A further satire occurs in number eight in which an elevator repairman jumps from the 83rd floor 'after the second plane hits' (*110*: p. 126). But he does not fall to his death. Instead he uncovers hitherto hidden 'superpowers' (*110*: p. 126) that allow him to hover in the air. Others have undergone such a transformation and they remain in the air above the 'collapsing buildings, like so many swimmers treading water' (*110*: p. 126). They then 'choose colorful pseudonyms and soar away together in formation to take vengeance on evil everywhere' (*110*: p. 126). This 'pitch', whilst resonant of Bush's rhetoric post-9/11, is also strikingly apposite given not only the rise of Super Hero film franchises in the subsequent decade but also in that Marvel Comics produced an issue of 'The Amazing Spiderman' that dealt directly with the terrorist attacks. This edition, published in 2002, entitled 'Revelations', opens with Spiderman surveying the wreckage of the WTC Towers: 'Some things are beyond words. Beyond comprehension. Beyond forgiveness' (*110*: pp. 3–4). What follows amounts to a speech/sermon spoken by Spiderman as he both witnesses the clean-up operation and helps, along with other Super Heroes the survivors.

Grossman's amusing satire at the expense of gung-ho foreign policy and fantasy wish fulfilment is strikingly accurate when one analyses 'Revelations' (the comic's portentous title indicating the tone of what follows). Spiderman's eulogistic register is filled with grandiose claims and declarations:

> The sane world will always be vulnerable to madmen, because we cannot go where they go to conceive of such things (RE: p. 6) . . . We are here. But with our costumes and our powers we are writ small by the true heroes (RE: p. 11) . . . What do we tell our children? Do we tell them evil is a foreign face? No. The evil is the thought behind the face, and it can look just like yours (RE: p. 18) . . . Whatever our history, whatever the root of our surnames, we remain a good and decent people, and we do not bow down and we do not give up. (RE: p. 20)

Whilst it might seem rather easy to mock such jingoistic language it is instructive to remember that Spiderman is, in effect, only articulating what many people felt in the immediate aftermath of 9/11. Indeed, Grossman's satire arguably anticipates, with a mixture of defensiveness and anger, how the attacks could both be re-presented through the familiar tropes of popular genre and how such tropes could be utilised to express political discourses. 'Revelations', in one reading, is so earnest, bullish and sentimental that it veers close to self-parody. The penultimate page depicts a group of mostly square jawed men staring resiliently ahead in uniforms ranging from the Police and the Fire Department, to the Armed and Naval Services and the FBI. The Superheroes stand behind them – including the Incredible Hulk and Captain America – and behind them all is a vast American flag. The final sentence is simply 'Stand tall' (RE: p. 23).

Grossman's other parodies include a science fiction thriller in which time travellers arrive from the future to save people before they die in the attacks; a nature documentary that follows a cumin plant's journey from Afghanistan to the kitchens of the Windows on the Worlds restaurant; a film of the events of 9/11 shown backwards (a concept that anticipates the montage ending in Safran Foer's *Incredibly Loud & Extremely Close*). It is in number five of the 'pitches' that Grossman most explicitly uses irony to critique the representation of 9/11. He writes of a performance piece where a poet describes the events 'in the form of a cycle of limericks'. Grossman goes on to write:

> The idea would be to self-consciously 'cheapen' the piece formally, to foreground its inadequacy and unimportance in the face of an inassimilable 'reality' by deliberately choosing a literary form incapable of expressing and 'meaning', e.g.:
> *As smoke billowed in the air*
> *The onlookers tore at their hair*
> *etc.* (110: p. 125)

Particularly in the examples of Beigbeder's *Windows on the World* and Armitage's poem/film *Out of the Blue*, these issues have great pertinence surrounding the representation of 9/11. Grossman cleverly alludes to the prevailing sense felt by many writers, that their words were 'inadequate' in representing an event of such historical and political significance. Indeed, many of the texts under scrutiny in this study suffer, at times, from Grossman's satirical accusations of tastelessness, sentimentality and aesthetic cliché. But such clichés of response, interpretation and choice of focus reveal ideological prejudices that have threatened to achieve complete hegemony over the years since the attacks.

Other pieces in *110 Stories* wrestle with the difficulties of writing directly about 9/11 and in many ways these writers are starting to clarify what will remain profound problems and challenges. Siri Hustvedt's 'The World Trade Center' focuses on the immediate linguistic force of 'World Trade Center' (*110*: p. 158) comparing its metonymic power to Auschwitz, The Disappeared and Rwanda. She describes the trauma experienced by children who live and go to school near the towers and then ends with an emotional peroration:

These are the translations of horror when it enters the mind and the body, and they seem to speak more directly to the truth than the elegant phrases we have been hearing lately, both political and literary. We have to talk, but we should be careful with our words. (*110*: p. 159)

The 'translations of horror' are the physical manifestations of trauma experienced by children unable to process what they have seen. And it is perhaps with Hustvedt's plea for caution that one senses something of the prevailing mood of Baer's collection. In many respects a critical study of 9/11 fiction is an analysis of how responses to the attacks have developed as time has gone on. Hustvedt's short essay is typical of so many of the pieces in *110 Stories* – personal and intimate, wounded by what has happened and yet tentatively optimistic that the city and its communities will recover. One is able to see how these urgent and hastily composed pieces with marked hesitancy struggle to make sense of, whilst contributing to, a literature that is at the time of the collection's publication still very much in its infancy.

Art Spiegelman, whose artwork adorns the cover of *110 Stories* and who in 2004 published *In the Shadow of No Towers*, a graphic novel about 9/11, writes of his 'unmediated' (*110*: p. 284) experience of the attacks. A resident of 'Lower Soho, on the outskirts of Ground Zero' (*110*: p. 284), Spiegelman makes a clear distinction between those who watched on TV 'last season's most compelling media event' (*110*: 284) and his own personal response as he and his wife rescue their daughter from a school immediately below the towers. Spiegelman then describes the process he went through as he tried to draw: 'Despite what felt like the irrelevancy of the task, it gave me a way to fend off trauma and focus on something. I wanted to find the awful (and awe-filled) image of all that disappeared that morning' (*110*: p. 286). At first his sketch emphasises 'the wondrous crystalline blue sky' and contrasts it with a drawing of the towers draped in a black shroud 'as if by Christo in mourning' (*110*: p. 286). And yet Spiegelman is dissatisfied with this image. He feels that 'Surrealism was inadequate to that moment, and the vividness of the color seemed to obscenely mock the blackness at the heart of the picture' (*110*: p. 286).

Spiegelman decides to desaturate the image until the sky is virtually black and it is this image that adorned the 24 September 2001 issue of the *New Yorker* (Spiegelman's wife is covers editor for the magazine). The artist believes that it is only in the use of such minimalism that he is able to avoid any 'insult to that somber moment' (*110*: p. 286). Again one is struck by Spiegelman's sensitivity in representing the attacks and his powerful sense of obligation to successfully memorialise the loss of life and the mournful symbolism of the fallen towers. But it is also revealing that less than a year later he feels that he has been afforded the 'luxury of trying to rescue and salvage' his original image (*110*: p. 286). Spiegelman deliberately compares this work to that of the 'rescue and salvage operation' that continues near his apartment. Hence, the role of the artist attempting to produce a work that will help people 'come to terms with their loss' (*110*: p. 286) is seen as being an important contribution to the more general 'rebuilding' of the New York streets and, by implication, of America as a whole. This discourse of 'healing', both personal and national, dominates the early responses to 9/11, in particular, of course, by American writers. But it is also interesting to note that Spiegelman's writing, even at this early stage, acknowledges a 'distance' that allows the artist gradually to move away from such a grieving period and potentially pursue other forms of representation.

Other pieces in Baer's collection offer perspectives on the attacks that range from the intensely personal to the historical. Jenefer Shute's 'Instructions for Surviving the Unprecedented (Break Glass in Case of Emergency, If Glass Is Not Already Broken')' details the experiences of a single person living on their own whose first few days following the attacks are spent in a mire of confusion and fear. In contrast, Paul D. Miller's 'Rio/Iguassu/Sao Paolo' finds common ground and metaphorical significance in the cultural, musical and social diversity in Brazil, a 'lesson in multiplicity' (*110*: p. 205) that he believes both connects with New York and suggests potential ways in which people can thrive within ethnically diverse communities. Tony Hiss' 'Finding the Center' charts a history of architectural change and development in Lower Manhattan culminating in the building of the WTC Towers in the 1960s. Amitav Ghosh's 'Neighbors' relates the story of Frank and Nicole De Martini, a married couple who both worked in the WTC. The couple are in the North Tower when the first plane hits but Frank De Martini decides to stay and help with rescuing others, urging his wife to take the stairway to escape. He perishes and she survives.

In conclusion, one is able to discern a development from McEwan's and DeLillo's impassioned, politically intemperate essays to the more personal, mournful work in *110 Stories*. Indeed, it is striking that there are very few moments in Baer's collection when the subject of revenge or retaliation is articulated. Temporal and geographical proximity evidently play a major part in the ways in which writers approached the subject and it is perhaps only with hindsight that McEwan's and DeLillo's work seems reactionary. Both writers went on further to contemplate 9/11, as has been seen in McEwan's *Saturday* and as will be subsequently analysed with DeLillo's *Falling Man*, and their reactions are certainly more nuanced than their initial essays proved to be. But these novels, in particular *Falling Man,* also underline, and are unable finally to resolve, many of the problems in representing the attacks in prose and poetry that the writers in *110 Stories* reflect upon. The study will now look at Martin Amis' work dealing with 9/11 and its aftermath, a writer whose response to the attacks shifts towards an examination of the forces behind the hijackers rather than those who died or who survived. Such a shift of emphasis reflects the increasingly troubled political landscape that has emerged in the subsequent years.

Chapter 2

'Total Malignancy . . . Militant Irony': Martin Amis, *The Second Plane*

Martin Amis' *The Second Plane: September 11: 2001–2007* (London: Jonathan Cape, 2008) collects together the majority of his journalism and stories inspired by the attacks. These include his first response published on 18 September 2001 through essays on terrorism and Islamism, Bush and Blair, the invasions of Afghanistan and Iraq and two short stories, 'In the Palace of the End' and 'The Last Days of Muhammad Atta'. Along with DeLillo and McEwan, Amis was one of the first novelists to write about the attacks in non-fiction pieces and one can detect a development of ideas from this writing to 'September 11' written in 2007. This 'political journey', as David Aaronovitch calls it, amounts to a move from 'the uncomprehending fug of ash, dust and speculation rising from Ground Zero' to a conclusion that 'an ideological struggle must be waged, in which the proper values of the West are championed'.[1] If Amis' work represents perhaps the most consistent, and certainly the most controversial, oeuvre thus far on the impact of 9/11 it is instructive to analyse the implications of this 'journey'.

Critics have, in increasingly inflammatory and contentious language, often received Amis' work within discourses of provocation and controversy and, if anything, *The Second Plane* has only added to this. It would be fair to say that much of the 'scandal' had more to do with Amis' perceived intolerant comments surrounding his appointment at Manchester University[2] and interviews promoting the publication of the collection than material actually included in *The Second Plane*. But Amis' thoughts on terrorism, Islam and the nature of the 'War on Terror' do inform his fictional writing here and it is instructive to see how his criticism and his fiction are intertwined. A question that emerges from this sense of cross-pollination is if Amis' criticism and journalism utilises the author's much vaunted prose style to augment his comments on 9/11 and its aftermath, what do his two fictions in the collection add to knowledge of the attacks? In other words, why write a short story when much of what one has already written has been articulated in non-fiction?

'The Last Days of Muhammad Atta' was published in *The Observer* on 3 September 2006 and is collected in *The Second Plane*. What is striking about the story is how much it resembles, as it were, an 'Amis-ian' fiction. He utilises very familiar tropes from his own creative writing in order to provide some kind of psychological insight into the mind of Atta but it is arguable as to what these actually add to the sum of knowledge concerning the motivations of the terrorists. John Updike, for example, was criticised by many for failing to illuminate the psychology of his fictional jihadist teenager.[3] Similarly, in DeLillo's *Falling Man*, Hammad can be seen as a familiarly 'DeLillo-ian' male protagonist whose faith and motivations for terrorism are understood within a perception of masculine self-discipline and spiritual renunciation. Likewise, aside from the documentary evidence that is currently extant – timelines, recorded phone-calls, Atta's will and testament, etc. – Amis describes his fictional Atta in motifs reminiscent of previous characters.

Amis's Atta, then, owes a great deal to other fictional men in the author's oeuvre. As Lionel Barber points out, Amis writes about the 'final apocalyptic act in overtly sexual terms'[4] and Sameer Rahim suggests that the story 'features a constipated terrorist who sounds a lot like Martin Amis'.[5] Throughout Amis' work, there is a consistent return to matters of the body – to defecation, to skin conditions, to hair loss, deteriorating teeth and impotence – and many of Amis' male characters endure humiliation and disgust at their own, and others' (mostly women's) corporeality. This is mainly utilised in satirical attack upon human self-importance and hubris. Amis' Swiftian 'excremental vision'[6] can be found in Charles Highway's romantic disillusionment with the titular object of his desire in *The Rachel Papers* (1973) when he discovers her soiled underwear; in Keith Talent's explicitly described excretions in *London Fields* (1989); and in *House of Meetings* (2006) the 'lowest' of the prisoners in a Stalinist slave camp are referred to as 'shiteaters'.[7]

This scatological trope reappears in 'The Last Days of Muhammad Atta' when Amis describes the hijacker's incontinence – 'he had not moved his bowels since May' (*SP*: p. 97) – and other maladies that he is suffering from. Indeed, just as Flight 11 is preparing to take off, Atta is afflicted by 'the ungainsayable anger' (*SP*: p. 118) of his stomach. He rushes to the toilets but they are closed because, as Atta knows, airplane facilities are locked until 'the plane levelled out' (*SP*: p. 119). Atta returns to his seat and acknowledges that even though he is committed to the 'core reason' (Amis' phrase for Atta's non-religious, non-political devotion to death and oblivion), this ideology 'couldn't carry the body'

(*SP*: p. 119). Here, with subtle irony, Amis satirises the abstractions and delusions of Atta's philosophy by reminding him, and the reader, of the undeniable fact of human corporeality.

Atta is afflicted with other very human complaints. He endures bouts of 'nausea' (*SP*: p. 97) and has a 'feverish and unvarying ache, not in his gut but in his lower back, his pelvic saddle, and his scrotum' (*SP*: p. 97). He witnesses his own sense of 'detestation' in his facial features as he contemplates them in the bathroom mirror (*SP*: p. 97) and he endures a constant headache that has 'established itself, like an electric eel, from ear to ear, then from eye to eye – and then both' (*SP*: p. 107). He dreads shaving because it forces him to contemplate his own face and later cuts himself, 'for the first time in his life' and is shocked by the 'apparently endless supply of blood' that spills out (*SP*: p. 99). Amis links these physical afflictions with Atta's very idiosyncratic motivations for becoming a suicide bomber and even as Atta has control of the hijacked plane his bowels are linked with transcendence: 'Now even the need to shit felt right and good as his destination surged towards him' (*SP*: p. 123).

This attention to the cloacal and to the general sufferings of Atta's body is also connected to Amis' description of the terrorist's commitment to jihadism. Atta, unlike, he feels, his fellow hijackers, cannot separate his mind from his body. The 'complete tranquillity' (*SP*: p. 100) that Islamist leaders have inculcated into the jihadists as an ideal state eludes Atta because he is incapable of 'sublimation': his 'fantastically acute' sense of his own body and its indelible relation to his mind stops him from this 'purity' (*SL*: p. 101). But he has, he believes, discovered the 'core reason' and although he is 'not religious' and 'not even especially political' this is 'the most charismatic idea of his generation'. The 'ferocity and rectitude' that Atta so admires in Islamism (presumably the 'single word' Amis alludes to but does not state explicitly) merely suits his self-loathing character, 'with an almost sinister precision' (*SP*: p. 101). But in the end Atta concedes that his ideology can't 'save' him from his body:

> Strapped in, Muhammad Atta managed the following series of thoughts. You *needed* the belief system, the ideology, the ardour. You had to have it. The core reason was good enough for the mind. But it couldn't carry the body. (*SP*: p. 119)

Atta's bodily self-loathing and his disgust with his life – 'his own he had hated' (*SP*: p. 124) – also mutates into a virulent misogyny, an aspect of Islamism to which he is also attracted. Amis takes his cue from Atta's infamous last will and testament from which he extracts quotations underlining Atta's mistrust of women, and particularly 'pregnant women' (*SP*: p. 99). He is scornful of the promise of virgins awaiting him in paradise (*SP*: p. 102), is horrified by the idea that the people he encounters in a descending elevator 'were all lovers, returning early to their beds' (*SP*: p. 103) and he fears the moment when he will have to disable one of the stewardesses, so he prepares himself with images of 'the opening of female flesh' (*SP*: p. 120) and 'the combination of women and blood' (*SP*: p. 121). Indeed, Amis implies that Atta may well have been a virgin at 33: he is fascinated and repulsed by the girlfriend of one of the other members of the 'Hamburg Cell' – 'how she must open herself up to him, with all her heaviness and darkness' (*SP*: p. 115) – and he concludes that 'romantic and religious ardour came from contiguous parts of the human being: the parts he didn't have' (*SP*: p. 115).

Atta's misogyny is a vital aspect to his character but this abhorrence of women is informed by a barely concealed lust. His aforementioned fantasies of what it will be like to kill one of the plane's stewardesses find their correlate in a memory Atta has stored from an earlier flight in 1999 returning from Afghanistan. Atta recalls that there was an altercation involving a group of men who insisted on praying in the one of the aisles. Despite the protestations of a male flight attendant, the passengers continue to kneel and pray. Atta then describes the arrival of a stewardess:

> Even Muhammad Atta at once conceded that here was the dark female in her most swinishly luxurious form: tall, long-necked, herself streamlined and aero-dynamic, with hair like a billboard for a chocolate sundae, and all that flesh, damp and glowing as if from fever or lust.

Atta, at this stage, can hardly control his erotic arousal:

> [T]hen she surged forward with great scooping motions of her hands, bellowing – '*Vamos arriba, coños!*' And the kneeling men had to peer out at this seraph of breast and haunch and uniformed power, and straighten up and scowl, and slowly grope for their seats.

Adding to his embodiment of her as akin to a plane – 'streamlined and aerodynamic' – and a mythological angel, Atta, contemptuous of the men's acquiescence, sees her face, in another aerial metaphor., 'of cloudless entitlement' and feels 'how badly he had wanted to hit her' (*SP*: pp. 120–1).

Amis' conception of Atta recalls other sexually frustrated, self-loathing and body-hating male characters such as Terry Service (*Success*, 1977), John Self (*Money*, 1984) and Richard Tull (*The Information*,

1995). Obviously, where Atta differs is that he is a historically situated, 'real' person who was directly involved in the 9/11 attacks. Amis has written historical fiction before – the threat of nuclear war in *Einstein's Monsters* (1987), the Holocaust in *Time's Arrow* (1992), the Soviet regime in *House of Meetings* (2006) – and has foregrounded the significance and debt he owes to detailed research. 'The Last Days of Muhammad Atta', as has been suggested, relies upon documentary evidence for Atta's movements and whereabouts in the months and years leading up to the attacks. Amis' fictional imagination is thus concerned with two, as it were, 'mysteries': Atta's personality, psychology, belief system and motivations; and the reason behind Atta's car journey from Boston to Portland, Maine on the morning of 10 September 2001.[8] Amis' insights into Atta's personality are, of course, highly derivative from his own work. A consequence of this is that, by his own admission, Atta is unlike the other hijackers. He feels little or no affection for them, even though he speaks admiringly of a 'brotherhood' (*SP*: p. 101) and rather cherishes the group's competitiveness with its 'nihilistic élan . . . [and] nihilistic insouciance' (*SP*: p. 107). We have noted that Atta is neither religious nor political and his sense of the 'core reason' is located in the failings of his body, his violent misogyny and his intense dislike of laughter, music and sex. Islamism is a suitable cause into which he can, so to speak, 'pour' his neurosis, paranoia and fear. Thus, in many ways, Atta is entirely atypical in comparison with other jihadists and perhaps this representation speaks more of Amis' own literary concerns than of an attempt to understand the terrorist mind. As Leon Wieseltier comments: 'He [Amis] believes that 2,992 more people would be alive today if 19 Middle Eastern men had only found some satisfaction of the flesh.'[9]

Clearly 'The Last Days of Muhammad Atta' is no act of literary ventriloquism – Amis has often been an 'intrusive author' both in the sense of his stylised, rhythmic, densely imagistic prose and in the sense that 'he' has sometimes appeared in his own fiction.[10] But there is a sense, perhaps, that the form and content of Amis' story, aside from its factual basis, inadvertently acknowledges its own failure in an attempt to understand the terrorist psyche. If Amis' Atta is, self-consciously, from the familiar tropes of a deracinated masculinity to the 'high' metaphor-laden style, another in a series of the novelist's favoured tormented male characters, then what is it, precisely, that the story is 'saying' about the attackers behind 9/11? A partial answer comes from Amis' fictional 'speculation' as to why Atta travelled to Portland, Maine on the day before September 11. It is through this scene – a filling in of one of the many mysteries and uncertainties surrounding Atta's character – and in other asides, that Amis reveals, again perhaps partly unintentionally, the guiding principle behind his description of a suicide bomber.

Amis has Atta visit a dying imam in a hospital in Portland, Maine. Here Atta recites quotations from the Koran that explicitly condemn murder and suicide. The imam then goes on to list American crimes with which Atta agrees. The imam then reaches for a 'half-empty eight-ounce bottle of Volvic' (*SP*: p. 111). At first it is left unsaid precisely what this gift signifies until Atta phones Ziad Jarrah, the pilot on the United 93 hijacking.[11] Atta tells Jarrah that he has received 'the holy water . . . from the Oasis' (*SP*: p. 115).[12] This water will, Atta has been told, absolve him of 'the atrocious crime . . . of the self-felony' (*SP*: p. 115). Jarrah asks Atta whether it comes in a special bottle and Atta replies that it came in a 'crystal vial' (*SP*: p. 115). As he waits to board the plane Atta takes out the bottle: 'The imam *said* it was from Medina. He shrugged, and drank the holy Volvic' (*SP*: p. 118).

Amis has always been an essentially satirical writer and his use of parody here points towards one of the central problems inherent in the story: how does this parody, which manifests itself elsewhere in 'The Last Days of Muhammad Atta' contribute to a knowledge of the attacks? In one sense these scenes parody religion and religious piety – rather than a 'crystal vial' the water comes in a commercial plastic bottle,[13] the mass-market object deflating the metaphysical symbolism of the 'holy' water. Atta's lack of concern with its origin and his subsequent lie to Jarrah underline Amis' assertion that the hijacker was not motivated by religious fervour.[14] Thus, Amis' satirical attack on Atta's 'faith', and faith as a whole, investigated in other essays in *The Second Plane*, dictates how he represents the terrorist psyche. Adam Mars-Jones has argued that Amis is 'locked into satire' and as such his work often slips into a 'discriminatory cartooniness'.[15] This insight sheds light upon the potential failings in Amis' representation of Atta – because Amis, along with many other American and British writers, cannot fully engage with the 'otherness' of the hijackers. Instead he relies upon trusted satirical tropes (excrement, sex, bodily decay) to parody Atta and his cohort of terrorists rather than attempting accurately to give them a voice in an attempt to gain some understanding of the attacks.

Of course, satire and parody are both routes to a kind of knowledge and Amis is under no ethical obligation to treat the terrorists, so to speak, 'seriously'. James Diedrick, writing about Amis's oeuvre, argues:

> The novels view the world through the magnifying glass of satire, which sees selfishness, duplicity, venality, and greed everywhere. The individual and collective ills exposed in these narratives would make for grim reading if not

for the transformative energy of Amis's comic voice, which employs exaggeration, parody, and irony to supply the civilized, civilizing perspective his characters typically lack.[16]

In other words, Atta does not, in effect he cannot, see the irony in the 'holy' water and its container because he lacks a 'civilizing perspective'. Amis has invariably utilised the first-person perspective in his fiction and it is often revealing in the novels and stories when he reverts to the third-person point of view. In 'The Last Days of Muhammad Atta' Amis employs a privileged third-person perspective and it is this 'distance' that Amis creates between himself and Atta, despite the story being 'seen' through his eyes, that also reflects Amis' satirical approach. This 'distance' allows Amis to comment on Atta's behaviour and ideas but it also exposes theories and opinions that inform his critical thinking and, finally, thwart an active engagement with the 'real' Atta (and by extension the events of 9/11).

These satirical asides rely on a certain portentous foreshadowing that undermines any sense of realism and betrays Amis' views that are articulated elsewhere in the collection. For example, Amis writes that Atta's name is 'itself like a promise of vengeance' (SP: p. 98), presumably playing on the proximity of the terrorist's surname to the verb 'attack'. There is no doubt that this is Amis' own reflection on Atta's name rather than Atta's himself. Likewise, when Atta has cut himself shaving, Amis intervenes: 'The themes of recurrence and prolongation, he sensed, were already beginning to associate themselves with his last day' (SP: p. 99). These 'themes' are actually the novelist's structuring devices rather than an effort to inhabit the terrorist's thought processes. Later, after Atta is asked to confirm the date of the attacks, Amis writes: 'And he was the first person on earth to say it – to say in that way: 'Nine eleven. September the eleventh' (SP: p. 105). Leon Wieseltier writes that the collection is still 'busy with the glamorous pursuit of extraordinary sentences' and that this preoccupation with style is 'an interruption of attention' and 'an invitation to behold the prose' and not the reality of the situation.[17]

There are other examples of Amis' self-conscious voice dominating the description and in the process creating a distance between the reader and the character of Atta. Here is an excellent example of this authorial interruption: 'And he didn't solace himself with the thought that this was, after all, September 11: you could still get to airports without much time to spare' (SP: p. 107). Amis is clearly 'here', in the text, and is reiterating an argument from his essay 'Terror and Boredom: The Dependent Mind' (SP: pp. 47–93). This conscious cross-pollination[18] between fact and fiction suggests something of the ongoing 'journey' that Aaronovitch identified was evident in the collection. But it also clarifies one of the problems in Amis' fictionalising of Atta's character; namely, that if this imagined Atta is both a recognisably 'Amis-ian' male protagonist and a vehicle for satire (or rather a vehicle for Amis' theories on Islamism), what is being said about 9/11? Put another way, if Amis' Atta is so forcibly shown to be different from his fellow hijackers, is the fiction revealing its lack of interest in or its inability to represent the reality of the attacks?

This tension can be found throughout the story. Amis refuses to bestow a 'genuine' faith on Atta, instead suggesting that the hijacker is filled with self-hatred, spiritual ennui and sexual confusion rather than religious fervour: 'If you took away all the rubbish about faith, then fundamentalism suited his character, and with an almost sinister precision' (*SP*: p. 101). This reflection stems more from Amis' non-fictional writing on Islamism rather than from any documentary evidence. In 'Terror and Boredom: The Dependent Mind', 'Iran and the Lord of Time', 'What Will Survive of Us' and 'Conspiracy Theories, and *Takfir*' Amis builds up his critique of militant Islam and these inform (or dictate) how he views the role of religion in 'The Last Days of Muhammad Atta'. Indeed, in 'Terror and Boredom: The Dependent Mind', Amis describes the plot of an aborted novella 'The Unknown Known' whilst delineating the research behind its creation. Amis' reasons for rejecting the story and the content of the story itself are highly revealing in regard to this relationship between fact and fiction. Furthermore, the essay underlines many of the problems that have been detailed concerning 'The Last Days of Muhammad Atta'.

'The Unknown Known' (its title taken from Donald Rumsfeld's notorious speech to the Department of Defense in February 2002) is a satirical novella in which Amis describes the life of Ayed, a Pakistani 'Islamist terrorist' (*SP*: p. 52). Ayed works in 'the "Prism"' (*SP*: p. 52), a terrorist cell in which plans are made for future attacks. Ayed's section 'is devoted to conceptual break-throughs – to shifts in the paradigm' (*SP*: p. 53) whilst he also struggles with his four wives.[19] Ayed's main contribution to this paradigm shift – and Amis' satirical focus – is a plan to 'scour all the prisons and madhouses for every compulsive rapist in the country, and then unleash them in Greeley, Colorado'[20] (*SP*: p. 55). Amis provides a psychological reason for Ayed's anxiety surrounding his wives (one of them is as young as nine): his father took his family to Colorado in the 1980s and there Ayed was 'humiliated' by his sisters' embrace of Western values: 'Before Ayed knows it, the women have shed their veils, and his sisters are being called on by gum-chewing *kafirs*' (*SP*: p. 65).

Ayed endures this for only so long: he hides himself away 'so that he [can] rail against the airiness of the summer frocks worn by American women and the shameless brevity of their underpants' (*SP*: p. 66) and, although the Prism considers 'killing them all' (*SP*: p. 66), instead Ayed returns home, joins the terrorist group and marries a number of women. Amis reveals, in an effort to shed some light on 'the art of fiction' (*SP*: p. 86), that his idea for the ending of the story came to him later because 'the subconscious had made a polite suggestion, a suggestion that the conscious mind had taken a while to see' (*SP*: p. 86). This 'polite suggestion' is manifested as a belt that Ayed buys in the USA – it 'consists of a 'weight strap' and the pommel of a saddle' (*SP*: pp. 86–7). Ayed uses it to sexually dominate his already unhappy wives. This belt, Amis intended, was to be used by Ayed in his 'conceptual breakthrough': he would be 'the first to bring martyrdom operations into the setting of his own home' (*SP*: p. 87).

As we know, Amis did not complete this story. He describes the abandonment of what he seems to feel was a promising piece as being dictated by 'wholly extraneous' (*SP*: p. 51) reasons. He adds that he was not writing under a 'fear of repercussion' but that he was 'receiving a new vibration or frequency from the planetary shimmer' (*SP*: p. 51). Despite being a frustratingly vague, even obfuscatory, explanation Amis does go onto clarify his position:

> The confirmatory moment came a few weeks ago: the freshly fortified suspicion that there exists on our planet a kind of human being who will become a Muslim in order to pursue suicide-mass murder. For quite a time I have felt that Islamism was trying to poison the world; and here was a sign that the poison might take – might mutate, like bird flu. Islam, as I said, is a total system, and like all such systems it is eerily amenable to satire. But with Islamism, with total malignancy, with total terror and total boredom, irony, even militant irony (which is what satire is), merely shrivels and dies. (*SP*: p. 87)

Amis followed this explanation in *The Second Plane* with a further clarification in the publication of the 'skeletal typescript' of 'The Unknown Known' in *Granta*:

> But in the end I felt that the piece was premature, and therefore a hostage to fortune; certain future events might make it impossible to defend. If I live to be very old, I may one day pull it out of my desk – at the other end of the Long War.[21]

As has been seen in relation to 'The Last Days of Muhammad Atta', the issue of satirising events surrounding 9/11 is deeply problematic. Amis' failure to finish 'The Unknown Known' is instructive and illuminating.

Of course, one should have no cause to doubt Amis' reasons for not finishing the story (the cynical response might simply be that the writer 'couldn't finish it' and has fashioned a political/cultural reason to disguise this aesthetic failure) but if one does then the sense that, in the face of Islamist terrorism, satirical devices are not suitable in fully engaging with the subject emerges. Or, to put it another way, 'fiction' loses its power in opposition to a reality that has surpassed it in terms of a 'negative' imagination: Amis feels that he cannot fictionalise an 'unknown unknown'; first, because the terrorist potential for increasingly insidious and 'evil' attacks far exceeds the imagination of a creative writer, and second, because the political and cultural sensitivities of the times demand that he cannot ethically continue with the story. If this is so, one must return to some of the reservations articulated surrounding the fictional and satirical elements of 'The Last Days of Muhammad Atta' and Amis' other 9/11 story, 'In the Palace of the End'.

'Terror and Boredom: The Dependent Mind' explicitly wrestles with this problem and finally concedes that historical fact 'defeats' fiction in that the 'imaginary' has been attenuated by the forces of the real. The essay also clearly emphasises Amis' reliance on documentary data:[22] around his description of 'The Unknown Known' Amis writes extensively about the life of Sayyid Qutb (the evident inspiration for the character of Ayed), the rise of the 'cult' of the suicide bomber, Islamist ideology, the invasion of Iraq and the nature of religion as a whole. In one respect, the essay demonstrates its own thesis – Amis shows how the historical evidence, as it were, 'feeds into' the fiction whilst always acknowledging that for these very reasons the fiction is 'impossible'. It is interesting to note that Amis – such a fierce opponent of clichés – should use one to explicate his moral position; in this instance, he writes that the potential story might well be a 'hostage to fortune'. *The Concise Oxford English Dictionary* definition of this common phrase is: 'an act or remark seen as unwise because it invites trouble'.[23] If 'The Unknown Known' with its satirical tropes and 'militant irony' had to be curtailed for ethical considerations, why is it permissible to write and publish 'The Last Days of Muhammad Atta' and 'In the Palace of the End'?

'In the Palace of the End'[24] can be used similarly to highlight these issues that Amis describes in 'Terror and Boredom'. A 'double'[25] working on behalf of Nadir the Next, the son of the unnamed country's[26] previous leader and who is now the new dictator, narrates the story. It is obvious that the regime is coming to an end and the narrator evokes a world outside of the 'palace' – where interrogations and torture routinely take place and the doubles are filmed having sex with female prisoners – that is in the midst of a brutal civil war. The narrator is only one of many doubles that, in the mornings, torture the prisoners in the 'Interrogation Wing' (SP: p. 31) and in the afternoons, in the 'Recreation Wing' (SP: p. 31) have 'filmed sex with . . . a series of picked beauties' (SP: p. 31). In one of the story's many ironic inversions, this 'filmed sex' is not, as was previously, principally about 'the snarling sodomisings, the raucous 'squad bangs'; rather, the doubles 'recline in luxurious apartments with our ladyfriends' and indulge in sensuous pleasures such as chocolate, poetry, music and physical intimacy (SP: p. 37). Following this they are filmed – presumably for the dictator's own pleasure – in an attempt to 'bring about multiple orgasm' (SP: p. 37) in the female prisoners.

Amis' tale appears to be largely based on stories surrounding Uday Hussein, one of Saddam's two sons, a man notorious for his criminal and psychotic excesses. Uday has been accused of being a murderer and a torturer, a serial rapist, a kidnapper and a man of fierce, sudden temper. He was also notorious for his insatiable sexual appetite.[27] Indeed, as has been shown with the two other 9/11 fictions, 'In the Palace of the End' feeds off an essay entitled 'The Wrong War'.[28] Amis describes Saddam Hussein's route towards power:

> He came up through the torture corps in the 1960s, establishing the Baath secret police, Jihaz Haneen (the 'instrument of yearning'), and putting himself about in the Qasr al-Nihayah ('the Palace of the End'), perhaps the most feared destination in Iraq until its demolition, after an attempted coup by the chief inquisitor, Nadhim Kazzar, in 1973. (SP: p. 27)

Again, as in the other 9/11 fictions, there is a solid basis in fact. Amis' 'Palace' can be interpreted then as a kind of allegory of Iraq – with ironic inversion Amis attempts to re-present the horrors of the Iraqi system to the reader. Many of the events described in the story have their correlates in the biographies of Uday Hussein and Amis, as it were, expands upon them and exaggerates them to make satirical points surrounding torture, masculine anxiety (particularly impotence) and Iraq itself.

The narrator essentially recounts his 'duties' throughout the days and months of torture and sexual excess that dominate and define 'the Palace'. The mornings are taken up with torture sessions taking place in 'a vast factory of excruciation: there the strappado,[29] here the bastinado;[30] there the rack, here the wheel' (SP: p. 32). Prisoners attempt 'instant suicide by the only means available – by the dental excision, that is to say, of their own tongues' (SP: p. 32). This self-mutilation has a correlate 'paradox' in that the 'tongueless ones' can 'neither proclaim their innocence nor (the far wiser course) trumpet their guilt' (SP: p. 32).

Such potential confessions are, the narrator points out, largely academic given that '99 per cent of those who enter the Interrogation Wing are eventually hanged'. The 'remainder are sent home fatally envenomed' so that they can 'sketch . . . write . . . [or] mime' stories of what they have endured which in turn help to spread 'respect for the essentially personal rule of Nadir the Next' (*SP*: pp. 32–3). 'Nadir', of course, means 'the lowest or most unsuccessful point'.[31]

The narration here most resembles Amis' *Time's Arrow* in which the workings of Auschwitz are recounted backwards so as to mirror the 'doubled' psychology of a Nazi doctor. Thus, 'killing' becomes 'healing' in this reversed universe – the sadistic doctor is transformed into a benevolent figure. Up until that point, the 'spirit' narrator has been perpetually confused as to the meaning of what the person he/she inhabits does. In the non-Auschwitz world the role of the doctor seems to be one of reinflicting wounds on patients rather than saving them. Indeed, in this 'upside down' world nothing makes logical sense. Until, the narrator realises in a series of ironic epiphanies, 'they' reach the Camp and everything appears to be 'explained':

> Enlightenment was urged on me the day I saw the old Jew float to the surface of the deep latrine, how he splashed and struggled into life, and was hoisted out by jubilant guards, his clothes cleansed by the mire.[32]

> A shockingly inflamed eyeball at once rectified by a single injection. Innumerable ovaries and testes seamlessly grafted into place. Women went out of that lab looking twenty years younger.[33]

Amis forces the reader to, as it were, 'turn' these images around and by doing this, the reader confronts the horror of the act in a radically new way. These reversed complexities of the narrative act as a device, through 'militant irony', to reassert the brutality and suffering endured in the Holocaust.

Likewise, in 'In the Palace of the End', Amis' narrator introduces elements of the Iraqi regime's hidden violence within the literary device of irony. As has been discussed previously, it is again a moot point whether this irony actively achieves its goal to make the reader 'resee' events. In 'The Last Days of Muhammad Atta' there is a lingering sense that Amis' previous non-fiction discussing Islamism and his unwavering commitment to satire arguably deflects away from a deeper understanding of the terrorists' psychologies. Amis' decision to abort the novella 'The Unknown Known' is perhaps further evidence of a slight doubt as to the efficacy of fictionalising such contemporary events. In 'In the Palace of the End' these doubts are further emphasised when one looks at its resonance with Amis' familiar preoccupations. Again, this centres on the theme of masculine insecurity.

In 'The Last Days of Muhammad Atta' Amis locates much of this insecurity in and on the body. This satirical trope is articulated in 'In the Palace of the End' with the doubles ordered to mirror the injuries that Nadir inevitably accrues over the years due to the 'increasingly frequent and desperate attempts on his life' (*SP*: p. 34). Whatever happens to Nadir must be replicated on the doubles:

> Similarly, every double lacks a right kneecap, a left heel, a left shoulder blade, and the fourth and fifth fingers of his left hand. We have all spent time in wheelchairs, on crutches, in neck braces, in traction. We are additionally subjected to periodic poisonings. More recently, we all had our hair scorched off (after a flame-thrower attack on the son of the dictator), and for a while a team of barbers and surgeons appeared every day to regulate the condition of our fuzz and blisters. (*SP*: p. 34)

These physical humiliations act as an allegory for the injustices endured by Iraqi people under Saddam's regime – they are enacted, as it were, on the 'body' of the nation. But, as with all of Amis' 9/11 fiction these are visited exclusively on the male body and thus the satirical aim of the writing is, perhaps inevitably, limited.

Amis's 'militant irony' extends to the sex sessions that have become parodies of traditional conventions of romance. As has been noted, rape and sodomy have been replaced by lengthy seduction scenes in which the narrator and his fellow doubles are obliged to make the female prisoners – 'young nurses, young secretaries, young schoolteachers' (*SP*: p. 38) – reach unsimulated orgasms. Mekhlis, a colleague, argues that he preferred the 'old days' (*SP*: p. 38) but the narrator has increasing doubts and is secretly relieved that he is no longer compelled to engage in torture and other acts of violence. The narrator describes one encounter where he 'romances' a 'young anaesthetist' with champagne, love songs and extravagant compliments. The woman is understandably terrified and he is aware of the 'cladding of hatred in her eyes' (*SP*: p. 39). He engages in three hours of 'unpunctuated cunnilingus' (*SP*: p. 39) but fails to stimulate the young woman who remains resolutely unmoved, her 'flesh as cold and adhesive as dry ice' (*SP*: p. 39). The narrator is resigned to the fact that the authorities will note this inability and that he will potentially run the risk of becoming a 'failed double' whose ultimate fate is death by 'lethal injection' (*SP*: p. 43).

As in so much of Amis' work the 'male vulnerability and flaw' (*SP*: p. 40) of impotence, both sexual and social, is the central ironic trope of the story. And again the question of what insight the author brings to Islam and its post-9/11 global significance arises. By focusing so narrowly upon the ironies of male heterosexual sexuality Amis runs the risk of potentially trivialising the subject, reducing issues of faith, nationality, despotism and political torture to overly familiar satirical jokes concerning masculine anxieties. Indeed, in the communal showers, the narrator describes the doubles as being 'all red and raw, like a convocation of colossal penises' (SP: p. 40). Along with all the many increasingly serious injuries that the doubles are forced to endure, they are also 'performing' for the pleasure of the 'Next' who is himself, it emerges, impotent. Nadir's 'inwrought wrath' (SP: p. 41) is directly linked to his sexual inadequacies: 'All his grown life, helpless, as in a dream, surrounded by naked women he could do nothing with' (SP: p. 44). Barely human and regularly humiliated the doubles act as conduits for the future tyrant's physical maladies and also his sexual frustration. The cruel inversion of consensual acts of love, lust and seduction are a 'mirror' – the doubles cannot bear to look at themselves and are constantly smashing them – of the previous regime of sexual barbarity.

Mekhlis' comment that 'rape is less boring, and much quicker, than the marathon "tongue work"' (SP: p. 42) emphasises, perhaps a little too aggressively, the inversion of conventional romance as a kind of 'torture' (for both man and woman). The narrator states that it is illegal to murder female virgins but that 'mass rape' (SP: p. 43) used to be the tactic that circumvented the law. But now the narrator and his fellow doubles, whose number is being depleted regularly, feel 'numbed' (SP: p. 42) by their actions and Amis begins to articulate a developing, if not fully formed, sense of compassion in the narrator's feelings towards his captors. This is most forcefully realised when the narrator ponders on the fact that pain is felt more urgently than pleasure:

> I am wondering . . . why the body's genius for pain so easily outsoars its fitful talent for pleasure; wondering why the pretty trillings of the bedroom are so easily silenced by the impossible vociferation of the Interrogation Wing; and wondering why the spasms and archings of orgasm are so easily rendered inert and insensible by the climatic epilepsy of torture. You don't need to dim the lights for torture, or play soft music. People will respond. You don't need to get them in the mood. Everyone's always in the mood. (SP: p. 45)

Much more successfully than his efforts to render the mind of a fundamentalist hi-jacker, Amis' contemplation of the effects of torture centres on one of the most controversial and disturbing developments in the post-9/11 world. Images from Abu Ghraib and Guantanamo Bay have become synonymous with the 'War on Terror' and Amis' satirical inversion, whilst initially limited in its focus on the bodily humiliations experienced by the narrator, another of the author's sexually anguished and physically deteriorating male characters, rather subtly invokes the growing awareness of the use of torture as a political weapon.

In her essay 'On the Torture of Others', Susan Sontag writes:

> Shock and awe were what our military promised the Iraqis. And shock and the awful are what these photographs announce to the world that the Americans have delivered: a pattern of criminal behavior in open contempt of international humanitarian conventions. Soldiers now pose, thumbs up, before the atrocities they commit, and send off the pictures to their buddies. Secrets of private life that, formerly, you would have given nearly anything to conceal, you now clamor to be invited on a television show to reveal. What these photographs illustrate is as much the culture of shamelessness as the reigning admiration for unapologetic brutality.[34]

Sontag's article appeared in the same year as Amis' story and both reflect a profound concern with the proliferation of torture and also of the phenomenon, hastened by the Internet, of images of this torture. Furthermore such acts of torture often had a perverse sexualisation about them as male bodies are photographed simulating fellatio, tied to a leash naked and buried together, their genitalia exposed. Thus, in one sense, the male bodies of these suspects are used as physical targets for revenge, frustration, contempt and boredom. But also, in the widely disseminated photographs, they inadvertently become symbolic of American foreign policy. Sontag writes:

> The torture of prisoners is not an aberration. It is a direct consequence of the with-us-or-against-us doctrines of world struggle with which the Bush administration has sought to change, change radically, the international stance of the United States and to recast many domestic institutions and pre-rogatives. The Bush administration has committed the country to a pseudo-religious doctrine of war, endless war – for 'the war on terror" is nothing less than that. Endless war is taken to justify endless incarcerations.[35]

Hence, part of this 'war' is fought at the level of interrogation, torture and sexual humiliation. The anonymous, naked bodies of the male suspects represent 'the exercise of extreme sadomasochistic longings'[36] that are intrinsic to the broader ideologies of the Bush administration's 'shock and awe' invasions – both militaristic and private. Militaristic in the obvious sense of the 'wars' in Afghanistan and Iraq and private in the sense of individual male bodies ritually scarred, beaten, humiliated and abused.

And it is here that Amis' story achieves a moving and powerful denouement in its evocation of human vulnerability. The narrator recognises the 'Next's' 'gravitation . . . to the tender' and his empathy for others grows. He goes on:

> When you have been hurt yourself, there awakens a part of you that doesn't want to hurt anyone. When you love something so intimately fragile as your own body, you don't want to hurt anyone. That's what I'm saying to myself, now, in the changing room. Please let me not have to hurt anyone. (*SP*: p. 46)

This incongruous compassion is a trope that runs throughout *The Second Plane* and reflects Amis' 'political journey' evident throughout the collection. If the two complete short stories are perhaps flawed in their representation of the terrorist/Islamist other they are also revealing in that they articulate the inherent difficulties – ethical, aesthetic, political – of finding ways to speak of motivations and ideologies that often appear impenetrable. If Amis' Atta remains constricted by the author's own very familiar obsessions surrounding male anxieties, in contrast the mournful narrator of 'In the Palace of the End' signifies the growing sense of disgust and anger that has arisen since revelations of torture have emerged. But more than this, despite the piecemeal nature of the collection a coherent response to 9/11 does begin to emerge, one that is both invigorating and controversial.

Undeniably, *The Second Plane* represents a concerted and often morally outraged attack on the tenets of radical Islamism in all its many mutations. In addition to the essays already alluded to in the Introduction there are reviews of Greengrass' *United 93*, Lawrence Wright's *The Looming Tower*, Bob Woodward's *State of Denial: Bush at War, Part 111*, Mark Steyn's *America Alone: The End of the World as We Know It* and Ed Husain's *The Islamist: Why I Joined Radical Islam in Britain, What I Saw Inside and Why I Left*. In these pieces Amis critiques Islamist thought as being defined by its misanthropy, misogyny, nihilism, anti-reason, anti-Semitism and its commitment to mass murder. And it is in the last essay in the collection, entitled 'September 11', that Amis sums up, six years later, his feelings about 'September 11'. After a perhaps slightly pedantic consideration of the linguistic ironies surrounding the contraction of the date September 11 into the numerical '9/11' Amis turns to what he perceives as the changed political climate he encounters when he returns to the UK after two and a half years spent living in South America. He describes his experience of appearing on the panel of BBC's *Question Time* when he expresses the opinion that the invasions of Iraq and Afghanistan have been largely successful. He adds that the West should be engaged in a 'hunt for the remnants of al-Qaeda' (*SP*: p. 199).

Amis, believing that his comments are 'tediously centrist' (*SP*: p. 199), is thoroughly surprised by the audience's response. Following an impassioned attack on American imperialism and its collusion with Islamists in Afghanistan, the audience applauds the suggestion that America should in fact be dropping bombs on its own citizens. Amis is appalled by what he sees as an abject example of the contemporary phenomenon of 'moral equivalence' (SP: p. 199) that determines the '100–per-cent and 360–degree inability to pass judgement on any ethnicity other than our own' (SP: p. 199). This reaction, he argues, is absurd in that it implies that Osama Bin Laden is somehow politically preferable to George Bush. Whilst it is easy to take issue with Amis' somewhat sanitised description of the state of Afghani and Iraqi society in the aftermath of invasion one can also see how Amis has arrived at such a position. For him it is clear who the enemy is and he mocks the idea that the terrorists are motivated by feelings of political disenfranchisement. Instead, Amis considers the Islamist ideology as being 'abnormally interested in violence and death' (SP: p. 201) and to have an 'organised passion for carnage' (SP: p. 201). He compares radical Islam to Bolshevism and Nazism and robustly argues against its 'pathology' that is, he argues, fundamentally a 'rejection of reason' (SP: pp. 202–3).

If indeed *The Second Plane* is reflective of an author's 'political journey' in the post-9/11 years it is telling that the collection ends with Amis' morally outraged, emotionally charged attack on radical Islamism. As has been seen in the previous chapter, many of the early responses to the attacks were written in hyperbolic language evoking, perhaps understandably, discourses of paranoia, anger, suspicion and a rueful sense that the world had become irrevocably divided between the 'West' and radical fundamentalism. Six years later Amis' tone has, if anything, become more apocalyptic still, as he laments that Islam's 'militant vanguard' (SP: p. 205) has turned towards a deepening of religious convictions the result of which, he argues, speaks of 'retrogression and revanchism . . . of a vehement and desperate nostalgia' (SP: p. 206). Amis' 9/11 non-fictions articulate a deepening resentment towards Islamism – and, more broadly, a distaste for religion as a whole. The two complete works of short fiction (and the aborted short story) are satires that attempt to incorporate such insights into issues surrounding male anxiety, vulnerability and repression. In this sense the fiction, by comparison, seems reductive in that it eschews politics and history in favour of parody and 'militant irony'. And whilst 'The Last Days of Mohammed Atta' arguably fails to bring any new insights into the psyche of a terrorist, 'In the Palace of the End' is perhaps more successful in finding a suitably bleak comic register with which to discuss the torture tactics of Hussain's Iraqi government.

Indeed Amis ends his essay, and the collection, with a final acknowledgement that writing about 9/11 and its aftermath is a continuing problem. He writes:

> September 11 entrained a moral crash, planet-wide; it also loosened the ground between reality and delirium. So when we speak of it, let's call it by its proper name; let's not suggest that our experience of that event, that development, has been frictionlessly absorbed and filed away. It has not. September 11 continues, it goes on, with all its mystery, its instability, and its terrible dynamism. (*SP*: p. 206)

If, then, *The Second Plane* remains an often flawed collection, in particular the fiction, it is also a fascinating reflection of a writer struggling to find ways in which to speak of the event. Undoubtedly satire and parody have a place in the 'Literature of Terror' – see Chris Morris' recent *Four Lions* (2010) for evidence of its efficacy – and Amis' efforts certainly suggest potential beginning points for treating 9/11 and its subsequent impact in more irreverent ways. But his description of the contemporary relevance of 9/11 as a global event that has not yet been 'absorbed' suggests that it will continue to draw artists to attempt to represent it. Its 'terrible dynamism' unquestionably continues and in the following chapter the study will look at a French novelist, Frederic Beigbeder, whose novel *Windows on the World* arguably takes the most creative and ethical risks in confronting the attacks.

Chapter 3

'You Know How it Ends': Metafiction and 9/11 in *Windows on the World*

There is a growing sense that the traditional realist novel struggles to accommodate the profound 'rupture' of 9/11. Furthermore, as will be argued later in the study in relation to a text such as *Man on Wire*, there is a developing suggestion that fictional realism might not be the most efficacious or suitable genre and that more hybrid forms – the graphic novel, the essay/memoir, the film-poem, conceptual art – are better suited to represent the attacks. *Falling Man* searches for appropriate metaphors in order best to capture the 'haunted', uncanny aftermath of the attacks and it is in the novel's most stylised moments that it is most successful. Safran Foer's *Extremely Loud and Incredibly Close* (2005), with its blending of linguistic and visual experimentation similarly points towards possible hybrid texts. This chapter will look at another novel, Frédéric Beigbeder's *Windows on the World* (2004), which self-consciously announces itself as a 'hyperreal' novel and represents 9/11 in a distinctive, controversial and formally daring way.

Before looking at *Windows on the World* in more detail it is instructive to see how a strictly realist novel such as Claire Messud's *The Emperor's Children* (2006) deals with the 'interruption' of 9/11. In a 431–page novel, the day of the attacks does not appear until page 370. This may well, in part, reflect Messud's writing process – that she was busy writing a novel about New York's cultural elite when the attacks occurred and, perhaps inevitably, the author felt compelled to include them in her novel. The effect that this has on the text is akin to a 'wake up call' to the characters – as such it provides a conveniently dramatic catalyst that alters the course of the characters' relationships. In this way the novel replays and redramatises a conventional view of the 1990s and 9/11: the self-absorption, consumerism and narcissism of the decade is 'destroyed' by the shocking rupture of the attacks.

The 'Emperor'[1] is Murray Thwaite, a radical journalist and cultural commentator whose 'children' are various people – family, friends, colleagues and rivals – who make up the privileged community. The novel explores the intergenerational differences between Thwaite's 1960s' political radicalism and the baby-boomers that follow in his hugely influential footsteps. Gradually, they challenge Thwaite, most notably his nephew, an ambitious young journalist, 'Bootie', who moves from disciple to rebel throughout the course of the narrative, challenge Thwaite. The aspiring writers and artists are variously seduced (both sexually and politically) and angered by Thwaite's imperious arrogance and sense of superiority. The interweaving relationships and professional travails of these characters are shattered by the attacks that loom over the narrative, which takes place from March to December 2001. The events of 9/11 both scupper ambitions – a cultural magazine's planned launch in September is suspended indefinitely – and provide an opportunity for escape – Frederick 'Bootie' Tubb, who has exposed Thwaite and subsequently has become something of a social pariah, is thought to have been in the towers and to have died flees to Florida and assumes a new name and persona.[2]

Thus 9/11 severely destabilises the class, wealth and property concerns of these insulated urbanites. How far Messud satirises these characters and their comparatively trivial pursuits is a moot point but it seems fair to say that 9/11 erupts into the narrative in an authentic way approximating the manner in which the majority of New Yorkers, and by extension the rest of America (if not the globe) experienced the attacks. Compared with Beigbeder's hyperreal metafiction, Messud's realism and temporal authenticity appears to treat the subject of the attacks with more gravity and to show more sensitivity towards those who perished on 9/11 (and those traumatised). But whilst such responses and representations make a historical sense given the profound wound that 9/11 caused in the collective American psyche, less memorialising and less honouring representations may actually shed more light upon the meanings of the attacks. One scene towards the end of *The Emperor's Children* highlights this dilemma and points towards a re-evaluation of Beigbeder's less conventional treatment.

Danielle Minkoff, a documentary filmmaker and friend of the Thwaites, has begun a tentative romance with the 'Emperor' Murray. He lies to his wife about attending a speaking engagement in Chicago and instead, on 10 September, meets Danielle in the city and invites her to take a helicopter ride to 'see it all from above' (*EC*: p. 368). Messud portrays this journey in lush, romantic language: she describes an 'intoxicated Rothko sunset' and 'everywhere the lights just flickering on, innumerable fireflies in the waning day' (*EC*: pp. 368 and 369). This epiphany is underlined when Danielle is filled with 'childlike wonder' at the sights she observes and Murray 'in his very heart [is] suffused with some hitherto unexperienced delight' (p. 369). Later, over supper, there is further foreshadowing:

> Danielle rose to put on music, a Spanish soprano singing Cantaloube,[3] her pure, agonized strains floating, their minor harmonies wavering in the small room, as if to remind them both that beauty and loss were inseparably entwined. (*EC*: p. 369)

The last clause of this sentence is Messud's authorial voice suggesting a shared feeling between the two. But the use of the phrase 'as if' denoting 'as would be the case if'[4] reveals how Messud relies upon the reader's knowledge of what will occur next – the following day is 9/11. Danielle and Murray's blissful ignorance is contained within the diegesis of the narrative whilst Messud's objectivity reflects a prior knowledge that the characters cannot share. The reader is also privileged by being made aware of how the characters' lives are about to be profoundly changed (and that the relationship is doomed).

In other words the Manhattan skyline and the music of Cantaloube move Danielle and Murray but Messud (and the reader) are in a position to interpret the pathos of this scene in context of what is about to happen. In one sense this merely reflects the characters' temporality but it also signifies a foreshadowing that relies upon the ominous reality of the terrorist attacks. Thus, Messud's narrative uses 9/11 to act as a catalyst for radical transformation of her novel. In one respect this seems realistic in that, for Danielle and Murray and the novel's other characters, 9/11 is an entirely localised catastrophe that violently intrudes upon their personal lives. But there is a deeper problematic in that, as it were, 9/11 does the work for Messud, giving her novel a gravitas it might not necessarily otherwise achieve. This is further compounded in the subsequent chapter – titled 'The Morning After' - in which Murray and Danielle wake up the next day in her apartment. Murray is the first to witness the attacks: ' "Look at that," he said. "They've got some colossal fire going. It must be a bomb or something" ' (*EC*: p. 370). Danielle turns on the television to confirm the reality and historicity of what she feels is 'sorcery' (*EC*: p. 371) happening outside her window. She experiences a sense of disorientation, 'as if they were simultaneously in Manhattan and anywhere on the planet' (*EC*: p. 370). Danielle is then comforted by the attacks' presence on screen:

> The sirens on the screen echoed, with a disconcerting lag, the sirens out the window. The cacophony on the television was more bearable, more reassuring, because it was contained in a little box; because unlike the sirens and

yelling and the visceral rumbles outside, you could imagine, at least, that you could just turn it off. Better to have them both going, to indulge the illusions that they could, if they chose to, call a halt to the whole catastrophe. (*EC*: p. 372)

Such reflections form part of perhaps one of the most dominant discourses surrounding 9/11 – their televisual/cinematic visuality versus the traumatic reality of the burning towers. Danielle is briefly calmed by the television images but as they watch events unfold Murray reveals that he should return to his wife Annabel (he tries to phone her but of course all the lines are down). Murray feels that he has no choice but to return to her and when he leaves Danielle looks down onto the streets and sees 'dust-coloured, bewildered people, some crying, drifting up the avenue, lots of them, like refuges from war, she thought' (*EC*: p. 373). It is important to note that 9/11 has not been explicitly alluded to – Messud is again relying heavily upon the reader's knowledge of recent history. Indeed, if, for whatever reason, a reader was unaware of 9/11 (which admittedly seems a very remote possibility), one wonders what kind of sense these chapters would make. Messud is thus able to describe what would otherwise be a fantastical narrative device with iconic images already loaded with significance:

> She had seen the *second plane*, like a *gleaming arrow*, and the burst of it, *oddly beautiful against the blue*, and the *smoke*, everywhere, and she had seen the *people jumping*, from afar, specks in the sky, and she knew that's what they were only from the TV, from the great reality check of the screen, and she had seen the *buildings crumble to dust* . . . (*EC*: p. 373; my italics)

These trigger images provide Messud with a ready-made vocabulary of 9/11 signifiers that bring the weight of historical reality into an otherwise fictional narrative. In particular Messud's use of the image of 'the second plane' – that Amis uses for the title of his essay collection – underlines how, rather than actively describing events directly from her characters' uncomprehending point of view, Messud uses a mixture of foreshadowing, semantic shorthand and a literary omniscience that would be unavailable to her if she had fictionalised a similarly huge catastrophe as a plot device to punctuate her novel.

Messud concludes these two chapters by returning to 'the Spanish woman singing last night'. Danielle feels sorrow for both Murray's departure and the devastation of the attacks themselves: 'there was nothing but sorrow and this was how it was going to be, now, always' (*EC*: p. 373). Hence, in one respect, the personal tragedies are metonyms for the wider suffering of those involved in the attacks.[5] On another level, 9/11, which is never mentioned, provides an effectively tragic and shocking 'plot development' for *The Emperor's Children*, one that in all probability could not have been bettered by anything in Messud's, or any other author's, imagination. The tragedy allows Messud dramatically to disrupt her own narrative with the force of the real historical. Indeed, if Messud had in fact fictionalised a similar event it may well have been accused of being a rather melodramatic *deus ex machina*. This is not to imply that Messud's use of 9/11 is cynical or exploitative but it does raise the question of how such a traumatising event can be accommodated within a realist fiction. As Kasia Boddy writes: 'When imagining how September 11 changed some lives forever, she [Messud] falls back on thriller-style plot devices and clichés about a "new world" (in short, on journalism).'[6]

Alfred Heckling goes further, arguing that along with the novel's other 'minor lapses' Messud 'draws attention to the greater issue of whether the events of 9/11 can be interpolated as a fictional scene'. Heckling goes on:

> Messud plunges straight into events as they were broadcast around the world, yet second-hand observations such as 'the plane, like a gleaming arrow, and the burst of it, oddly beautiful against the blue' read less like perceptive fiction than further unnecessary additions to the mounds of descriptive journalism that followed the event.[7]

Indeed, Messud appears to be making a broader literary point about the continued efficacy of the realist novel – in the tradition of Tolstoy – and its ability to dramatise ordinary lives set against the reality of history. 'Bootie', for example, is reading David Foster Wallace's *Infinite Jest* (1996), an infamously dense, difficult and erudite postmodern novel. He has chosen it largely because of the cultural hype surrounding the text as a 'definition of the zeitgeist' (*EC*: p. 51) but is confused by its intricacies and the novel remains unfinished.[8] Hence *The Emperor's Children* distances itself from such allegedly frivolous and self-indulgent 'exercises' and argues through its narrative for a journalistic realism. But as has been seen, Messud can find no language to add to the already established signifiers of 9/11 and because of this its appearance towards the end of the novel seems slightly opportunistic. The observations about television and reality are familiar, as are the cluster of trigger images. Likewise the trope of 'innocence' being smashed by the 'experience' of the attacks has become a cliché, in large part thanks to the Bush administration's rhetoric.

So if *The Emperor's Children* fails to accommodate 9/11 – in that there is an 'excess' of reality that the novel appears to confront but in actual fact shies away from – perhaps there is a larger point to be made about the inability of the realist genre fully to incorporate the intensely visual and historically unique attacks. Despite Messud's parodying of David Foster Wallace, one might argue that postmodern tropes could aid the author in more fully capturing the unsettling, uncanny, 'spectacular' nature of 9/11. *Windows on the World* announces itself as a 'hyperreal'[9] novel and consistently revels in games, metafiction, jokes, parodies and philosophical musings on the significance of 9/11. Unlike *The Emperor's Children* or other realist novels such as Jay McInerney's *The Good Life* (2006), Beigbeder's text is explicitly focused on the attacks: the novel's title comes from the name of the restaurant that was on the 107th floor of the North Tower. Indeed, Beigbeder's novel is partly set in the restaurant on the morning of September 11 and includes scenes involving people trapped and dying in the smoke and wreckage that are highly unusual outside of journalism and testimony.

Hence Beigbeder, by his own acknowledgement, takes a potentially enormous risk by including such scenes. Despite a number of critical reservations – Josh Lacey calls these sections 'just schlock' and argues that 'Beigbeder is simply incapable of writing a conventional narrative or creating autonomous fictional characters'[10] – Beigbeder utilises a number of devices in order both to represent the events of 9/11 and also constantly to challenge his own right to do so. *Windows on the World* self-consciously interrogates itself throughout and a list of the ways in which it does so will be useful when examining its techniques:

1) The novel is structured in chapters titled after each passing minute, running from 8.30 am through to 10.29 am.[11] Thus the novel begins sixteen minutes before the first attack and ends one minute after the collapse of the North Tower.

2) These chapters alternate (with six exceptions) between two narrators:

   a) Beigbeder himself writes from the perspective of living in Paris one year after the attacks. In a series of essays that combine autobiography, philosophy, cultural critique, satire, protest and personal observation. Beigbeder (a TV celebrity in France)[12] writes, one year after the attacks, about the difficulties in writing about 9/11. He also argues that he is, as it were, obligated to write about the subject and continues to probe his own personal life, the aftermath of the May '68 protests, the cultural/political/social sphere of the 1970s, the connections between America and France, art and other artists and intellectuals.[13]

   b) The self-consciously fictional character Carthew Yorston who, with his two young sons David and Jerry, is in the 'Windows on the World' restaurant when American Airlines Flight 11 slams into the North Tower. Carthew describes their attempts to escape the burning tower whilst also reflecting on his relationship with a lingerie model, Candace (who Beigbeder, when in New York, tries to pick up: one of many links between the fictional and non-fictional parts), the plight of his sons, memories of his life and his American heritage.

3) Beigbeder utilises photographs, apparently authentic addresses and phone numbers, lists and references to his own public and private life further to authenticate his chapters. He also uses a number of other typographical innovations such as a pastiche of an immigration questionnaire, a self-accusatory list in the style of Zola's 'J'accuse', apparent edited sections and a penultimate chapter where the sentences are shaped to resemble the Twin Towers (the time 10:28 used vertically to recall the North Tower's distinctive antenna).

We can see from this overview of the structure and basic components of the novel that Beigbeder takes great aesthetic and ethical risks. The author consistently acknowledges these risks – indeed he cleverly (some might say disingenuously) anticipates any accusations of self-indulgence, cynicism, narcissism, trivialisation, bad taste or exploitation by readily raising these issues himself. In doing so, Beigbeder offers a self-contained, self-reflexive defence by pre-empting a reader's reservations. The book begins, 'You know how it ends: everybody dies' (WW: p. 1), thus acknowledging that there will be no redemptive narrative arc. And similarly, at the end of the novel, Beigbeder declares that 'in leaning on the first hyperrealist attack, my prose takes on a power which it would not otherwise have. This novel uses tragedy as a crutch' (WW: p. 301). He also writes that 'this thing happened, and it is impossible to relate' (WW: p. 9) and emphasises the fact that 'even if I go deep, deep into the horror, my book will always remain 1,350 feet below the earth' (WW: p. 124). Through these comments, therefore, *Windows on the World* provides its own meta-commentary, exposing its fictionality whilst also straining for verisimilitude. As Steven Metcalf puts it:

> Pick your favourite anti-French epithet, throw it at Frédéric Beigbeder, and chances are it will stick. Beigbeder is a moral dandy, a hipster nihilist, a publicity hound, a jerk, a self-impressed renegade and that most boring of all boring clichés, a celebrity intellectual bored by boring clichés.[14]

Beigbeder frames his fictional story – that risks sentimentality and even bad taste – by reminding the reader of his own obsessions, indulgences and failures. This makes the novel seem almost hermetically sealed and, thus, resistant to criticism.

The chapters written from Carthew's point of view are similarly self-conscious despite their 'meticulous realism'. As we have seen throughout this study, descriptions of events inside the towers have been rare – *Falling Man*'s last chapter is another exception. The vast majority of representations have resisted the urge to, as it were, 'go inside' the burning towers. This may well be due to certain factors: taste – the sense that peoples' experiences within the towers, whether victims who perished or people that survived, are sacrosanct and that fictionalising necessarily trivialises or misrepresents real traumatic experiences; impossibility – the sense in which these experiences are 'unimaginable' and therefore not available to language or the written word. In one sense this 'silence' respects those who died and those who narrowly escaped and honours their lives and their experiences through interviews and individual testimony. The role of the 'existential witness' has become increasingly important in the writing of history, arguably accelerated by the Holocaust and the subsequent war crimes trials in which many Nazis were convicted, in part, thanks to recorded witness testimony. This has also been true in the 9/11 aftermath where survivor testimony has been culturally and politically significant.[15] Indeed, witness and survivors' voices were utilised in the trial of Zacarias Moussaoui,[16] one of the 9/11 conspirators sentenced to life imprisonment in 2006.

In such a context, as Beigbeder is thoroughly aware, the potential problems of a novelist (and a French one) fictionalising experiences within the towers are many, varied and complex. He does acknowledge his reliance upon eyewitness accounts,[17] in particular the original article that was the basis for the subsequent full-length book *102 Minutes: The Untold Story of the Fight to Survive Inside the Twin Towers* (2005). Hence, on one level, the fictionalised account of Carthew and his sons is heavily indebted to actual historical record. It is important to note that Carthew is speaking 'from beyond the grave' – he likens himself to Lester Burnham, the central protagonist in Sam Mendes' *American Beauty* (1999) – and that he looks back at what he experienced with posthumous insight, sadness and even irony. The self-conscious, metafictional elements allow Beigbeder to produce a fictionalised character (who at times seems rather implausible) inhabiting a real-time historical moment. But, of course, this reality is always understood within the parentheses of fiction and Beigbeder's *roman à clef*. There are moments when the author and Carthew directly communicate with each other and both address the reader. Indeed, increasingly, sometimes it is hard to ascertain who is speaking; the two voices merge at times and share similar attitudes, insights and are even historically linked.[18]

Hence Carthew and Beigbeder share a sense of hindsight and context for the 'surprise' of the attacks. In the realist novels we have looked at, the sudden 'jolt' of the planes' arrival replicates the actual experience of the attacks themselves. But coupled with this self-consciousness – the novel's playful status as a self-reflexive fiction – are scenes of realism that are heavily dependent upon knowledge gained from witness/survivor testimony. Carthew phones his estranged wife; he and his sons attempt to escape down the stairwell but access has been cut off; he witnesses severely burned people and endures the intense heat, smoke and acrid stench; there is an increasing collective despair as the towers burn and the environment becomes intensely dangerous; Carthew witnesses people jumping from the towers. These descriptions come directly from actual witness reports and thus provide *Windows on the World* with another layer of verisimilitude along with Beigbeder's confessional, candid observations. He goes to great lengths to establish authenticity in his chapters that achieve a dual purpose: both to underline the essential fictionality of Carthew's sections whilst also emphasising that such experiences did occur.[19]

In this respect *Windows on the World* uses postmodern literary (and philosophical) techniques in order to emphasise the traumatic reality of the attacks. But, as some critics have argued, Beigbeder, despite appearances, finally ends up 'looking away' from the full horror of what happened inside the towers. The 'real' that Beigbeder describes within the WTC – so reliant is it upon extant testimony – suffers from an unexpected sentimentality and an equally surprising reticence. Josh Lacey writes: 'But if you are going to attempt to write the unwritable [sic], why give up at the vital moment?' He goes on: 'He [Beigbeder] has chosen to peer into the abyss, then closed his eyes.' So here the accusation is that Beigbeder, despite his extensive self-ironising, self-aggrandising, self-heroising commentary on the 'impossible', redundant and potentially insensitive task he has set himself, finally shies away from the full trauma of the victims' plight. As is familiar from the novel, and as has been shown so far, Beigbeder alerts the reader to this very fact. In the voice of Carthew, Beigbeder writes of 'tabloid television' (*WW*: p. 265) and its cowardice in refusing fully to report reality:

> What? This carnage of human flesh is disgusting? It is reality which is disgusting and refusing to look at it, more so. Why did you see no pictures of our dislocated legs and arms, or severed torsos, our spilled entrails? Why did the dead go unseen? It was not some ethical code of practice, it was self-censorship, maybe just censorship, period. (*WW*: p. 266)

He adds – although it is fairly plain that this is Beigbeder speaking: 'People should have the courage to look at us, just as we force ourselves to witness the images in *Nuit et Brouillard*' (WW: p. 266).[20]

Beigbeder deals most forcefully with the central issue that informs his novel – that of how it is possible to write about the attacks – as the chapters' minutes edge closer to the collapse of the North Tower. He writes:

> From here, we can penetrate the unspeakable, the inexpressible. Please excuse our misuse of the ellipses. I have cut out the awful descriptions. I have not done so out of propriety, nor out of respect for the victims because I believe that describing their slow agonies, their ordeal, is also a mark of respect. I cut them because, in my opinion, it is more appalling still to allow you to imagine what became of them. (WW: p. 276)

So here Beigbeder reveals that he is now retreating from his own convictions and that his decision not to include explicit descriptions is not so much ethical as dramatic: he wants the reader to imagine, or rather reimagine, what he has chosen to 'edit' out.[21] The ellipses that he refers to occur in subsequent chapters:

> The helicopters flew past is, watched us dying.
>   (Paragraph cut). (WW: p. 277)

> In Windows on the World, the customers were gassed, burned, and reduced to ash. To them, as to so many others, we owe a duty of memory.
>   (Page cut.) (WW: p. 278)

> [And after Carthew and Jerry have jumped]

> We three are the burning phoenix which will rise from its ashes. Phoenix isn't only in Arizona.
>   (Page cut.) (WW: p. 306)

In one crucial respect Beigbeder is unable to describe scenes inside 'Windows on the World' because there were no survivors from the 107th floor – hence the only remaining evidence can be culled from phone calls made from the restaurant. In a sense these apparent edits are merely one more literary trick – Beigbeder implies that he has written these sections and actively cut them from the main body of the text. Arguably the more likely scenario is that these 'censored' scenes are used to indicate the 'unspeakable' reality that Beigbeder has been self-consciously acknowledging throughout the novel: 'This thing happened, and it is impossible to relate' (WW: p. 9).

In the chapter '10:24' Beigbeder writes:

I truly don't know why I wrote this book. Perhaps because I couldn't see the point about speaking of anything else. What else is there to write? The only interesting subjects are those which are taboo. We must write what is forbidden. French literature is a long history of disobedience. Nowadays, books must go where television does not. Show the invisible, speak the unspeakable. It may be impossible, but that is its *raison d'être*. Literature is a 'mission impossible'. (*WW*: p. 301)

In a novel filled with paradoxes this is perhaps the most fundamental one – Beigbeder is a confirmed ironist. The novelist's urge is to 'speak the unspeakable' and deliberately to confront taboos whilst on the other hand recognising the 'impossibility' of doing so. This is a factor that defines the literary and journalistic texts that we have looked at in this study – these are concentrated around the ability of writers to represent the 'spectacular' visuality of the attacks through language. This can perhaps be succinctly understood through common phrases of disbelief associated with 9/11: 'I couldn't believe my eyes'; 'Words fail me'; 'I can't put into words what I saw'; 'It was beyond words', etc. There is then a profound feeling that 9/11 – or more precisely the synecdoche of the film footage of the WTC attacks – stands for itself, as a 'documentary' of the attacks, as news footage, that 9/11, so to speak, *is* the image and vice versa. If so, of course, the need or impulse to redescribe – either in language or image or a combination of the two – is a definitive problem, one might even say crisis. Beigbeder's novel is self-reflexively aware of this crisis and he all but admits that he too has failed (whilst valorising his own failure).

Frank Furedi alludes to the crisis in *Invitation to Terror: The Expanding Empire of the Unknown* (2007). He writes that 'we lack the conceptual tools with which to grasp the new, unprecedented and complex dimensions of an elusive phenomenon [terrorism]'.[22] He quotes Ulrich Beck who has described 9/11 as standing for 'complete collapse of language'[23] and goes on to argue:

If indeed we lack a language to interpret contemporary reality, it has consequences that go way beyond linguistic difficulties. Language is the most important source of symbolic meaning in everyday life. And if we are genuinely lost for words it has serious implications for our ability to interpret experience as a society.[24]

The implication of these thoughts is that the catastrophe of 9/11 and its subsequent global impact have contributed to surpassing contemporary language by the rapidity and unexpectedness of its traumatising images. It is useful to evoke the metaphor employed by Sidra DeKoven Ezrahi who, following Lyotard, wrote of the Holocaust as an earthquake. As

Ernst Van Alphen clarifies: 'Auschwitz, writes Ezrahi, has become a met-aphor of the earthquake that destroyed not only people and buildings, but also the "measure" through which destruction can be gauged.'[25]

If we, for a moment, are able to substitute 'Auschwitz'[26] with '9/11' we can perhaps see the attacks as a similar kind of 'earthquake' that has resulted in Beck's 'complete collapse of language'. Hence, conventional language, or rather pre-9/11 language, is unable fully to describe the profound rupture that it represents. Van Alphen illuminates this point:

> The destruction of the ability to measure destruction results in Auschwitz's fundamental ambiguity as a historical site and event, as well as a symbol: forever caught in the ambiguity of its signifying force, Auschwitz can never be more than a symbol of what can no longer be symbolized. For we have lost the measure to decide of what Auschwitz is a symbol.[27]

In a sense, this is what Beigbeder's novel wrestles self-consciously with: that a new poetics, a 'literature of terror', has to be constructed in order to represent 9/11 because 9/11 has destroyed previous discourses that might have been used to speak about it. In a literary context this is a concern surrounding the linearity and narrative coherence of the realist novel as opposed to more postmodern tropes of fracture, hybridity, self-reflexivity, irony, pastiche and hyperrealism. If the attacks on the Trade Towers act as both 'historical site' and 'symbol' and if a new poetics is required to understand its 'signifying force', does *Windows on the World* contribute to this task? And also, given that Beigbeder is fully aware that the 'symbolism' of 9/11 remains ambiguous, what can be 'said' about the event that it has, as it were, not already 'said'?

The self-conscious, metafictional elements of the novel do perhaps suggest a way in which the enormity of 9/11 can be spoken about.[28] In some respects this strategy recalls the first journalistic reactions by McEwan, DeLillo and Amis that were looked at in the Introduction. The individual, localised, personal response to the 'symbolic' is matched with a broader appreciation of the historical significance of the attacks. Beigbeder does not hide his largely ambiguous motivations and shows himself in an often highly unflattering light but he does also show how the vast majority of people 'experienced' the attacks – through television images. In a sense the novel explores the highly mediated popular culture that dominates many lives – Carthew's sons regularly imagine/hope that they are in a film and that their father will reveal himself to be a super-hero (*WW*: pp. 138–9). Beigbeder is committed to American popular culture – at one point he lists his favourite American writers, musicians and film directors (*WW*: p. 17) – and suggests that the structure and form of *Windows on the World* is a fairly accurate representation of how an individual versed in the media and contemporary visual culture reacted to 9/11. In this respect the only way to apprehend the reality of the attacks is self-consciously to fictionalise characters who would plausibly have been in the towers on September 11 and constantly call attention to this artifice whilst, mostly, adhering to historical document.

As to what can be said about 9/11 that the event itself hasn't already signified, Beigbeder suggests that, even though he recognises his own failure at adding anything new to the sum of knowledge, the enormity of the 'spectacle' demands that it must be written about in some way or other. A particular scene in the novel can be used to tease out what Beigbeder is saying and how his blurring of fact and fiction corresponds with the real and the symbolic aspects of 9/11. Gradually Beigbeder moves physically closer to Ground Zero and as he does so there is a sense of gradual intermingling of the author and Carthew. At times it is hard straightaway to tell who is narrating. In the '9:35' chapter the narration is initially objective as the narrator observes Jeffrey, one of the people who is trapped, helping his colleagues traverse the restaurant, finding water from vases to douse napkins and tearing down curtains to wave from the broken windows. In the second paragraph (on the opposing pages each paragraph is a single block – denoting the towers) Jeffrey decides to jump. He grabs a curtain in the vain hope that it will help him to parachute to safety but the curtain catches light and Jeffrey plummets to his death – thus recalling perhaps one of the most taboo images from 9/11, that of people jumping/falling from the towers.

The point of view changes to Beigbeder when he writes:

> I would have liked to be able to say that he made it, but people would simply criticize me for the same reason they criticized Spielberg when he had water gush through the nozzles in the gas chambers.[29] Jeffrey didn't land gracefully on his toes. Within seconds his derisory piece of fabric became a torch. Jeffery literally exploded on the plaza, killing a fire-fighter and the woman he was rescuing. Jeffrey's wife got the news of his death from his boyfriend. She found out he was bisexual and that he was dead in the same instant. If I'd hoped to tell charming stories, I picked the wrong subject. (WW: p. 207)

In microcosm, this paragraph captures the essence of Beigbeder's poetics of 9/11 and suggests the ways in which *Windows on the World* gestures to new knowledge of the attacks (albeit knowledge of a decidedly problematic nature). Beigbeder highlights what is fiction and what is fact by clearly delineating them, but also deliberately blurs these distinctions as well. Jeffrey begins the paragraph as a fictional character; then he enters into the realm of the real – as one of the people who jumped or fell from the towers; and then he dies as a fictional character again and in the process signifies a cruel irony that is both apparently fictional[30] and yet also a familiar trope of 9/11 discourse (that of chance, serendipity and bleak irony). Beigbeder adds another intertextual layer when he alludes to Spielberg's *Schindler's List* (1993) and its controversial fictional tactics in relation to the representation of the gas chambers. This, as with many other areas of the novel, is disingenuous.

Beigbeder suggests that he isn't sanitising the truth as Spielberg has, in some quarters, been accused of doing. In the film, women have their hair cut and are sent to the showers – the film plays upon the audience's knowledge and the sequence is dramatically edited to eke out suspense. We are first taken into the showers with the other prisoners and then, as Michael Rothberg describes 'the door slams shut, the camera appears at a peep-hole, suggesting an entirely different identificatory position'.[31] Rothberg goes on:

> The camera then returns to the shower room and moves between a bird's-eye view and more subjective angles, as the music swells and the women are ultimately given a reprieve from death. The camera's movement inside/outside and above/within the scene of death indicates contrary desires to 'testify' within an impossible space and to distance the film from what has been judged socially unrepresentable.[32]

Beigbeder's sequence works along similar lines. The initial objectivity – these are scenes that Carthew is unable to witness – akin to an authorial omniscience, describes Jeffrey 'inside' the restaurant (the 'impossible space'). The figurative 'camera' (a not wholly inappropriate metaphor given the novel's attention to cinema and television) then 'cuts' to outside the tower to observe Jeffrey preparing for his 'jump'. His descent is then described from the perspective of those who watched on the ground and on TV as people fell to their deaths. The prose now is situated 'outside' Beigbeder's fictional space and enters into the discourse and history and reality before switching finally to the point of view of the author commenting on his own role in representing this sequence.

One can see how *Windows on the World* wrestles with the many problems that 9/11 presents to the fiction writer. But one can perhaps also begin to appreciate how Beigbeder fashions a hybrid form that is sufficiently open to self-questioning, irony, self-reflection and that possesses an awareness of its own limitations. Indeed, as has been implied, the fictional sections of the novel are arguably the least convincing and the most unsatisfying. But if such fiction ultimately 'fails' the novel is also aware of the reasons for such a failure. Beigbeder reaches the new restaurant opened by the 'Windows on the World' owner and starts a conversation with an employee. He speaks of his American descendants who were related to John Adams and Daniel Boone and of his American grandmother whose name, he asserts, was 'Grace Carthew Yorstoun' (*WW*: p. 304). Beigbeder then declares that his cousin died in the September 11 attacks. This, he reveals, is untrue:

> I don't know why I lied like that. I wanted to move him. Cowardice makes you a pathological liar. Carthew Yorstoun was my grandmother's family name. Take out the 'u' and you have Carthew Yorston, a fictional character. (*WW*: p. 305)

Here the fictional and documentary elements of the novel meet, as Beigbeder emphasises the extent to which he has throughout manipulated the reader and created a questionable verisimilitude. In one way it is as if Beigbeder is, as it were, confessing to the comparative flimsiness of his fictional creation in comparison with the magnitude of the real event. It also underlines how the novelist acknowledges the ultimate failure of his text fully to come to terms with the attacks.

In conclusion one is able to see how *Windows on the World* mixes non-fiction and fiction in order to produce a work that is consistently self-aware, reminding the reader at every step that Beigbeder is both author and (part) subject of the text. Anticipating criticism of certain artistic decisions and a number of potentially controversial statements, *Windows on the World* is structured in such a way that it can appear rather self-indulgent, glib, pretentious and, at times, surprisingly sentimental. These are all charges, of course, that Beigbeder acknowledges, and, to some degree, even embraces. But, as was previously discussed, a strictly realist novel such as *The Emperor's Children* can appear somewhat mendacious in its use of 9/11 as a convenient dramatic device to, as it were, 'wake up' the characters and by comparison Beigbeder, to his credit, admits to many of his failures, both artistic and moral, in representing the attacks. Indeed, the author's (in)ability to do this is arguably the central point of the novel. Its hybrid intermingling of various discourses – autobiography, essay, satire, fiction, etc. – allows for such a self-conscious analysis to take place. By adopting such tactics Beigbeder provides an implicit critique of realist fiction's suitability to re-present the attacks. It also allows him to say things about 9/11 that more 'respectful' texts avoid, an issue that is further explored in the following chapter's focus on Armitage's *Out of the Blue*.

Chapter 4

'A Wing and a Prayer': Simon Armitage, *Out of the Blue*

Simon Armitage's film-poem *Out of the Blue* was shown on Channel Five on the anniversary of 9/11 in 2006.[1] It has subsequently been published in 2008[2] alongside two more long poems dealing with the Allied Forces victory on 8 May 1945 and the Cambodian genocide. Armitage has written such poetry before, most notably in the 1000–line work *Killing Time* (1999) that was published to commemorate the Millennium. As has been seen throughout this study, 9/11 poses many complex problems for prose writers and it is instructive to look at how Armitage responds to the attacks in verse.[3] One of the central dilemmas for fiction writers has been how to accommodate the attacks into a fictional narrative. The enormity of the event – its traumatic incomprehensibility – potentially unsettles the 'flow' of a conventional linear realist narrative and as such the more conventional novels have arguably struggled to reconcile the reality of 9/11 within a fictional milieu. This chapter will explore Armitage's poem (with reference to the differences of the TV film) in light of these problematics and will analyse how the poem uses clichés, rhythm, metaphor and verse structure to evoke the attacks. How does *Out of the Blue* contribute to a 'literature of terror'?

The poem is written ostensibly from the point of view of an English futures trader who works in the North Tower of the WTC. It follows him from his journey to work and his thoughts as he surveys New York from the vantage point of his office window, then the planes attack and the narrator describes his predicament as the tower burns. In some respects this recalls *Windows on the World* in that it, rather unusually, goes inside the towers, positioning the reader as a victim/survivor in the 'real' time of the immediate aftermath of the attacks. The poem is comprised of thirteen sections and a coda that ends by declaring, 'everything changed. Nothing is safe' (*OB*: p. 33). On the one hand the poem situates itself within a familiar discourse of grief, sadness and fear – many

of the anthologies of 9/11 poetry are explicitly concerned with honouring the dead and paying respects to the 'tragedy'.[4] But, like Beigbeder,
Armitage risks accusations of tastelessness and exploitation by using a
fictionalised character and placing him within the reality of the attacks.
Windows on the World uses, perhaps partially defensively, a number
of self-reflexive and self-conscious literary devices to contextualise the
descriptions of traumatic events within a hyperreal narrative. How successful Beigbeder's strategy might be is a moot point but is it similarly
possible for a poem, no matter how self-consciously commemorative it
might be, to incorporate the shock of the attacks?

The poem's title is just one of many clichés that Armitage uses and
these surprisingly hackneyed phrases are a beginning point to elaborate
on how *Out of the Blue* negotiates these problems. Dotted throughout
are such examples as 'up with the lark' (*OB*: p. 10), 'a peach of a sun'
(*OB*: p. 12), 'hell lets loose' (*OB*: p. 15), 'a wing and a prayer' (*OB*:
p. 19), 'they'll wind back the film' (*OB*: p. 23), 'spinning a web' (*OB*:
p. 25) and 'loses heart . . . gives up the ghost . . . hell-for-leather' (*OB*:
p. 27). Armitage appears to be using these clichés – conventionally one
would assume that a poet would be striving to find new imagery to
write about such a well-known subject – to underline the fact that, for
him at least, everything has indeed changed, including much over-used
language. The poem attempts to ironise these clichés, showing how
they have been recharged with new significance after the attacks. The
title, for example, connotes the suddenness and unexpectedness of the
hijacked planes whilst also referring to the famously blue skies of the
morning of September 11: the planes came 'out of the blue (sky)'. On
the one hand, of course, these clichés help to make the poem potentially more accessible – Armitage has been referred to as the 'poet
laureate in waiting'[5] and his poetry is on the GCSE syllabus[6] – but
they also, damagingly, threaten to reduce the attacks to mere word
games.

There are times when Armitage's use of clichés comes perilously close
to facetious humour (despite the poem's overall mood of memorialising
sadness). In '7' Armitage attempts to mirror the rising panic of those
caught inside the towers with a long paragraph – its shape signifying a
tower – made up of severely truncated sentences:

Rescue services now on their way. What with? With what – with a magic
carpet? A thousand foot rope? Stand back from the door. They're saying its
war. Don't break the glass – don't fan the flames. Outside it's air. Outside it's
sheer. *A wing and a prayer* . . . It's daddy, ask mummy to come to the phone.
Call home. No way. Get out on the roof. Go north. Go up. *A wing and a
prayer.* Outside it's sheer. Outside it's air. (*OB*: p. 19; my italics)

Armitage's use of 'a wing and a prayer' is a useful indication as to how he – as with the use of 'out of the blue' – intends the phrase's meaning to be altered given the context of 9/11. *The Oxford Dictionary of Idioms* defines the phrase as meaning 'with only the slightest chance of success'[7] thus suggesting that the people inside the tower are mostly doomed to perish.[8] But Armitage also implies that it has taken on a different connotation in light of the attacks: the synecdoche 'wing' indicates the hijacked planes whilst the metonym 'prayer' alludes to the Islamist fervour of the hijackers. The improbable 'success' of their mission had a similar 'slightest chance' and hence with the use of a familiar and accessible idiom Armitage loads 'wing and a prayer' with added significance. Put another way, it is simply a rather weak pun: it conflates the hijacked planes and religion with the hopeless situation of the stranded office workers. The result attenuates the traumatic reality of the events into a cliché with the intention of reinvigorating it and reinvesting it with new meaning.

As we have seen, the writers under discussion in this study have consistently wrestled with the hegemony of signifiers that have arisen surrounding the representation of 9/11. These 'trigger words' are often comparatively neutral, even banal, but are loaded with added layers of meaning in relation to 9/11. Nouns such as 'smoke', 'dust', 'ash' have been utilised by writers in response to the iconographic images from the footage of the attacks as have 'falling', 'plane', 'fireman' and even 'tower'. Such words have accrued significance thanks in part to their repetition and ubiquity but also because of their signifying weight aided by the plethora of TV and amateur film. In this context, Armitage's poem adds two more signifiers – contained within a clichéd idiom – 'wing' and 'prayer', to the growing lexicon surrounding 9/11. Similarly, Armitage uses the familiar metaphor of 'spinning a web' to allude to the phone-lines stretching from the towers and connecting up family and friends. He refers to these lines as being like 'tightropes' (*OB*: p. 25), perhaps an allusion to Philippe Petit's famous walk between the Twin Towers and also as a symbol of the imagined life-lines that phone contact suggests which is ultimately, movingly, illusory given the individuals' inevitable demise.[9] Again, the poem asks the reader to re-examine a phrase perhaps overly familiar from poetry and to reinvest it with a changed significance.

Armitage continues this use of clichés when he writes in '11' – all of the sections are written as concrete poems, their shapes signifying the vertical lines of the two towers – 'The tower to the south / now loses heart, / now sieves itself through itself. / Just gives up the ghost' (*OB*: p. 27). By anthropomorphising the building Armitage is able to invest it with 'heart', signifying something that is alive and capable of 'giving in' to death. The biblical allusions in 'give up the ghost' are also suitably full of suggestive meaning. In *The Dictionary of Phrase and Fable* Brewer writes:

> The idea is that life is independent of the body, and is due to the habitation of the ghost or spirit in the material body. At death the ghost or spirit leaves this tabernacle of clay, and either returns to God or abides in the region of the spirits till the general resurrection. Thus in Ecc. Xxi. 7 it is said, 'Then shall the dust return to the earth as it was: and the spirit shall return unto God who gave it.'[10]

The South Tower, here imbued with a 'heart', is now a 'material body' that relinquishes its 'ghost' and dies. One can delve further and suggest that the 'spirit' of the tower is a metaphor of the people who die instantly when the building collapses – in perhaps an optimistic (even sentimental) trope that they will 'survive' and return to God whilst the tower crumbles into 'dust'. Armitage continues this motif in the same section when he writes of on-lookers fleeing the scene: 'And people . . . New Yorkers in spate, / a biblical tide flowing north, going safe . . .' (*OB*: p. 28).

Armitage actively uses clichés and common phrases in order to keep the poem accessible to a wide audience but also as a way of examining how such idioms can be reinvigorated by the events of 9/11. But, of course, they remain clichés and as such they carry with them connotations of being trite, hackneyed and over-familiar. Armitage himself has commented on his use of clichés and his defence of his use of them is quoted in Ian Sansom's 'Cliché!: The Poetry of Simon Armitage':

1. It's my voice: that's how I speak.
2. It allows me to get nearer, or associates me more clearly with the speaker in the monologues [he is speaking in 1991].
3. Most idioms of catchphrases are images of some type, and whilst I'm not exactly 'revitalising' them I am asking them to work a little harder, not just perform their common function, but introduce a second, sometimes literal or sometimes punning element.
4. They contain a good deal of music and rhythm which isn't disharmonious with the way I'm trying to construct poems.
5. I've said before that I don't hold with the view that cliché represents a bias against the truth, in terms of there being only one truth, or poetry owning the franchise on truth.[11]

Sansom writes that Armitage's use of clichés and everyday phrases is an example of a particular contemporary trend in poetry. He suggests that some of Armitage's early work 'excelled in the rewriting and the reinvention of idiom-clichés and hackneyed phrases'[12] but that this tendency has stymied his output in recent years. Indeed, Armitage often uses these phrases as a way of embracing provincial dialects and as such he associates himself with the quotidian. This aspect of his work arguably accounts for much of the poet's popularity and allows him to introduce humour and parody into his language. Sansom celebrates the 'natural exuberance' of these often witty allusions to the 'kaleidoscopic elements of everyday speech' but also suggests that they have quickly ossified into 'a laboured sincerity' that settles for 'the loud, the easy and the obvious'.[13]

Out of the Blue uses these phrases so that their 'common function' is challenged and altered in some way by the events of 9/11. The 'punning element', for example, of a reversed or partially altered cliché can be seen in '9' in which the arrival of the second plane is described. Indeed, this section is something of an exemplar of what Armitage has described as his approach to voice and speech patterns and his willingness to use clichés. The narrator is 'fighting for breath' (*OB*: p. 23) when United 175 flies into the South Tower: 'I sort of swayed, sort of thing, / sort of swooned, that fear / when something designed to be far / comes illogically near' (*OB*: p. 23). The use of the idiomatic 'sort of' connotes everyday speech and suggests a confluence between narrator and poet that Armitage describes as one of his primary intentions. The following line with its rhyming 'fear/near' contains a more recognisably 'poetic' insight – 'something designed to be far / comes illogically near' – implying the point of view of the poet himself. Armitage utilises cinematic/ photographic allusions - 'a snapshot only / frame by frame by frame' (*OB*: p. 23) to work towards the turning point of the poem: 'I actually thought there's got to be some mistake: / they'll wind back the film, / call back the plane, / they'll try this again. / The day will be fine, / put back as it was' (*OB*: p. 23). Rhythm aside, this is an unoriginal observation that has been used in many 9/11 texts that we have looked at in this study. But arguably, as Armitage seems to imply in his defence of 'everyday speech', this could reflect very accurately what many on-the-spot witnesses thought as they watched the attacks.

Conversely, this would seem to be an observation that people watching the events on TV considered rather than those actually in and around the towers. Hence it feels much more like Armitage's own reflection on seeing the events filmed and as such is merely a cliché, a rather tired comment that has been used so many times before that its over-familiarity deadens any sense of a useful addition to thinking about 9/11. The following lines exacerbate this: 'This time they'll steer! / Because lightning never strikes once, / let alone twice, / and no two planes just happened to veer / through mechanical fault / or human error, / one after the other' (*OB*: p. 24). The initial ironic exclamation – again signifying common speech patterns - is followed by an inversion of the common phrase 'lightning never strikes twice in the same place'. Here lightning is used as a metaphor of the likelihood of a plane crashing into a skyscraper once *or* twice and confirms the poet's belief that clichés can be used not only to 'perform their common function, but introduce a second literal, or punning element'. The poem relies upon the reader's prior familiarity with a much-used cliché and then upsets its 'common function' by setting it within the iconography of 9/11.

There is an intriguing problematic at play here that has critical implications not only for Armitage's poem but also for the 'Literature of Terror' as a whole. A question that has continually been asked in this study is that if the visual evidence of the footage of 9/11 – that has become a virtual synecdoche for the entire events of the day – then what more can a fictional text 'say' that hasn't already been 'said'? *Out of the Blue*'s determined use of common phrases suggests that in times of stress and trauma individuals and even communities fall back on clichés in order to make sense of what they are experiencing. The poet's avowed intention is to write as he himself speaks and in doing so he aligns himself with the 'ordinary individual', in this case an English futures trader[14] who has a family and is 'humanised' by mementos of his past and the reality of his powerlessness. A case can be made then that Armitage argues that the formerly familiar, even comforting meaning behind such banal, everyday utterances has been 'turned upside down' by the attacks. The poem ends – 'Everything changed. Nothing is safe' (*OB*: p. 33) – and it is tempting to suggest that this despairing conclusion includes clichés that held within them truths that have now, after 9/11, been irrevocably subverted. Their 'safety' – what Samson refers to as their 'folk wisdom'[15] – and their sense of tradition has been destroyed and by interspersing the text with them *Out of the Blue* enacts their changed status. But a wider problem emerges when one considers the idea that this insight is itself a cliché – the oft-repeated discourse that 9/11 has 'changed everything'. In other words Armitage's clichés confirm a particular set of hegemonic ideological assumptions: the social, political and cultural centrality of 9/11, its iconic power, its long-lasting sense of trauma, surprise and shock, its status as historical beginning point/end point.

In an essay on the *Collected Poems* of John Ashbery, Dan Chiasson writes:

> In a famous exchange with the poet Ann Lauterbach, Lauterbach exclaimed, 'Oh, Mr Ashbery, I love clichés,' to which Ashbery replied, 'And they love

you.' Clichés and stereotypes are Ashbery's expressive unit . . . Cliché is language that has been repeated so often it becomes infinitely repeatable. It 'loves us' because it is inevitable; we 'love it' as a way of mastering, by ingenious bricolage, the language that saturates us anyway.[16]

Thus, one reading of *Out of the Blue* is that Armitage seeks to represent 9/11 as a challenge to the 'mastering' technique of using clichés. Its infinite repeatability is both adhered to – Armitage values the new truths that these phrases may still contain – and challenged – will the phrase 'wing and a prayer' now only make people think of 9/11? This reading supports the poem's 'bricolage' of common speech and poetic imagery as a way of articulating the confusion and fear as the attacks occurred. A revealing example of this effect can be found in the poem's coda that is written in 2006 from the poet's perspective: 'what peace can be said to be water-tight' (*OB*: p. 33). This is one clause from a stanza-length sentence asking whether anything – from a 'false alarm' to a 'structure', a 'case or bag' to a 'column' and a 'floor' (*OB*: p. 33) – can be trusted as it was before the attacks. Initially the use of a metaphoric 'water-tight' peace seems like a rather banal, journalistic phrase. But in context of this, as it were, 'revitalising' of the cliché within poetry, in light of Chiasson's analysis of Ashbery's and Sansom's denunciation of Armitage's over-reliance on everyday phrases, the poem suggests that the phrase itself 'water-tight' is no longer reliable given the enormity of the attacks.

But even given this – and it is a moot point whether Armitage's clichés can be so neatly reclaimed as original insights into post-9/11 language – there are moments when, to echo Sansom, the poem merely seems to rely, perhaps rather lazily, on clichéd images. In section '13', for example, the narrator posthumously describes the day after the attacks – again recalling *Windows on the World* – before the poet's authorial voice, as it were, 'steps in' and declares: 'Five years on, nothing in place: / the hole in the ground / still an open wound, / the gaps in the sky still empty space, / the scene of the crime still largely the same . . . / but everything changed' (*OB*: p. 32). The use of 'open wound' alludes to the personification of the towers, a motif throughout the poem, but also signifies the 'wounded' state of the nation. Likewise 'scene of the crime' reminds the reader that Ground Zero, whilst symbolising the attacks and the space left by the fallen towers also underlines the fact that a 'crime' has taken place. But rather than reading these clichés as having been revitalised by their context one can argue that instead they merely reiterate trite observations. The 'wounded' and 'criminal' aspects of 9/11 have been well documented and Armitage seems content simply to repeat them in order to evoke pathos. Little or nothing newly insightful has been created.

Why continue to resort to phrases and images that have been largely dulled by repetition? This may be partly explained by Armitage's admission that he himself speaks in this way and by implication that there is an honesty and sincerity inherent in using everyday, familiar language. Conversely, though, one can argue that by embracing such commonplace language the poem risks reducing the enormity and massive suffering of the attacks to platitudes and clichés. Rather than 9/11 revitalising these overly familiar phrases instead there is perhaps a prevailing sense that the poet inadvertently concedes that there is little or nothing new that one can say that the events themselves haven't already demonstrated. Throughout the study it has been shown that writers have struggled with the representation of 9/11, in particular within the conventions of realist fiction. The combination of trauma, taboo and historical significance put a certain ethical and aesthetic pressure on fiction that in many cases remains unresolved. *Out of the Blue*, whilst original in its structure and in some of its imagery, attempts to use clichés in order to comment on the fundamentally changed world post-9/11. This undoubtedly adds to the poem's accessibility (and perhaps popularity) but it also relies upon already existing responses and attitudes that have found themselves articulated in the wider culture. Hence the poem 'works', in part, because its message – 9/11 was a tragedy – is already a dominant, if not *the* dominant, discourse and the language used to express this is often clichéd.

An intriguing answer to these issues can be found in the Channel 5 film of Armitage's poem, performed by Rufus Sewell. With its mix of intimate close-up monologues, dramatic music, 9/11 footage, slow-motion, montage and recordings of telephone calls from the towers, *Out of the Blue* provides a vastly different experience from that of the published poem. Indeed, the film makes much more emotional sense than the poem but also highlights the dilemma of representation that the poem simply cannot come to terms with on the page. It seems self-evident to state that the film benefits from using real footage from the WTC attacks but this fact is at the heart of the poem's central dilemma – how to describe these attacks in verse. But what becomes much clearer in the film is that the poem – through the character played by Sewell – is commenting more on the footage of the WTC attacks themselves than, as seems more the case in the printed text, actively attempting realistically to 'go inside' the towers. It is clearer as well that Sewell is speaking (direct to the camera) posthumously. This gives the film a more marked elegiac tone and emphasises the complex temporality of the poem that again is less convincing on the page. Increasingly, and tellingly, the film relies heavily on the use of real footage of the attacks, particularly in the second half when the viewer is presented with the iconic images whilst the voice-over, read with the actor's skills of vocal modulation, pace and intonation, comments on the pictures rather, as is the case with the printed poem, than appearing to dramatise the attacks in verse. In this instance the use of clichés also feels much less problematic.

Armitage has been quoted as saying of his intentions for the film-poem: ' "For this new poem I was interested much more in bereavement [than political comment] . . . I also wanted it to reflect what was happening that day inside the towers. To give those inside a voice." '[17] But what emerges as the primary difference between the printed poem and the film is that it is apparent that the use of 9/11 images is crucial in providing a power and a context for the perspective of the poem that the text singularly lacks. And this fact underlines the central dilemma for writers in their often self-conscious suspicion (or dawning recognition) that their words are insubstantial in comparison with the spectacle of the filmed footage. As we have seen with Armitage's printed poem, there is a persistent sense that the poem's message – explicitly 'bereavement' and in particular empathy with the sixty-seven British people who died in the Towers – and its use of clichéd everyday phrases, remain incommensurate with the enormity and complexity of the attacks. The film is much more successful at commenting upon the footage – the language does not attempt to re-present the attacks but rather more successfully complements the montage of images, adding poignancy to scenes that have entered the historical consciousness of global culture.

The film gradually merges voice and image together and it is this hybridity – its provocative mixture of poetic monologue and real footage – that both highlights the film's achievements and conversely the printed poem's shortcomings. Indeed, it is in this correspondence between Armitage's words and footage of the hijacked planes' attacks, the burning towers and their subsequent collapse that *Out of the Blue*, perhaps unconsciously, acknowledges the implicit hierarchy of the visual image and the spoken word. This is more than a case of privileging the film simply because of its added immediacy and emotional charge. *Out of the Blue* carefully acknowledges the primacy of the footage and at certain moments precisely marries poetic image with real film, in effect acknowledging that the poem, without the intrinsic power of the visual, cannot withstand the imprinted memory of the filmed attacks. Indeed, in a sense, the poem is indivisible from its direct correlation with the attacks and as such the visceral power of the footage, rather than being potentially lessened by the use of clichés and the poem's arguably rather banal reflections on the importance of the attacks, is reinvigorated by the defamiliarising use of poetry rather than the familiar soundtrack of either a reporter's commentary or voices from witnesses and survivors. The ways in which the film acknowledges this relationship between poem and image are instructive and revealing about the broader dilemmas in 9/11 representation that are seen throughout this study.

Initially the film has a rather loose, non-literal, relationship between word and image. Section '2', beginning with 'Up with the lark, downtown New York' is matched with generic footage of busy crowded Manhattan streets and Sewell's trader making his way up to his office.[18] When he mentions the objects on his desk – 'here is a rock from Brighton beach, / here is a beer-mat, here is the leaf' – rather than cutting to actual images of them, the camera remains on Sewell's face. This technique is also used when Sewell recites what his colleagues are doing around him in the ensuing chaos after the first plane has hit and in '7' in the narrator's panicked monologue that includes the aforementioned 'a wing and a prayer'. But by contrast, when the second plane attacks the film turns to the actual footage and by doing so the directly matched poetry achieves a far more nuanced power: as the plane crashes into the South Tower Sewell reads, 'that fear / when something designed to be far / comes illogically near'.

So, in effect, the film 'saves' the poem and lends it a gravitas that it so singularly lacks on the pages. But it also underlines, of course, the central dilemma for imaginative writers when confronted with the enormous visual symbolism of the attacks. *Out of the Blue*'s use of a skilled actor reading the poem aloud mixed with visual imagery evoking the attacks – along with real footage – creates an often extremely persuasive representation of 9/11. As will be seen in the next chapter concerning the book and the film of *Man on Wire*, the use of visual imagery is often able to 'deal' with the attacks in a way that literature struggles to achieve. But as has already been noted, it is this struggle that the 'Literature of Terror' consistently addresses. If the printed poem *Out of the Blue* finally fails to develop its tropes, motifs and metaphors beyond the realms of memorialisation and cliché, the film/poem seems in part to be a tacit acknowledgement of the need to supplement the written word with the more immediate impact of visual images. And, as such, the hybrid, and rather unusual, film/poem provides an intriguing text with which to discuss the 'presence' of 9/11 in representations.

Chapter 5

'A Certain Blurring of the Facts': *Man on Wire* and 9/11

At first it might seem strange to include a chapter on a film that does not mention the attacks on 9/11 once. But James Marsh's *Man on Wire* (2008), a documentary detailing the audacious cable-walk between the two towers of a 24–year-old Frenchman Philippe Petit in 1974, is 'about' 9/11 in many intriguing and subtle ways.[1] Indeed, it is the very absence of the attacks in the film that allows the audience to contemplate the 'presence' of the towers as Petit finally succeeds in his spectacular 'crime/work of art'. As Bryan Appleyard writes:

> A mood of anticipatory sadness and nostalgia for a pre-9/11 world suffuses the film. We see the towers being built, the construction mess foreshadowing the wreckage after the planes hit. Most important of all, we see the wonder and joy of the New Yorkers as they stare up at Petit on his wire. He made these office blocks, in spite of their architecture, beautiful – and now they are gone.[2]

In this respect the film can be seen as a redemptive narrative that deliberately avoids mention of 9/11 and instead seeks to, as it were, 'rebuild' the towers and encourage the audience to contemplate Petit's remarkable feats rather than the terrorist attacks. It is because of this that Appleyard suggests that *Man on Wire* may have succeeded in its engagement with 9/11 where others have failed.

Appleyard goes on to suggest that *Man on Wire* improves upon previous 9/11 representations because the film 'says nothing and, as a result, says a very great deal'.[3] This is precisely because 9/11 'doesn't happen'.[4] Appleyard argues that 'art and 9/11 have been locked in a passionate embrace' and it is this tension – between the 'spectacle' of the attacks and their subsequent aesthetic re-presentation – that defines all such efforts to dramatise the events. Appleyard contends that it is still too soon for artists successfully to 'capture the experience' and that in fact 'perhaps the best answer is to say nothing'.[5] He suggests that 9/11 art, rather than being explicit and realist, needs 'a certain blurring of the facts' and cites Francis Coppola's *Apocalypse Now* (1979) as an example of a text that 'said something about that war [Vietnam] that was both true and unsayable in any other way'.[6] Appleyard further suggests that artists' proximity to the events means that they cannot successfully focus, indeed he uses ocular metaphors to make his point: 'When blinded by a bright light, you need to half close your eyes to see what is really going on – and, as yet, we can't quite do that with the burning towers.'[7] Given the fact that *Man on Wire* does not look, as it were, at 9/11 at all it is intriguing to explicate the ways in which it 'says nothing' and yet 'says a very great deal' about the attacks.

The 'passionate embrace' that Appleyard evokes is the tension between the spectacular visual symbolism of 9/11 and the urge to re-present it in art. This question has been crucial throughout the present study and, perhaps surprisingly, *Man on Wire* offers a possible solution to this tension. The film never alludes to 9/11 directly but the event is implicitly, even conspicuously, 'in' its narrative by the presence and solidity of the towers. It is perhaps useful to see the film – again leaving the audience to make the connections themselves – as a 'reversal' of 9/11, almost akin to Amis' *Time's Arrow* (1991), Christopher Nolan's *Memento* (2000) and the photographic montage at the end of Safran Foer's *Extremely Loud and Incredibly Close*. Rather than replaying the footage of the attacks – that, as we have seen, is an act of virtually reliving the trauma over (and over) again – *Man on Wire* emphasises the construction, 'permanence' and completion of the towers and by doing so encourages the audience consistently to contemplate their absence.

The film celebrates, as it were, the solidity (and architectural ambition, even beauty) of the WTC as does Petit's walk. It also draws attention to the space between them – Petit refers to it as the 'void' – a space that, of course, no longer exists. In documentary footage we see the towers being constructed (they were designed by Minoru Yamasaki and work was officially begun in 1966)[8] and at one point one tower is significantly taller than the other, again recalling their destruction in 2001. Once more one is able to think of these aspects of the films as *Man on Wire*'s tactic of 'reversal'. Indeed, the temporal scheme of the film is complex and underlines its relationship with 9/11, which remains unspoken. A working plan may help in this analysis:

1. 'Now': Contemporary interviews with the main protagonists.
2. 'Then': The actual day of the walk – 7 August, 1974.[9] This is dramatised through a combination of reconstruction (that self-consciously
   is shot in the style of a heist thriller), home movie footage, still

photography, news montage and the testimony of witnesses and colleagues.

3. 'Before': The time before the walk – reaching back to when Petit first saw a picture of the towers (as they were being built), his days as a circus and street performer and the long months of planning and preparation.

4. 'After': This is the comparatively brief aftermath of the walk that combines Petit's ecstasy of success with his friends' dual sense of awe, and at times, palpable sadness.

These time frames are interwoven throughout the film and build towards the climax of Petit's successful walk between the towers. And it is this mood of celebration and youthful exuberance in *Man on Wire* that most separates it from other texts under scrutiny in this study.

The aspects of Petit's extraordinary achievement that the film celebrates are also reversals of 9/11 tropes:

1. Petit's walk itself – its intrinsic beauty and audacity, the bravery required and also a sense of 'innocence' about the entire enterprise.

2. The Towers, and by implication their absence. Added to this is the knowledge that Petit is now unable to replicate his walk. Other parts of the film contribute to this: photographs taken by Petit's colleagues of offices, corridors and stair-wells, all of which are empty, uncannily foreshadowing the thousands of people who would later work there and also images of crowds escaping the burning towers;[10] photographs of Petit scouting for the best vantage points on top of the South Tower; one eerie photograph taken from the ground looking up at Petit walking across the rope with a plane flying above him; labourers who worked on the towers for years giving interviews to Petit's team – masquerading as journalists – assuring them of the buildings' permanence and strength.

3. More tangentially the film and memoir are a celebration of, or even a lament for, an 'innocence' associated with 1960s' idealism. Petit's original plan begins as a dream or vision and it is developed in an improvisational and ad hoc manner. The construction of the towers is similarly seen as an example of visionary ambition.

Hence, the film resonates with the knowledge that all of this is over because of the attacks. Thus it is both celebration and nostalgic lament[11] but, crucially, despite implicitly mourning the destruction of the towers, *Man on Wire* fulfils Appleyard's theory that 9/11 representations should, so to speak, 'half close their eyes'. A more speculative but perhaps more accurate description would be to suggest that the film is 'haunted' by 9/11, haunted in the sense of being 'persistently and disturbingly present'.[12] There are other examples of this throughout the film and Petit's memoir and they further suggest the ways in which 9/11 is subtly foreshadowed.

A black shape is seen by the gathering crowd below and for a few brief moments, as Petit begins his walk, there are immediate fears that it is Petit's falling body (he was dressed in black for the event so as to be more noticeable against the sky). It quickly transpires that this is in fact a floating black shirt but the connection with 9/11's falling bodies is apparent, again without any explicit commentary. Petit's highly important first step (both symbolically and for his safety) onto the wire encourages the audience to contemplate the vast height that Petit is precariously about to traverse and the other 'first steps' that people were forced (or chose) to take to escape the suffocating smoke. The plan itself, filmed in the dramatic reconstructions in the manner of a heist thriller, hint at the 'other' plan of Islamist terrorists who plotted for many years.[13] Indeed, the audience is consistently reminded that Petit and his team of helpers are committing a 'crime' and that all along what they have planned is illegal. The, at times, almost comically lax security in the towers that Petit and his enthusiastic amateurs find relatively easy to circumvent and subvert reminds the audience of the terrorists as well. Security has been one of the most dominant discourses in the 9/11 aftermath, mostly focused around perceived failures in procedure, communication and speed of response by the authorities.[14] Petit's ability to circumvent the WTC security systems implicitly alludes to the terrorists' success in avoiding detection and their relatively modest tools. As Petit points out, his 'crime' was 'beautiful' and 'benign' in stark contrast to the destructive and violent crime committed by the terrorists.

It is important now to connect these comparisons – the ways in which *Man on Wire* reverses the terrorist attacks – by discussing one of the most controversial and potentially divisive areas of 9/11 discourse: namely, the theories surrounding the attacks as 'spectacle' and even 'art'. This provocative and apparently insensitive, for some morally bankrupt, view has been voiced by a number of individuals and despite its initial premise seemingly espoused simply to shock there are valuable insights within the idea that require further analysis. On 16 September 2001, the German composer Karl Heinz Stockhausen, whilst being interviewed in Hamburg before a festival of his work was quoted as saying that 9/11 was 'the greatest work of art that is possible in the whole cosmos'.[15] Stockhausen was widely lambasted for these comments – that he claims were taken out of context and therefore misunderstood

– and his subsequent career suffered as a result (he died in 2007). But in these, perhaps off-hand, comments there are the beginnings of a way of interpreting the visual spectacle of the attacks in terms of the 'artistic'. The English artist Damien Hirst contributed to the controversy when he asserted that the 'thing about 9/11 is that it's kind of an artwork in its own right. It was wicked, but it was devised in this way for this kind of impact. It was devised visually.'[16] He goes on to argue:

> You've got to hand it to them on some level because they've achieved something which nobody would have ever have thought possible, especially to a country as big as America.
>   I think our visual language has been changed by what happened on September 11: an aeroplane becomes a weapon - and if they fly close to buildings people start panicking. Our visual language is constantly changing in this way and I think as an artist you're constantly on the lookout for things like that.[17]

Again, of course, one must perhaps take these comments as another of Hirst's deliberately provocative comments – many contained within his artistic output. But as with Stockhausen – and implicitly in Petit's memoir and James Marsh's film – one senses that an important issue is being raised and perhaps misunderstood in a culture still dominated by a mood of mythologising, honouring and even sacralising 9/11. As has been seen, the majority of 9/11 art has sought to commemorate the event and has mostly avoided explicit representations or the more controversial aspects that potentially threaten to destabilise hegemonic discourses. An emblematic example of this social, cultural and artistic urge is Oliver Stone's *World Trade Center* (2006). The film is suffused with sentimentality, quasi-mystic imagery and surprisingly aggressive masculinist/military politics. The film's hermetic narrative presents an overly sanitised and maudlin view of the attacks and ends seemingly justifying the invasion of Iraq. As Peter Bradshaw argues:

> There are some films so awful, of such insidious dishonesty and mediocrity, that their existence is a kind of scandal . . . Stone never puts a foot right. He uses lumberingly misjudged state-funeral camerawork and elegiac music actually before, and during, the horrific attack itself, smothering its dramatic impact in a hundredweight of scented cotton wool.[18]

So Stone's film fails in its two crucial functions: as an earnest dedication to the bravery and dedication of those who attempted to help others in the attacks; and as an entertaining, mainstream action-adventure movie. Indeed, the generic conventions and expectations – a disaster/rescue narrative with a suitably redemptive ending – reduce the real-life characters and their situations to cliché and stereotype, thus, paradoxically, cheapening the apparent urge to offer a celebration of the NYPD and other services that lost individuals in the attacks.

To return to Stockhausen's and Hirst's provocative statements about the 'art' of 9/11, and keeping in mind the counter-spectacle of Petit's walk, one can argue that Stone's aesthetic decisions actively dehistoricise, mythologise and even distort the reality of the attacks. So committed is the film to honouring the lives of these characters[19] that it risks demeaning their travails by fixing their experiences within a risible and mawkish narrative. If *Man on Wire* 'says nothing' explicitly about 9/11 but, because of its symbolic reversals, starts to 'say a lot' then *World Trade Center*, despite being explicitly concerned with a real historical story, 'says very little' that is new, profound or adds knowledge to the poetics and politics of 9/11 discourse. There are a vast number of groups, institutions and organisations that act as resources and disseminators of information for victims and survivors' families and for those who wish to be included in commemoration. But if art is to continue to wrestle with the implications and meanings of 9/11 perhaps one must look beyond already familiar discourses of tragedy, mourning and redemption and acknowledge less conventional representations. This is certainly true of the complex reversals evident within *Man on Wire* but other future fictions might engage in political, aesthetic and ethical ideas that include misanthropy, anger, disgust and ambivalence in relation to 9/11. *Windows on the World* alluded to some of these responses – as do, say, *The Mercy Seat* and Kalfus' *A Disorder Peculiar to the Country* (2006) – but an important article by Daniel Cottom suggests other provocative ways in which 9/11 might be spoken about.

Cottom's essay 'To Love to Hate' (2002)[20] examines the work of artist Chris Burden and, after contextualising Burden's oeuvre, relates it to the events of 9/11. Burden's 'misanthropic' provocations include shooting at a recently departed airliner in Los Angeles (he was judged to have been out of firing distance so avoided prosecution), a 'mock monument' listing the names of dead Vietnamese immediately in front of the Washington War Memorial, and having a bullet shot into his own arm (he was ordered to see a psychiatrist). Cottom historicises these and other 'works' within an artistic and philosophical tradition of misanthropy. He identifies this as an important, if undervalued, theme in the history of Western art. He describes the 'terrific suggestiveness' (LH: p. 119) of Burden's '747'[21] and goes on to argue that Burden is a 'reckless immoralist so devoted to aesthetic sensations ... that he is heedless of the human consequences of his pursuits' (LH: p. 119). Cottom sets Burden's provocation (it is immortalised in a black and white photograph) within traditions of Dadaist *épater les bourgeois* acts, Beckett's mordant vision and Adorno's suggestion of Baudelaire's 'protest against morality' (LH: p. 122). Rather than art being valued as a medium enforcing and implicitly celebrating humanity and human values (that the art is beautiful, that it has intrinsic 'worth', that an audience benefits from engaging with it morally and aesthetically), Burden, Cottom suggests, reflects a more cynical, misanthropic and potentially destructive poetics that has its eclectic antecedents which include Swift, Molière, Dorothy Parker and Schiller.

Cottom writes of Burden's extreme, excessive misanthropy:

> [His] performance leads us to see the constitutive misanthropy at work in the very conception of art: its appeal to the realm of the *unhuman* [sic], which includes not only the domains of brute material events and of cultural representations but also of identifications with things such as leaders, gods, consumer goods, *planes, skyscrapers, and movies*. (LH: p. 123; my italics)

One senses the anticipatory echoes of 9/11 here, a fact that is underlined when Cottom evokes the work of Dread Scott whose installation 'Enduring Freedom' (2002) offered an alternative symbol of mourning in light of the attacks, recalling the names of Afghanis who have suffered in the subsequent war.[22] It is Cottom's use of the word 'unhuman' that is perhaps most crucial here, the sense that as Burden fired his pistol at the plane overhead he 'was like those uncanny things-in-the-act-of-becoming-art that are no longer objects, exactly, as they appear to their makers or audiences' (LH: p. 122). The most extraordinary example of this would, Cottom suggests, 'involve bystanders watching symbols being attacked and, as thousands die, imagining they are watching a movie' (LH: p. 122). One can infer from Cottom's allusions that he is working towards a way of responding to Burden's 'unhuman' art through the symbolism of 9/11. Furthermore, the terrorists themselves may well have planned and executed the attacks with commensurate 'unhuman' designs, foreseeing the 'spectacle' of the hijacked planes slamming into skyscrapers as a kind of destructive 'art', utterly indifferent to the inevitable loss of life, blinded, as it were, by the catastrophic symbolism.

Cottom contemplates the ways in which Burden's '747' does not adhere to conventional definitions of art:

1. No audience – or rather no prepared audience (it is unclear as to who took the photograph but it is attributed to Burden himself).
2. No curtains or music to signify a beginning or an end.
3. No object was produced to display in a gallery – save the photograph (and Burden's personal testimony).

4. If the act were 'successful' there would have been a terrible catastrophe for which Burden would have been solely responsible (LH: p. 123).

In other words the 'art' of Burden's act – it is, certainly on one level, intended as such – demands that one must establish a new aesthetic and ethical vocabulary with which to describe it. Burden's real act was not 'watched' or observed conventionally and, it can be inferred, is more important than any subsequent representation. Evidently, as with much of Burden's work, it cannot and was never designed to be repeated. It stands alone, a perverse, potentially dangerous, morally questionable but also, arguably, compellingly transgressive act that evokes – or re-enacts – terrorism.[23] In some ways Burden appears to be responding to other acts of real terrorism that were prevalent in the late 1960s and 1970s – it thus becomes a Baudrillardian simulacrum of a terrorist 'spectacle'. As Cottom goes on to argue, this aspect of Burden's misanthropic, nihilistic act uncannily anticipates the 9/11 attacks – or, more specifically, the footage of the WTC attacks and their aftermath.

Cottom writes of 9/11 resembling a movie but one that offered no 'comfort' and whose real deaths were less about 'strategic' reasons than 'symbolic' reasons (LH: p. 133). Here it is possible to start to interpret 9/11 as a shocking challenge and a major disruption of the 'flow' of mediated images. In the 'society of the spectacle', where disturbing images are quickly and consistently accommodated into the crowded sequences of mediated reality, both the artist and the terrorist are confronted with the central problem of how their 'art' or 'act' can, however briefly, grab an audience's attention. Within this framework we can thus set the three spectacles upon a continuum:

1. The 'spectacle' of Petit's walk between the towers is an 'artwork' that celebrates human ingenuity and imaginative/physical daring whilst also celebrating the solidity and structural aesthetics of the WTC Towers. His successful feat inspires awe and a sense of the unimaginable.
2. At the other end of the spectrum is the 'spectacle' of the hijacked planes slamming into the Two Towers. The terrorists' symbolic inversions of passenger planes and skyscrapers instigate fear and awe and are similarly witnessed within the realm of the unimaginable.
3. Acting as something of a conduit between these two spectacular 'events' is Burden's '747'. The self-confessed 'artist' fires a loaded pistol at a departing airliner, therefore potentially risking many lives

and his own imprisonment. This act invites disgust, perhaps, but also a certain sense of awe and disbelief.

It is perhaps clearer now how Burden and Petit's 'spectacular events' invite symbolic connections with 9/11.[24] All three 'events' utilised objects of contemporary capitalist society – skyscrapers, airplanes, guns – to create stunning spectaculars that symbolise, respectively: human ingenuity, violence and destruction; and a merging of the first two in Burden's 'art/terrorism'.

Stockhausen's and Hirst's apparently tasteless and trivialising comments linking 9/11 with art can thus be seen in a slightly different light. As Cottom goes on to argue, they were not alone in this acknowledgement of the 'symbolic' rather than 'strategic' impulses behind the attacks. The American novelist Jonathan Franzen also raised this issue in *The New Yorker*. His feelings, when watching the events unfold, included 'an admiration for an attack so brilliantly conceived and so flawlessly executed or, worst of all, an awed appreciation of the visual spectacle it produced.'[25] Franzen calls the terrorists 'death artists' who 'were rejoicing over the terrible beauty of the towers' collapse'.[26] His use of the phrase 'terrible beauty' is significant here because it alludes both to the violence and the undeniably compelling spectacle of 9/11, that it is 'beautiful' despite its, or perhaps even because of, its murderous intent. Cottom alludes to other similar observations by Marshall Bermann[27] and Herbert Muschamp whose article 'The Commemorative Beauty of Tragic Wreckage' (2001) is worth looking at in more detail further to contextualise the subject. Muschamp writes about the early debates amongst various groups about what to do with the ruins of the towers. He describes them as 'architecture'[28] or rather ruins that recall architecture, in particular the work of Frank Gehry. With a degree of irony, Muschamp refers to a 'major new work'[29] that has recently appeared in New York. He goes on:

> If you believe that beauty begins in terror, then it is not sacrilege to speak of the beauty of the remaining walls. Nor is Gehry's architecture the only work that has constructed an aesthetic context for them. A substantial body of literature has been dedicated to the contemplation of ruins. The Neoclassical tradition sprang from within the imaginations of those who meditated on stone fragments of the ancient world. That is why 19th-century architects went to Rome. Piranesi's engraved visions of fantastic classicism should be required study for those now gazing on ground zero.[30]

Muschamp argues that these ruins would make a fitting memorial to the collapsed towers and those who perished in the attacks. But as can be seen, he also sees the aesthetic connections between the ruins and architecture.

As with the other comments by Franzen, Stockhausen and Hirst, there is a mixing of art and terror in Muschamp's words that echoes the works of Petit and Burden. Muschamp writes:

> Ultimately, however, the Walls are walls, or, rather, the blasted skeletons of walls. It's hard to imagine a more potent architectural symbol, particularly as we confront a high-security future in which walls, borders, boundaries and other varieties of exclusion and restricted access are likely to play a prominent role.[31]

Thus, the ruins of the towers have their own intrinsic signifying force. An implication of this argument is that any other future works of architecture that might replace the ruins (when the buildings' remains would be taken away as merely 'wreckage' and then cease to have meaning beyond waste material) would, by definition, be superfluous. The ruins also have 'aesthetic context' within the fragmentation and complex formal experimentations of Gehry's architecture. A more speculative, but no less compelling, reading is of the original WTC Towers representing modernist architecture – functionality, man-made materials, non-traditional structures – and the ruins representing postmodernist architecture with its commitment to eclecticism, spectacle and hybridity. Muschamp suggests that the 'art' of the towers resides in the memory of their former solidity and commanding size and concomitantly in the ruins of their destruction. A similar formula connects and also separates Petit's walk and Burden's shooting at an air-liner: the first celebrates the towers and the tightrope walker's ingenuity; the second 'risks' disaster and revels in misanthropy.

Cottom's essay argues that such responses to 9/11, far from being trivial or deliberately amoral, actively help to reveal the 'aggression against humanity, the unhuman motivation, that we find in art' (LH: pp. 134–5). He argues further that the towers were re-presented as souvenirs, in exhibitions, shrines, videos, comic books and art installations and that there is a strain of 'beauty in destruction' (LH: p. 134) in these responses. He writes of the 'compulsiveness' he himself experienced as he watched the footage repeatedly, recalling, as it happened, the art of Chris Burden. He stresses that these feelings – arguably shared by many – were inevitable because 'politics will be aestheticized' and that art, with the theme of misanthropy, is the necessary medium through which the event can be better understood (LH: p. 134). Cottom acknowledges 9/11's 'unique and almost unbearable pathos' (LH: p. 134) but also argues that it is inevitable 'that people should have felt compelled to imagine, momentarily, that all this was art rather than yet another experience of its death in life' (LH: p. 135). Such remarks recall Petit's walk – the very real possibility of his death hangs over proceedings but its eventual success (and intrinsic beauty) reverses the memory of those who fell or jumped from the towers on September 11.

'He is Consoling, She is Distraught': Men and Women and 9/11 in *The Mercy Seat* and *The Guys*

As has been seen throughout this study, marriage and male/female relationships have been a common motif in much 9/11 writing. Some critics have argued that this is a kind of 'retreat', accusing American writers of turning away from the political ramifications of the attacks and returning to the novelistic conventions of the minutiae of heterosexual relationships. Marriage has, of course, always been a primary concern for novelists and perhaps one can argue that, say in the case of *Falling Man*, this trope has been used as a microcosm for the wider preoccupations of post-9/11 America. As has also been argued, most forcefully by Susan Faludi, discourses surrounding 9/11 have been dominated by cultural anxieties concerning masculinity and femininity. Two plays,[1] Neil LaBute's *The Mercy Seat* (2003)[2] and Anne Nelson's *The Guys* (2001)[3] examine 9/11 exclusively through dialogues between men and women whilst at the same time reaching very different conclusions. Indeed it is tempting to see the two plays as unconsciously responding to each other as one looks at selfishness and individualism and the other celebrates selflessness and heroism in light of the 9/11 attacks. But as we will find, the first play's cynicism about human behaviour runs parallel with the second play's equally forceful (and narrow) sentimentality to such an extent that both responses have their problematics.

The Mercy Seat dramatises an often heated and bad-tempered conversation between Ben Harcourt, a World Trade Center worker and his boss Abby Prescott, with whom he is having an affair, on the day after September 11. Ben's family believe that he has died and he is keen to perpetuate this lie and make a new life with Abby. As Ben refuses to answer his perpetually ringing phone, the two argue the rights and wrongs of this plan and more broadly debate the tensions between altruism and self-interest:

ABBY Because it makes me curious, that's all. (*Beat.*) When I was out there, walking around, staring at people . . . I suddenly wondered how you feel about it. I mean, *really* feel about what's happened.
BEN I feel like everybody does. / I do!
ABBY I don't think that's true. / No, uh-uh. (*Beat.*) 'Cause after the shock of it, okay, after the obvious sort of shock that anyone goes through . . . your first thought was that this is an opportunity . . .
BEN Yeah, but I meant . . . for us. / Just as a *possibility* for *us*
. . .
ABBY Who does that?! / Who in their right mind is going to see . . . *this* . . . as having 'unlimited potential'? (*MS*: p. 11)

Thus, set against the backdrop of the immediate aftermath of 9/11 – the set is covered in white dust – Ben and Abby examine, in LaBute's words, 'the "ground zero" of our lives, that gaping hole in ourselves that we try to cover up with clothes from The Gap, with cologne from Ralph Lauren, with handbags from Kate Spade' (*MS*: p. x).

The play's title[4] suggests that Ben is seeking to atone for his 'sins' – indeed, at the very end of the play, after Ben has confessed that he had planned to end the affair on the morning before the attacks, Abby tells him that she will show him 'some mercy' (*MS*: p. 68) and not reveal his whereabouts. Whether, of course, she actually means this as an act of forgiveness is evidently a moot point given the fact that she angrily leaves Ben alone as he prepares to answer his ringing phone and tell his family that he is alive. Thus, initially, it is tempting to see Abby's apartment as 'the mercy seat': Ben decided to drop in on Abby rather than go to work and was being fellated when the planes crashed into the towers. Abby 'saves' him and by doing so inadvertently provides Ben with an excuse to turn his back on his marriage and his family and create a new life. The play explores the moral quandary that the attacks have presented the couple with and also dramatises the power relations between Abby and Ben: she is his boss and their affair – which is already three years old – has been troubling her for some time due to its secrecy and possible professional exploitation.

As will be seen later in this chapter LaBute's play contrasts vividly with Nelson's *The Guys* which settles for a sentimentalised view of its firefighter lead and his camaraderie with his colleagues. Nelson's play is unapologetically redemptive and ends with an uplifting message of solidarity and empathy. *The Mercy Seat* is concerned with the exact antithesis of this celebration of 9/11 heroism – Ben is shown to be opportunistic, narcissistic and selfish in contrast to Nelson's Nick who is dignified, generous and sensitive. The two playwrights are very different as well: LaBute's play can be understood in context of his previous and subsequent plays and screenplays[5] whilst *The Guys* is Nelson's first play (she is a journalist by trade). LaBute's work has often been controversial and many critics have written about his perceived misanthropy and misogyny. Jumana Farouky writes: 'LaBute refuses to judge any of his characters. He likes nothing better than to test how fine the line between good and bad can be and look at how suddenly someone – anyone – can trip over it.'[6] But David Edelstein, writing about LaBute's film version of his play *The Shape of Things*, argues:

> In LaBute's movies, people are either clueless dupes or psychotic manipulators, while art is meant to rub your face in unpleasant 'truths'. And I think he takes a little too much pleasure in that nose-rubbing, which might be why some critics (and a lot of women I know) called him a 'misogynist'.[7]

The Mercy Seat explores themes that have informed LaBute's work, in particular the on-going tensions inherent in heterosexual relationships, and can be seen as contributing another scathing judgement on the confusions and misunderstandings these couples are routinely immersed in, invariably with bleak, downbeat conclusions. As LaBute admits:

> I tend to write about small groups of men and women (friends, lovers, co-workers, family), locked in some kind of gender struggle. These are the politics that interest me, and I scour over them like Herman Melville's Bartleby sitting at his little wooden desk. In the course of a decade of writing, however, I have also tried to look at religion, race, art, national tragedy and a host of other social ills . . . I have a capricious streak in me that likes writing about the unexpected, messing about with what my audience might want to see or hear or experience - and I think of these as positive qualities.[8]

This work is thus a further instalment in LaBute's fascination with the often selfish and even mercenary ways in which men and women relate to each other. The relationship between Abby and Ben is characterised by often sharp and invariably cruel invective as they pick apart the mechanics of their affair set against the aftermath of 9/11. So as an illustration of LaBute's preoccupations *The Mercy Seat* is an exemplary text, a fact that the playwright concedes in his Preface: 'Above all else, this play is a "relationship" play, in the purest sense' (*TG*: p. ix). But of course it is a play that is also 'about' 9/11 or at least has the attacks as a kind of backdrop to the duelling couple. LaBute writes:

> And while I don't think of this piece as a significant response to the attack, the particulars of the plot mechanics could have been put into motion only by the catastrophic events of that notorious Tuesday. (*MS*: p. ix)

September 11 then, in Labute's words, 'hangs like a damaged umbrella over the events of *The Mercy Seat*' (*MS*: p. ix) and provides the play with a starting-off point in order to investigate 'how selfishness can still exist during a moment of national selflessness' (*MS*: p. x). LaBute started writing his play in early 2002 and so cannot have had knowledge of the number of cases of fraud that have arisen in the intervening years since 9/11. But in one sense *The Mercy Seat* anticipates these stories that include the embezzling of national funds, defrauding relief programmes, lying about being married to a victim of the WTC attacks and claiming to be a survivor of 9/11.[9] Ben proposes to Abby that given the assumption that he was inside the WTC and that he had died, they are presented with an opportunity to exploit his 'death' and 'set up house' (*MS*: p. 60) in 'another state' (*MS*: p. 59) with new names.

How does *The Mercy Seat* respond to the 9/11 attacks and what does it 'say' about them in relation to the play's combative couple? As has been alluded to earlier in the chapter the play's title has a religious basis (LaBute is a Mormon)[10] and questions of 'mercy' and 'grace' are at the centre of the play's morality. Abby's apartment fulfils the role of the 'seat', a resting-place away from the confusion and palpable terror on the New York streets outside. One of LaBute's epigraphs[11] underlines this religious interpretation: 'Approach, my soul, the mercy-seat, / Where Jesus answers prayers; / There humbly fall before his feet, / For none can perish there' (*MS*: epigraph). In the Bible the Mercy Seat is the place where a blood sacrifice is presented (above the Ark of the Covenant) and where God 'would mediate His rule on the earth as a representation of the real throne in heaven'.[12] There are further religious connotations surrounding the etymology of the noun mercy that include 'atonement' and 'propitiation'.[13] Thus it seems fairly clear that Ben seeks atonement for his 'sins' – he readily admits that his life has been 'screwed up':

> I always take the easy route, do it faster, simpler, you know, whatever it takes to get it done, be liked, get by. That's me. Cheated in school, screwed over my friends, took whatever I could get from whomever I could take it from. (*MS*: p. 32)

Ben claims that his relationship with Abby represents a riposte to these examples of his previously desultory experience and that 9/11 – referred to as 'apocalyptic shit' – is an opportunity for him to atone:

> I see a way for us to go for it, to totally erase the past – and I don't think that makes me Lucifer or a criminal or some bad man because I noticed it. I really don't. We've been given something here. A chance to . . . I don't know what, to wash away a lot of the, just, rotten crap we've done. More than anything else, that's what this is. A chance. I know it is. (*MS*: p. 32)

This chapter will return to Abby's rejection of Ben's interpretation of events but for now this extract demonstrates how LaBute's play utilises Christian doctrine in order to explore contemporary male/female relationships.

It is tempting to interpret, within this religious discourse, the dust covering the apartment as a version of a 'blood sacrifice' and therefore Ben is in effect asking Abbey to release him from his guilt. The 'apocalypse' – 'from the verb *apokalypto*, to reveal'[14] – of the attacks provides Ben with this opportunity to receive 'mercy' from his old life and self. R.W. Rasband, in an essay positioning LaBute as a 'Mormon artist' writes:

> LaBute shows us how ironically painful it is to live in the presence of the mercy seat, to know our actions have eternal consequences and that we can't take the easy way out without abdicating our souls.[15]

Thus, in this religious reading, throughout the play Ben is asking for his sins to be absolved at the 'mercy seat' – and not only his own sins, for he suggests that Abby has also been 'dishonest' (*MS*: p. 33) in maintaining the affair and also that she has been leading a 'less than desirable' (*MS*: p. 62) life that continually makes her miserable. These tropes of atonement and mercy that define the play are also highly significant aspects of Mormon belief:

> Part of the work of salvation has been done by the atonement of Jesus Christ, in that all human beings are guaranteed resurrection, but to attain the full quality of eternal life, human beings also have work to do. Mormons believe that people arrive in this world without sin, but that they soon misbehave and need to be saved from the consequences of their own actions. To live close to God, a person must have dealt with all the sins in their life. People have a choice of what sins they commit, and they have a free choice of what to do to put things right.[16]

Despite Ben's efforts to convince Abby of his plan – which LaBute constantly points out is an essentially self-serving one – he is left at the end of the play contemplating his ringing phone, at the end of which is undoubtedly his wife desperate for news. He thus has 'a choice of what sins' he will commit.

On one level then, 9/11 acts as a starting point for Ben's 'work' in atoning for his sins and Abby acts as a sounding board for his self-analysis. Conversely, if one is comfortable reading the text within a religious context – Nelson's play is also informed by a religious sentiment, in her case 'praise' rather than 'atonement' – Abby herself seeks atonement for what she sees as her own sins. The 'mercy' she shows Ben at the end of the play – she promises not to tell anyone of his whereabouts as she leaves the apartment to return to work– suggests that she has been more successful in her 'free choice of what to do to put things right'. It is here, in Abby's atonement, that the play's religious motif seems most problematic. After Abby has accused Ben of only having sex 'doggie-style' (*MS*: p. 42) and hence of never looking her in the eyes (Ben concedes that this may be because of guilt) (*MS*: p. 43) she describes her thought processes as Ben makes love. She says it is 'like it's being done to you' (*MS*: p. 44) and that she often slips away to think of other mundane things. But, she confesses, she mostly imagines that it is Ben's wife behind her with 'one of those, umm, things, - those, like, *strappy* things that you buy at sex shops . . . going to town on me' (*MS*: p. 45). In Abby's imagination she is being punished and that she 'probably deserve[s] it' (*MS*: p. 45). This contemplation inspires Abby to speculate upon this 'dream's' meaning:

> Maybe that's what Hell is, in the end. All your wrongful shit played out there in front of you while you're being pumped from behind by someone you've hurt. That you've screwed over in life. Or worse, worse still . . . some person who doesn't love you anymore. No one to ever look at again, make contact with. Just you being fucked as your life splashes out across this big headboard in the Devil's bedroom. Maybe. Even if that's not it, even if Hell is all fire and sulfur [sic] and that sort of thing, it couldn't be much worse than that. (*MS*: p. 45)

The carnal imagery in this vision of Hell is telling in that the play overall takes a rather moralistic and prudish view of sex and sexuality – Rasband refers to LaBute as a 'fire-and-brimstone moralist'.[17] Indeed, Ben avoided being in the towers because he had stopped off at Abbey's apartment and he received oral sex whilst the attacks occurred.[18]

Thus, in effect, Abby reveals that her guilt surrounding her relationship with Ben has been a constant and that she feels that she should – if only figuratively – be punished for her 'sins'. Her vision of 'Hell' is sexual humiliation – rather unconvincingly she cannot name the dildo that she imagines Ben's wife to be wearing – a kind of anonymous abjection that connotes her shame at having succumbed to a 'piece of ass' (*MS*: p. 39). Abby alludes to her life as being ejaculated 'across this big headboard in the Devil's bedroom', a strikingly bizarre image that suggests something of her self-disgust. She urges Ben to atone for his deceit and selfishness by contacting his family to let them know he is alive and also to inform his wife of his adultery. By doing so, she hopes, both will be, as it were, 'saved': 'I don't wanna carry all that shit around, I'm not willing to do that!!' (*MS*: p. 64). What becomes problematic about this trope of the characters' attempts to find 'mercy' is that it is increasingly clear that Ben is a decidedly unworthy individual – as opposed to Nelson's almost saintly Nick in *The Guys* – and that Abby's atonement at the climax of the play only occurs when she discovers that Ben was actually planning to end the affair and return to his family. His surprise arrival at her flat and their subsequent sexual liaison (inadvertently 'saving' him from 9/11) were apparently the result of Ben's decision to tell Abby face-to-face that he was ending their relationship rather than phoning her. In a sense, his sexual opportunism 'saved' him – Abby's sexual favour was done to 'encourage' (*MS*: p. 67) him to phone his wife.

The telephone is thus a significant object in the play – and has great symbolic weight in 9/11 discourse. Not only does Ben's mobile ringing consistently punctuate the drama but the play's climax turns on a final call. Abby finally persuades Ben to 'make the call' (*MS*: p. 65) he was preparing to make the day before, assuming that it is going to be to his wife to confess his cheating. The stage directions describe the ensuing action:

> **ABBY** *crosses back toward the kitchen and sits on the edge of a stool near the counter.* **BEN** *takes a deep breath, then dials a number and waits. After a moment,* **ABBY**'s *phone begins to ring. She looks up, startled, and mimes to* BEN: '*What should I do?*' *She starts to panic, but* **BEN** *motions for her to take the call.* (*MS*: p. 66)

Ben reveals that it was in fact Abby that he was planning to call to end their affair but decided instead, because he was close to her apartment, to 'stop in and talk to her [Abby]' (*MS*: p. 66). Ben never had any intention of phoning his wife – 'I wasn't going to phone home, Abby, I can't do that' (*MS*: p. 67) – and made a sudden decision to propose running away together following the news of the attacks. He was able almost to convince himself of his plan but because of Abby's pressure for him to confess he declares that he has no choice but to end their relationship. Within the play's engagement with religious ethics (or perhaps more accurately Mormon ethics), Ben's inability to atone for his marital deceit leaves him bereft and morally bankrupt.

Indeed, Ben is quite explicit in his rejection of atonement:

> If you'd taken this . . . meal ticket . . . of ours, then great. I'd've worked in a fucking *lumberyard* the rest of my days to be with you, but if you wanna make me come clean about what I've done, purge all my sins for some un-fucking-fathomable reason . . . I mean, if I'm publicly forced to choose between those little girls' hearts and your *thighs*, well then, there's just not much question. (*Beat.*) Sorry, Abby, I'm really very . . . I don't know. Just sorry. G'bye. (*MS*: p. 67)

Ben's response is typically disingenuous in that he appears to be saying that he would be happy to run away with Abby as long as he isn't compelled, or forced, to confess openly to his affair to his wife. Abby, although understandably reluctant to commit her future to Ben, seems at least partially interested in his plan but insists that he atone by calling his family rather than using the attacks as an excuse to escape. Ben describes their 'opportunity', granted to them by the coincidence of 9/11 and Ben's decision to visit Abby rather than tell her over the phone, but it is obvious that the 'opportunity' only came about because Abby offered sexual favours – 'a last suck for good luck?' (*MS*: p. 67). In other words, it appears that Ben's highly conflicted ethical position is entirely cir-cumstantial – *if* he had phoned Abby rather than visiting her he would, presumably, have told her that he wanted to end the affair (and by impli-cation he would have been in the WTC when the planes attacked); *if* Abby hadn't given him a blowjob ('a little incentive' (*MS*: p. 8) as Abby refers to it, as the planes crashed into the towers) Ben would not have formulated his plan for them to run away; *if* Abby had agreed, without insisting he call his family, Ben would have 'worked in a fucking lumber-yard' to be with her. Because she insists on his atonement he decides to return to his wife – or at least contemplate it as Abby leaves him.

Despite Abby's apparent consideration of the plan and her surprise that Ben had intended to end the affair, LaBute quite clearly prefers her to the venal Ben. Throughout the play the audience is reminded that Ben is a fairly contemptible character who remains unredeemed at the climax. Abby, who alludes to his previous selfishness and immaturity (she is twelve years older than him), interrogates his ethical position in relation to his fortuitous 'survival' and his sense of public duty. Abby wants 'to see if you have a decent fucking bone in your body' (*MS*: p. 9) and wonders 'how you feel about it. I mean, *really* feel about what's happened' (*MS*: p. 11). Abby presses Ben, speculating whether his first response – that here was an opportunity for them – has overtaken a potential urge to 'go pitch in down at a hospital, or hand out food' (*MS*: p. 13). In other words she questions the balance between his civic (and human) responsibility and his adherence to his own pleasure. Ben argues that he cannot put into words how he feels and that he can't leave the apartment and offer his help because 'we've got to look at the implica-tions here. What it means to *us*, our future' (*MS*: p. 15). He goes on to connect his individualism up with a broader national trait:

> [D]o you honestly think we're not going to rebound from this? And I don't just mean you and me, I'm saying the country as a whole. Of course we will. We'll do what it takes, go after whomever we need to, call out the *tanks* and

shit, but we're going to have the World Series, and Christmas, and all the other crap that you count on in life . . . I'm saying the American way is to overcome, to conquer, to come out on top. And we do it by spending and eating and screwing our women harder than anyone else. (*MS*: p. 16)

Ben's monologue could almost be a post-9/11 and pre-Iraq invasion speech by George Bush or a senior figure in his administration and LaBute implicitly equates Ben's machismo (which is shown to be a façade) and self-interest with the political atmosphere of the time. Abby, although herself compromised by the affair, at least shows the beginning of her personal atonement and a sense of camaraderie with her fellow New Yorkers outside the 'mercy seat' of her home.

Increasingly Abby is disgusted by Ben's lack of conscience about using the attacks as a way of being able to run away from his responsibilities, and in this she is very much LaBute's moral surrogate on the stage. Rather than hiding and turning his back on his family Abby pleads for him to do some 'work' (in the Mormon sense of the term), actively to involve himself in contacting his family or even offering his services to help, but he isn't, as he freely admits, 'that kind of guy' (*MS*: p. 15). In one sense the play dramatises the awakening of Abby's own conscience[19] in response to Ben's selfishness. She concedes, for example, that earlier when she witnessed a woman diligently taping 'Have You Seen Him?' (*MS*: p. 14) photocopies of what appears to be her missing son she didn't offer to help – 'I had the . . . groceries and everything' (*MS*: p. 15). By the end of the play she leaves the apartment: 'I'll go to work, I guess. I'm going to walk over to our office and find out what's happened up there . . . see if I can . . . something' (*MS*: p. 68). LaBute shows that Abby's developing sense of her own ethical conflicts, her act of 'work' – of atonement – demands that she move beyond the narrow confines of their relationship (that is gradually revealed to be unsatisfying) and reconnect with the immediate issues of the city and its inhabitants. Ben, on the other hand, is far more concerned with being financially 'buried' (*MS*: p. 57) by his wife in a potential divorce than he is with the other 'buried' at Ground Zero.

Another element that LaBute explores is that of power relations between men and women – articulated here within a professional/corporate milieu. This trope follows on from LaBute's first film *In the Company of Men* (1997) in which two male executives, the confident and assertive Chad and his more socially anxious friend Howard, bitterly resentful of their recent romantic failures,[20] hatch a vengeful scheme to find a woman they can punish. They pick on a deaf[21] secretarial assistant, Christine, who the two men simultaneously date until she falls in love with Chad. Howard, who has genuinely fallen for her, angrily informs her of their plot and she confronts Chad only to be cruelly humiliated. Chad, cheerfully proud of his scheme, is promoted and Howard, who realises he too has been duped, demoted.[22] The film is a critique of macho, corporate culture and the two executives' sexual exploitation of a female subordinate links Chad's and Howard's misogyny with rapacious corporate politics. Although much less acerbic, *The Mercy Seat* reveals professional tensions between Ben and Abby and alters the conventional power dynamic by making the male character subordinate to the female character. But Ben is very much a 'cousin', as it were, of Chad and Howard and he reveals much about his ambivalent attitude towards Abby being his manager.

It gradually becomes apparent that Ben is far from secure in their relationship and despite being often arrogant and aggressive is some-times vulnerable to Abby's satirical asides concerning his lack of cultural knowledge.[23] He is keenly aware of their respective professional status:

> **BEN** I don't work under you.
> **ABBY** No?
> **BEN** No, I do not. I hold a position that supports yours.
> **ABBY** Yes, you do.
> **BEN** . . . is subordinate to yours, maybe.
> **ABBY** True.
> **BEN** I get paid less.
> **ABBY** Quite a bit less.
> **BEN** *Somewhat* less. Right, that's all true . . .
> **ABBY** But . . .?
> **BEN** *But* I'm not 'under' you. You do not tower over me in some literal or figurative way.
> **ABBY** This may be drifting toward semantics . . .
> **BEN** No, it's not. I have a point and it's not. (*Beat*.) I am your colleague. Your co-worker. Your partner. (*MS*: p. 21)

Such fears suggest that Ben is much less comfortable in his masculinity than he would like to appear and there is a hint here that professional jealousy and/or ambition have influenced his affair with Abby. He reveals that their sexual relationship is perhaps intimately linked with their respective professional positions – 'you have never, in your infinite wisdom, seen fit to *promote* me' (*MS*: p. 22) – and as tensions grow this resentment becomes clearer. As will be seen Nelson's *The Guys* is a tacit critique of women who are committed to their careers, indeed Abby embodies the kind of woman who Nick, the fire captain, suggests is incapable of 'being led' and is too independent to 'give in' to a man in a symbolic dance. In *The Mercy Seat* Ben is very much the 'junior partner' in his relationship with Abby and evidently resents her authority. Abby teases Ben about this – 'you like fucking the boss' (*MS*: p. 35) – and Ben argues back that if she didn't want the affair to continue she would have ended it because she is 'that kind of woman' (*MS*: p. 36).

Ben's lets slip his sexual/professional jealousy:

> **BEN** . . . You don't like some assistant at work, they're outta there in twenty minutes. You don't fancy a *salt shaker* in the cafeteria it's changed. If you didn't want us coming here, or sneaking off at conferences and me banging the shit outta you, we wouldn't be doing it.
> **ABBY** Really?
> **BEN** Yeah, really. I mean, you're the fucking 'guy' in this relationship, let's not kid ourselves . . .
> **ABBY** Okay, Ben . . .
> **BEN** Ms Prescott sports the Haggar[24] slacks around here.
> **ABBY** Well, *somebody's* got to!
> **BEN** Yeah, but somebody doesn't have to be an overdominating cunt about it . . . (*Beat.*) Sorry, shit, I didn't mean . . . you know . . .
> **ABBY** Oh, I'm sure you meant that in the best possible way.
> **BEN** No, I just . . .
> **ABBY** As you always say, Ben . . . whatever. (*MS*: pp. 36–7)

On the one hand, according to Ben, Abby's professional power is admirable in the sense that she is able to make her own decisions and she is largely in control of her workforce and office environment. On the other hand she is 'an overdominating cunt' who 'wears the trousers', refuses Ben promotion and enjoys the erotic/power charge of sleeping, in secret, with a younger man. But Abby is more worried about 'sexual harassment' (*MS*: p. 38) and the hypocrisy of her seminars on an 'empowered workplace' (*MS*: p. 39), reminding Ben that he is not the only one who is risking important aspects of their life: 'After everything I've worked for, the *pounds* of shit I've eaten to get where I am . . . to blow it all on a piece of ass' (*MS*: p. 39). Indeed, Abby forces this issue of the conflation of lust and professional ambition when it emerges that the two of them had been up for the same promotion that Abby herself achieved. She suggests that Ben's aforementioned taste for the 'doggie-style' position is actually an expression of sexual domination: 'You don't think it's just a little bit of "I'm gonna let the ol' gal have it for getting a promotion over me"?' (*MS*: p. 41). If Abby were to agree to Ben's plan she would be forced to give up her 'seniority' and her 'pension plan' (*MS*: p. 60) and an implication of the narrative is that Ben is partly inspired by the fact that once they had fled their old lives they would be more 'equal partners'.

In direct contrast to LaBute's analysis of masculine selfishness in context of 9/11 *The Guys* is essentially a celebration of conventional gender roles that the attacks have generated in certain discourses. Anne Nelson's Preface to *The Guys* is an emblematic piece of local New York 9/11 writing. Nelson emphasises the authenticity of the project and in so doing defines the play as an act of community solidarity:

> I hadn't written a play before, but I was motivated to capture what I had observed and experienced through my conversations with the captain. I also wanted to try to help the theater. I loved the sound of what Jim had described . . . It was the sort of enterprise that had drawn me to New York in the first place, and part of me felt – not entirely coherently – that if we could somehow keep it alive, it would deprive the attackers of another victory. (*TG*: pp. xxi–xxii)

The 'captain' (he remains anonymous) in question is a NYFD chief who is helped by Nelson – a journalist – to compose eulogies for the many men from his company who died in the 9/11 attacks. Nelson is invited to visit the firehouse and afterwards she is struck by the mood of mourning and by the chief's stoicism in the face of such loss: 'The captain impressed me deeply. I thought that I had never met anyone so generous. I realized that generosity was the essence of the job – a firefighter's work was about saving lives, and the more often and effectively he did it, the happier he was' (*TG*: p. xix). 'Jim' is Jim Simpson, the husband of Sigourney Weaver, who runs the small Flea Theater, situated seven blocks from the WTC that has been severely affected by the attacks and is facing financial problems. Simpson suggests that Nelson should write a play based on her experiences with the fire chief – a task she completes in an extremely short space of time - and *The Guys* is the result. It was premiered on 'Tuesday, December 4, 2001, twelve weeks to the day after the World Trade Center attack' (*TG*: p. xxv).

Thus Nelson emphasises the personal, collective and commemorative impulses behind the writing and production of the play. In stark contrast to the cynicism about some human behaviour evident in *The Mercy Seat*, *The Guys* is predicated on empathy and admiration for the firemen and a commitment to public service. An intriguing contrast can be made with Beigbeder's *Windows on the World* in which the author constantly acknowledges his lack of personal connections with the attacks: he is a French intellectual; he didn't know anyone involved; he is narcissistic, cynical, spoiled and can only write about the attacks in a playful, postmodern and metafictional way (whilst also fabricating a personal connection to his own fictional character). The reader is thus persistently reminded of the artificiality of the novel – indeed, Beigbeder castigates himself for his insincerity (despite the sentimentality that gradually becomes apparent towards the end of the narrative). *The Guys*, on the other hand, is presented as a personal, genuine and kind-spirited gesture both to help a struggling theatre affected by the attacks and to provide a paean to the fraternity of New York fire fighters who died (and those confronted with their deaths). The intuitive way in which Nelson wrote the play adds to this sense of artless sincerity:

> I only wrote at night, liberated by the license of sleep deprivation. I have never written anything in such an uninterrupted fashion. No outline, few preconceptions, no notion of what would be the beginning, middle, or end. I just typed forward. I think it helped that I had no certainty it would ever be produced. (*FM*: pp. xxii–xxiii)

The 'uninterrupted fashion' in which Nelson writes *The Guys* suggests an almost unmediated outpouring of sentiment, bypassing aesthetic and intellectual concerns and relying instead upon emotional engagement and autobiographical truth.

Nelson has subsequently written other plays[25] but she prefers to emphasise the emotional investment – by her and by others – of this particular play, its communal production and its cathartic 'working through' of trauma and grief. Hence, of course, the critic is presented with something of a dilemma: how to interpret the play without the weight of sincerity and sentiment and to offer a cogent reading of its tropes, motifs and meanings. Nelson acknowledges this problem when she writes that some critics were 'puzzled' by the play and how it could be placed within accepted theatrical aesthetics. She explicitly states that it was written 'to confront our city's devastation in a humane fashion and to help the theater company' (*TG*: p. 63). She goes on to write about the responses to the production by 'psychiatrists, psychologists, and counselors' who themselves were involved in treating people in the aftermath of the attacks and who responded to the play in terms of the 'therapeutic':

> After a number of conversations along this line, we reflected that both theater and psychology traced their vocabulary back to the Greeks: *drama* and *psyche* to start with, but also *catharsis*, *crisis*, and *therapy*. A play couldn't cure anyone. But it could bring people together in a dedicated space and allow them to experience emotion together. From my limited knowledge of the ancient Greeks and their theater, this wasn't so far from their intent. (*TG*: p. 63)

In this sense Nelson's play bears comparison with other responses to 9/11 that were produced in the immediate aftermath (see Introduction) in that it is unashamedly personal and inflected with the collective response of shock and trauma. Nelson describes the 'strange intensity' (*TG*: p. 64) in the theatre as she watches the play night after night and how she was 'reliving the loss' (*TG*: p. 64) each time. She adds that the 'reactions in December were very raw' (*TG*: p. 64).

As can be seen from these comments, the aesthetic and formal aspects of the play are barely mentioned at all. Instead Nelson privileges the solidarity, selflessness and commitment to rebuilding that she sees as joining together a traumatised city. Nelson goes further in her revealing Afterword to give an over-view of NYFD culture (highly reminiscent of the ways in which the Naudet brothers spoke of the men in Firehouse 7 in their documentary *9/11*): the different echelons within the firefighting community; the importance of professionalism and loyalty; the often complex and eclectic private lives of the firefighters; the social and cultural commitment felt throughout the department, in particular an awareness of their significance to the wider community. This celebration of the department is then intimately linked with the history of the city (*TG*: pp. 68–71) and finally there is a journalistic over-view of the immense loss of life and its profound impact upon local firehouses. Nelson actively joins the 'clearing up' process at 'Ground Zero' and ends by suggesting that rather than simply moving on and seeking 'closure' (*TG*: p. 79) from the attacks 'we' should instead ask ourselves what 'we' have learnt: 'One place to start could be the simple but demanding lesson of the firehouse: Honor belongs to those who "use their talent for the betterment of the company"' (*TG*: p. 79). Here 'company' acts as a synecdoche for the global community, alluding to the fraternity of the firefighters as an inspiration for everyone.

There is a sense here that these extensive supporting pieces both contextualise the writing and performing of the play (and its basis on fact) and also serve to fix its meaning. The 'suggested reading' and 'acknowledgements' add to this fixing of meaning. The play, these extra-textual notes attest, serves its own intended purpose to console, grieve and stand as a testimony to the 'guys' that died. In other words, the play is merely a vehicle that directly mirrors events in real life and for these honourable reasons should be read and understood as such. Whilst these sentiments are self-evidently worthwhile and whilst it is entirely reasonable, not to say crucial, that art is able to perform a useful social function, is it possible to read the play in any critically informed way that could potentially release other readings? Inevitably it is rather challenging to try and resist Nelson's own, evidently sincere, commentary on the play. It is as if the play is closed to any further interpretation and that Nelson herself helps to fend off any negative comment or awkward question about its characters and themes. As was seen, for example, in Messud's

The Emperor's Children, the use of 9/11 granted the novel a ready-made tragedy to provide its narrative with a suitably large historical event in order to add gravitas to the characters. The author relies upon the reader's knowledge of the events and is freed of any explicit reference to 9/11; instead 'it' merely happens, with heavy symbolic foreshadowing, and Messud does not need to describe 'it'. Likewise Nelson's play is predicated upon certain dominant discourses of grief and trauma and is presented to the reader as an ideologically neutral homage to the bravery of the fire-fighters. But on closer inspection *The Guys* is anything but ideologically neutral.

As has been alluded to elsewhere in this study, Susan Faludi's *The Terror Dream: What 9/11 Revealed about America* is one of the most revealing and insightful analyses of the impact of the attacks. Her descriptions of the charged political landscape post 9/11 is useful in its deconstruction of a number of compelling mythologies that rapidly arose in the aftermath. One of these – the myth of the heroic firefighter – is especially pertinent to a reading of *The Guys*. Through Faludi's critique of this myth one can begin an enquiry into the politics of Nelson's play and also, concomitantly, a deeper appreciation of its problematic poetics. As Bruce Weber writes, in an otherwise highly favourable review, *The Guys* is not an 'artful or literary piece'. He goes on to say that Nelson 'shows all the earmarks of a talented writer who is lacking in experience and who could certainly make use of time for a rewrite' and that the 'writing slides noticeably as the play proceeds, and the last couple of eulogies are considerably less inspiring'. But, he adds, 'such a conventional assessment doesn't do justice to the show'.[26] This chapter will thus proceed to analyse *The Guys* in relation to Faludi's understanding of the mythic firefighter and also in response to the play's formal and thematic weaknesses. Indeed, the two issues are subtly intertwined – ideology and art inform each other throughout Nelson's work.

Faludi writes of the 'magnification of manly men' that occurred in the immediate aftermath of 9/11.[27] This recelebration of certain masculine myths – that Faludi sees as a direct backlash against feminism – found its apotheosis in the figure of the heroic, brave and selfless firefighter that emerged in the popular press and on TV. The firefighters became, Faludi points out, the 'new supersoldiers' in the post-9/11 cultural discourse and were lauded as almost legendary figures that, conveniently for what Faludi identifies as a collective, media-inspired retreat to American archetypes, were exclusively male.[28] The firefighters are subsequently referred to as 'knights in shining fire helmets',[29] as being 'like the cowboys of yesterday'[30] and as 'America's Real-Life Superheroes' who might eclipse fictional Superheroes such as Spider-Man.[31] This mythologising, Faludi argues, had a distinct political agenda that was taken up by President Bush and was endorsed by individuals such as the designer Ralph Lauren:

> I have always been inspired by America and its heroes – the cowboy, the soldier and now the firefighters, police officers and rescue workers [many of whom, of course, were women]. There is one common thread in every hero. They are ordinary Americans, they come from nowhere, make their mark, get knocked down and rise up again.[32]

But more than this appropriation and 'glorification' of an American male stereotype for ideological purposes was a correlative that Faludi calls a 'contemptuous double slap – to the "soft" male and the feminist who supposedly made him what he was, or rather, wasn't'.[33] Thus the mythic male firefighter was imbued with a whole host of traditional male attributes – physical strength, bravery, practicality, stoicism, fraternity – and these were then used in a counter-movement explicitly proclaiming the death of feminism and a rebirth, as it were, of traditional gender roles.

Faludi points out that this backlash against feminism found its expression through other stereotypes and myths such as its perceived obsolescence in light of the enormity of the attacks, the 'heroisation' of Bush, Donald Rumsfeld and other male politicians and public leaders, the widows of the 9/11 dead portrayed as 'perfect virgins of grief'[34] and the alleged return, by many women, to domesticity. The NYFD firefighters were themselves increasingly bemused, and in some cases angered, by this ideological battle being waged over their status. As Faludi argues, this heroic 'soldier' image accorded to firefighters was a dangerous distortion. It was claimed that these 'Green Berets in red hats' had saved thousands of lives:

> That was a claim the surviving firefighters themselves would regard as preposterous. Of the sixteen to eighteen thousand occupants of the World Trade Center that day, 95 per cent of those who died were on the upper floors, beyond reach of rescue, and most of those on the lower floors rescued themselves without uniformed help. The grim truth is that the human toll would have been significantly lower had the firefighters never entered the buildings (about three times more firefighters than office workers died in the floors below the impact of the planes).[35]

This awkward realisation, Faludi writes, had been successfully buried beneath the weight of admiration for the 'rescue mission' and although individual firefighters continually attested not only to the futility of entering the towers but also the consistent failure of communication equipment[36] the mythologies continued to dominate political and cultural life. As Faludi herself points out, Nelson's *The Guys* was produced in this atmosphere and contributed to the 'erasure of women from ground zero'.[37]

It is now perhaps possible to return to the text itself to see how it articulates many of the discourses that Faludi delineates and to understand better how the weak poetics of the play contribute to them. A useful place to begin is with Nelson's epigraph for the published text of *The Guys* that is a quotation taken from Gerard Manley Hopkins' poem 'Pied Beauty' (the poem was written in 1877 but wasn't published until 1918). It is worth including the entire poem with Nelson's extract highlighted:

> Glory be to God for dappled things—
> For skies of couple-colour as a brinded cow;
> For rose-moles all in stipple upon trout that swim;
> Fresh-firecoal chestnut-falls; finches' wings;
> *Landscape plotted and pieced—fold, fallow, and plough;*
> *And áll trades, their gear and tackle and trim.*
>
> *All things counter, original, spáre, strange;*
> *Whatever is fickle, frecklèd (who knows how?)*
> *With swíft, slów; sweet, sóur; adázzle, dím;*
> *He fathers-forth whose beauty is pást change:*
> *Práise hím.*[38]

Hopkins' poem is a hymn to the beauty of God[39] and ends with an exhortation to 'praise him' because of his 'creation' of nature. Nelson's elision of the poem's opening four lines evidently rids her epigraph of the subject of God and instead suggests that 'the guys' of her play are akin to the farmers who 'plot' and 'piece' the land with their 'gear and tackle and trim'. These agricultural men are intimately linked with the natural beauty of God's world and by implication Nelson suggests that the firefighters are themselves attuned to sublime rhythms of the world. 'He', in the original poem obviously signifies God and it seems apparent that Nelson deliberately equates 'the guys' with a supernatural deity. Thus, despite the ever-changing 'pied' aspects of nature – the 'moles' and 'stipple', the 'fickle' and constantly fluctuating climates – God remains 'past change' and thus should be 'praised'. Likewise, the NYFD firefighters, despite their losses in 9/11 remain constant and immutable and also should be praised.

So at first it appears that Nelson secularises the poem, shedding the explicit allusion to a Christian god. But this reading is complicated by the last two lines that refer to the NYFD firefighters who seem to be both

mortal men of 'trades' with 'their gear and tackle and trim' and also
likened to a god who 'fathers-forth' the world and as such we should
'express respect and gratitude towards'[40] them. This is an unusual and
slightly bewildering suggestion but it does indicate how Nelson wants
the reader to think about the 'guys' spoken about by Nick in the play.
For her they are to be venerated in part because they are skilled and
central to human life but also because in light of 9/11 they have achieved
some kind of deified superiority. This view evidently alludes to Faludi's
assertion that firefighters were mythologised in the immediate aftermath
of the attacks. But it also highlights the sentimental and ultimately
rather mawkish portrayal of Nick and his colleagues whom he eulogises.
The 'guys' are venerated because of their commitment to the job, their
bravery and selflessness, but also because of their working-class camaraderie, their jocular masculinity and their 'ordinariness'. Increasingly in
the narrative Joan (who is essentially Nelson herself) is seduced by this
vision of the NYFD culture and indeed, to some degree, the play's trajectory is akin to a conventional romance – the two characters are attracted
to each other, Joan fantasises about dancing with Nick, and the play
ends in silence with them both looking at each other: 'He is consoling,
she is distraught' (*TG*: p. 60).

Thus the characters change roles: Joan spends most of the play offering support, gently encouraging Nick to open up about his feelings
and reassuring him that she will help him work through his memories.
Nick is initially hesitant and finds difficulty in articulating but gradually, thanks to Joan's sensitive interventions, has the strength to attend
a memorial service and with more assurance reads out the last eulogy.
By this stage Joan is visibly upset and even angry and looks to Nick to
console her. In light of the gender issues Faludi raises it is possible to see
Nelson's play as a retreat into conventional stereotypes. Joan represents
the nurturing, maternal 'woman' whose role is to help Nick who needs
her feminine emotional openness to unlock his feelings about the 'guys'
who have died. Indeed, it is telling to read the stage directions towards
the play's climax. Nick is dressed in 'uniformed funeral attire' and he
reads 'in a simple, unpretentious, dignified way'. He is confident and 'in
control' (*TG*: p. 56). In contrast Joan is 'defiant' and then 'desperate'
(*TG*: p. 58) before finally 'she wilts' (*TG*: p. 59) and ends the play 'distraught' (*TG*: p. 60). Joan, completely seduced by Nick and his stories
of his colleagues' lives, ends the play in deep grief: 'I want them back. I
want them back. All of them. That's all I'd settle for. I want them back,
just the way they were. I want them all back, together again. That's final'
(*TG*: p. 58).

What is intriguing then about *The Guys* is that its narrative is determined by a sentimentalised view of both genders. Nick's task of eulogising his colleagues – Bill, Jimmy, Patrick and Barney - inevitably means that the details he shares with Joan about their lives remain rather banal and are always generous. At one point Joan addresses this issue after Nick has been speaking about his missing colleague Patrick O'Neill. Nick has referred to him as a 'leader' (*TG*: p. 32) who 'the men looked up to' (*TG*: p. 32) and a 'real straight arrow' (*TG*: p. 34) who led a 'full life' (*TG*: p. 34). Joan asks if Patrick had a flaw because Nick's description has been so complimentary. Nick replies that 'he was a perfectionist' (*TG*: p. 42). Joan acknowledges this but wonders whether this is a flaw or simply an example of him being 'human' (*TG*: p. 42). Thus Nick and Joan are constrained by the need to 'praise' the men, as is the play itself. As Claire Fox argues: 'Oh how I longed for an evil or corrupt firefighter to emerge, or one who ran away. This might have allowed some drama to emerge, some sense that art was happening on stage instead of testimony, and mawkish testimony at that.'[41] Throughout the play Nick struggles to articulate his memories of the men but can offer only rather trite and bland insights into their lives. As Fox argues, this makes for a dramatically arid play without conflict or ambiguity. The use of Hopkins' 'Pied Beauty' at the start of the play makes more sense in this context – the poem's urge to 'praise him' dictates the only way that *The Guys* can speak about its protagonists.

Nick does question the mythologising of NYFD firefighters – 'I keep hearing all these speeches from the politicians on TV. The pictures in the papers. Hero this, hero that. I don't even recognize them' (*TG*: p. 12) – but is unwilling to look too closely into his colleagues' lives. Joan encourages him to emphasise the 'ordinary' (*TG*: p. 12) aspects of Bill's character but because of the one-dimensional nature of the eulogy Nick resorts to platitudes: 'He was real good with the younger guys' (*TG*: p. 13); 'he was proud of being Irish' (*TG*: p. 14); 'He loved New York' (*TG*: p. 14); 'He was never mean' (*TG*: p. 15). Joan then hands Nick the notes she has taken and he reads back what she has written. Joan's more polished eulogy repeats Nick's sentiments: 'Bill was a quiet hero' (*TG*: p. 16); 'He was absolutely dependable' (*TG*: p. 16); 'But Bill was always looking out for the young guys' (*TG*: p. 17); '[he] was steady and professional' (*TG*: p. 18). One of the central themes of the play is the question of translating grief into language but here, and elsewhere in the narrative, Joan's re-presentation of Nick's description of Bill merely reiterates, all but precisely, what has already been said. Joan admits, when Nick compliments her work, '[t]hey're your words. I just put them in order' (*TG*: p. 17) but Nick insists on the value of her 'craft' (*TG*: p. 17). As can be seen in these examples, it is rather difficult to locate how Joan's 'craft' manifests itself given that her eulogy perfectly mirrors Nick's reminiscences. Nelson's 'play' itself adds another layer of repetition that creates an atmosphere of inertia and of turning away from difficult truths towards the consolation of cliché and platitude.

As Nelson has attested, *The Guys* was designed as a therapeutic play and it can be argued that these understandably lachrymose stereotypes are the result of the air of mourning that dominated the weeks after 9/11. But the play's sentimentality, whilst perhaps easy to forgive in the context of the fate of a local theatre and the community surrounding it militates against the sense of conflict and confusion that arguably *The Mercy Seat* more adroitly addresses. The need to 'praise' overwhelms the potential drama and the play's conservative gender politics adds to the hagiographic content of the eulogies.[42] One can see how the gender relations between the two characters develop in a crucial scene in Act II. Nick has struggled through his memories of 'straight arrow' Patrick and is visibly drained by his efforts. Joan, keen to brighten the mood between them recalls attending a 'tango wedding party' (*TG*: p. 35) the previous evening. Joan evokes the scene:

> And the women were all dressed up, with their hair up, wearing little high-heeled shoes with pointy shoes. You don't see that anymore. When they got going on the dance floor, their feet just flashed. It was so beautiful. It was like a dream intermission in the middle of – all this. (*TG*: p. 35)

She reveals that 'on the eleventh, the groom was flying in from the West Coast, and the bride was working downtown' (*TG*: p. 35) but eventually they were together and they 'had this incredible evening. It was beautiful. They were beautiful. They made us all beautiful. For a few hours' (*TG*: p. 36). As we have seen, *The Guys* partly resembles the trajectory of a chamber romance and it is here, when Nick reveals that he dances himself, that the play is at its most idealised.

In what is subsequently revealed to be a dream sequence, Nick and Joan get up from their chairs and start to dance a tango. Nick tells Joan that 'the people are great' (*TG*: p. 36) where he dances and that one time he danced with his teacher who he describes as being 'perfect' (*TG*: p. 36). Through dialogue and stage directions the two characters tentatively begin to dance. Nick takes the lead and by doing so the dynamics of their relationship change – the dance represents a kind of 'swap over' as Joan is increasingly affected by Nick's eulogies whilst Nick is gradually emboldened by his sessions. It is an undoubtedly romanticised scene and Joan's acquiescence – she puts up her hand to his, he takes it with a 'firm and pliant' (*TG*: p. 37) grip – signifies her growing dependence on Nick to help her through their shared mourning. Nick underlines the importance of synchronicity in dancing:

> Sometimes it's real hard for these modern women, you know. They're professionals, they're educated, they're used to being in charge. But when you're dancing, you got to be able to follow. You've got to be able to feel the lead. (*TG*: p. 37)

It seems evident that Nick is speaking about Joan and tacitly suggesting – in what is in fact Joan's own romantic yearning – that she 'just follow' (*TG*: p. 37) him and that she shouldn't 'look down' (*TG*: p. 38). Implicitly Joan seems to be unconsciously longing to 'give in to' Nick, unquestionably sexually but also because his vision of masculine solidarity – emphasising traditional male values – has seduced her. The implication of this dream sequence recalls Faludi's insight into the anti-feminist 9/11 backlash that called for women to return to domesticity. Joan moves from her capable professional role as a therapist manqué to an adoring conventional 'old fashioned' woman who willingly submits to Nick's equally traditional masculinity.

Thus both plays utilise male/female relationships in order to explore the immediate aftermath of 9/11 but in markedly different ways. What is intriguing about the texts, beyond their sexual politics, is that they concern themselves with two opposing qualities – selfishness and empathy – and how these are related to 9/11. DeLillo's *Falling Man*, that will be analysed in the following chapter, is similarly focused on a marriage and also deals with characters' impulses towards helping others in a time of personal and national crisis whilst grappling with how the attacks expose problems in their own lives.

'Everything Seemed to Mean Something': Signifying 9/11 in Don DeLillo's *Falling Man*

Don DeLillo's *Falling Man* (2007)[1] begins with the immediate aftermath of the WTC attacks:

> It was not a street anymore but a world, a time and space of falling ash and near night. He was walking north through rubble and mud and there were people running past holding towels to their faces or jackets over their heads. They had handkerchiefs pressed to their mouths. They had shoes in their hands, a woman with a shoe in each hand, running past him. They ran and fell, some of them, confused and ungainly, with debris coming down around them, and there were people taking shelter under cars. (*FM*: p. 3)

The novel's central character, Keith Neudecker, emerges from the 'smoke and ash . . . office paper flashing past . . . otherworldly things in the morning pall' (*FM*: p. 3) carrying a briefcase (that is subsequently revealed to belong to Florence Given with whom Keith later has a desultory affair). As Keith makes his way through this 'world' he sees 'figures in windows a thousand feet up, dropping into free space' (*FM*: p. 4) and 'faces in collapse' (*FM*: p. 4) and then, as the North Tower collapses he hears 'a soft awe of voices in the distance' (*FM*: p. 5). In these early descriptions – that 'haunt' the rest of the narrative – DeLillo establishes a set of motifs familiar from 9/11 representation: falling people, smoke and dust, chaos, defamiliarised objects. In a novel predicated on connections, doubles and parallels the image of a shirt 'lifted and drifting in the scant light' (*FM*: p. 3) anticipates *Falling Man*'s concluding lines: 'Then he saw a shirt come down out of the sky, He walked and saw it fall, arms waving like nothing in this life' (*FM*: p. 246).

Thus DeLillo presents the reader with an utterly changed, collapsed, 'fallen' dystopian city and establishes a mood of uncanny sadness that permeates the novel. As has been seen in the study's Introduction, DeLillo's initial responses to the attacks in journalistic pieces were characterised by a profound sense of wounded psyches, traumatised communities and civic violation.[2] There was, of course, a palpable sense of anger in DeLillo's non-fiction but, by the time of *Falling Man*'s publication in 2007, this anger has been replaced by an overwhelming mood of mourning and melancholy. The novel is essentially concerned – as in other 9/11 texts such as *The Good Life*, *The Mercy Seat* and *A Disorder Peculiar to the Country* – with the deterioration of a marriage and utilises 9/11 as a catalyst for the couple to re-evaluate their relationship. The reader gradually discovers that Keith and Lianne's marriage was all but over before the attacks and despite their, admittedly muted, efforts to rekindle conjugal intimacy they drift further apart in the following months. Interspersed with chapters from both Keith and Lianne's perspectives are chapters describing the point of view of one of the 9/11 hijackers, Hammad.[3] He trains with al-Qaeda, is a member of the 'Hamburg Cell' with Mohammad Atta and 'meets' Keith, as it were, in the North Tower as the plane hits. In perhaps the most discussed sequence of the book, DeLillo unites Keith and Hammad in one sentence:

> A bottle fell off the counter in the galley, on the other side of the aisle, and he [Hammad] watched it roll this way and that, a water bottle, empty, making an arc one way and rolling back the other, and he watched it spin more quickly and then skitter across the floor an instant before the aircraft hit the tower, heat, then fuel, then fire, and a blast wave passed through the structure that sent Keith Neudecker out of his chair and into a wall. (*FM*: p. 239)

Falling Man is suffused with other similar eerie parallels and connections that we will look at throughout this chapter but as in Amis' *The Second Plane*, DeLillo's writing on 9/11 is inflected with tropes and themes familiar from his oeuvre. Also in common with Amis, DeLillo writes about 9/11 within discourses surrounding masculinity. If Amis, in his 9/11 short fiction, suggested various ironies about Islamist masculine identity, DeLillo interprets the attacks as emasculating Keith and by extension, America as a whole. For example, Keith was a member of a poker group who met regularly but who then dissipate and finally disband. Keith is deeply nostalgic when he recalls the men's camaraderie – he associates this with a kind of innocence before the 'fall' – but also, crucially, he admires the seriousness of purpose and the necessary discipline required to play. This leads him to the world of professional poker, a career change Keith all but drifts into and that takes him to Las Vegas. This commitment and dedication mirrors Hammad's religious fervour and obsessive focus on the 9/11 plot. Keith's emasculation takes him away from his wife and family and allows him to continue to be introspective, emotionally detached and still grieving in parallel with

Hammad's exile from his country leading towards his own 'epiphany' in his martyred death.

This crisis in masculinity that makes up a major aspect of the novel can be read in the other male characters, particularly in respect of uncertain nomenclature. These include: 'Bill Lawton' (actually Bin Laden but his name has been westernised by children who mishear it and collectively mythologise his imminent arrival in New York); Ernst Hechinger, Lianne's mother's German art-dealer lover who, after a radical political youth changes his name to Martin; and David Janiak, who is later revealed to be the man who performs as the novel's titular 'Falling Man', a street installation in which he is seen hanging from various buildings in an apparent homage to the falling bodies on 9/11. Hammad's religious passion – inspired in no small part by Atta himself (in Hamburg and in Florida) – is informed by his guilty sexual fantasies. He masturbates (*FM*: p. 80) and wonders about a woman he knows who 'had dark eyes and a floppy body that liked contact' (*FM*: p. 81). As he willingly surrenders to Islamist philosophies and prepares himself for his exalted death, he is still burdened with lust:

> Two women rustling through a park in the evening, in long skirts, one of them barefoot. Hammad sat on a bench, alone, watching, then got up and followed. This was something that just happened, the way a man is pulled out of his skin and then the body catches up. He followed only to the street where the park ended, watching as they disappeared, brief as turning pages. (*FM*: p. 176)

Hammad turns his back on the promise or possibility of real human contact[4] in favour of an abstract, but passionately felt, idea in a similar way to Keith, who renounces his former life and retreats to the mathematics, statistics and routine of poker.

Hammad, unusually given his fellow jihadists' piety and chastity, does have sexual relations, or appears to, with a woman called Leyla. In many ways this relationship's apparent disconnectedness correlates with Keith's brief affair with Florence. Hammad enjoys the fact that she makes him feel 'more intelligent' and revels in the fact that his association with the 'cell' means that he must remain 'mysterious, a circumstance she found interesting' (*FM*: p. 82). He hopes to learn English from her and continues to dream of 'some huge future landscape opening up, all mountain and sky' (*FM*: p. 82). DeLillo suggests though, that whilst Hammad is drawn to women he is also simultaneously trying to escape them and what they symbolise to him:

> He did a little lusting after the roommate when he saw her ride her bike but tried not to bring this craving into the house. His girlfriend clung to him and

they did damage to the cot. She wanted him to know her whole presence, inside and out. They ate falafel wrapped in pita and sometimes he wanted to marry her and have babies but this was only in the minutes after he left her flat, fleeing like a footballer running across the field after scoring a goal, all-world, his arms flung wide. (*FM*: p. 82)

Hammad and Keith thus share a devotion to self-discipline, or more accurately the two men share a desire to escape the self. Both seek to renounce the material world and lose themselves in a 'cause' or a 'sport' (both, in very different ways, involve risk and chance). Hammad dreams 'of the rapture of live explosives pressed to his chest and waist' (*FM*: p. 177) and when he sees 'rivers and streams' and holds a stone in his hand all he observes is 'Islam' (*FM*: p. 172). Keith achieves a 'measure of calm, of calculated logic' (*FM*: p. 211) when he plays cards and he enters a kind of trance where 'there was nothing outside, no flash of history or memory' (*FM*: p. 225) to intrude upon his thoughts. As Laura Miller suggests, this is part of DeLillo's aim to show how the two men are pursuing an almost transcendent release from the world that will make them 'pure and free'.[5] This 'connection' between the two men, culminating in the attack on the Twin Towers, is only one of many connections that DeLillo stresses throughout the novel. This is part of the text's urgent attempts to 'make sense' of the attacks, seeing a certain kind of pathology in the masculine mind that leads to Keith's sense of confusion and trauma and Hammad's desire to cause massive death and catastrophe.

In one respect this is reminiscent of much of DeLillo's previous writing, in particular his portrayal of Lee Harvey Oswald in *Libra* and, as Toby Litt points out, the Moonies in *Mao 11*.[6] Indeed, the character of Hammad bears much resemblance to Oswald and this comparison sheds some light on perhaps the central motif of *Falling Man*: ambiguity surrounding ontology, identity and nomenclature. Michael Johnstone refers to this as 'ontological insecurity'[7] and argues that this has become an increasingly important trope in DeLillo's work. Oswald trains to become 'Oswald' and is partly a figment of other peoples' imaginations and ambitions – a metaphor that aptly mirrors the mysteries and lacunae evident in the real Oswald's life. Hammad, likewise, 'becomes' another person through his complete immersion in radical Islam and the 'magnetic effect' (*FM*: p. 174) of the 9/11 plot: 'He sat in a barber chair and looked in the mirror. He was not here, it was not him' (*FM*: p. 175).

This 'ontological insecurity' can be found throughout *Falling Man*, suggesting a sense of profound 'slippage' in the defining of character and self. Linked to this trope is the recurring problem of the ambiguity of meaning inherent in signs and symbols. Throughout the novel characters are confronted with things that appear to signify particular meanings but they continually resist precise definitions. Evidently the 9/11 attacks are part of this dilemma: in effect DeLillo's novel grapples with the signifying force of the attacks. The performance artist 'Falling Man', for example, appears on the streets of New York suspended in mid-air from various buildings. This provocative act[8] appears deliberately to evoke perhaps the most controversial set of images from 9/11.[9] Lianne witnesses one of his performances on an elevated roadway at Grand Central Station:

> A man was dangling there, above the street, upside down. He wore a business suit, one leg bent, arms at his sides. A safety harness was barely visible, emerging from his trousers at the straightened leg and fastened to the decorative rail of the viaduct. (*FM*: p. 33)

This art/spectacle/performance seems to be 'speaking' about 9/11 and Lianne, as she watches, considers what it is 'saying':

> There were people shouting up at him, outraged at the spectacle, the puppetry of human desperation, a body's last fleet breath and what it held. It held the gaze of the world, she thought. There was the awful openness of it, something we'd not seen, the single falling figure that trails a collective dread, body come down among us all. And now, she thought, this little theater piece, disturbing enough to stop the traffic and send her back into the terminal. (*FM*: p. 33)

This art installation's silence – it is 'saying' nothing but at the same time has remarkable symbolic power – mirrors the 'silence' of the infamous photograph of the unnamed falling body. Both have 'awful openness' to them, a sense of proliferating readings that coalesce around a 'collective dread' that the attacks produced. Lianne recoils from the knowledge that the 'Falling Man' stunt embodies, a 'turning away' from reality that informed the concomitant cultural retreat from the 'taboo' of the original photograph.

Throughout the novel there are many recurrences of this dilemma of reading into signs and symbols in the aftermath of 9/11. DeLillo suggests that this 'world' has been radically ruptured and as such this motif is summed up when Lianne later observes: 'Everything seemed to mean something. Their lives were in transition and she looked for signs' (*FM*: p. 67). The 'Falling Man' performance pieces seem to 'mean something' about 9/11 but it is never really clear what that meaning is. It is as if the huge, overwhelming symbolism of the attacks has made everything in its wake alive with new and elusive content. The characters search for co-ordinates and for a language to articulate this changed world but struggle to achieve mastery over the accumulating signs and symbols. This is emphasised the second time Lianne encounters the 'Falling Man'. She, along with others, sees him clamber down onto the tracks of the elevated railway, dressed in a blue suit. At first, because previously his performances have been in busy areas where there were large crowds, Lianne worries that this individual is actually a real suicide but she soon realises his identity and finds herself helplessly watching as he prepares to throw himself off the tracks just as a train approaches. Lianne imagines the passengers 'jarred out of their reveries' who 'would only see him fall out of sight' (FM: p. 165), unaware that he was fixed with a safety harness.

She then considers his motivation, realising that people on the train would pass on what they saw on their mobile phones:

> There was one thing for them [the passengers] to say, essentially. Someone falling. Falling man. She wondered if this was his intention, to spread the word this way, by cell phone, intimately, as in the towers and the hijacked planes. (FM: p. 165)

But, as throughout the novel, Lianne cannot be certain that this is the case: 'Or she was dreaming his intentions. She was making it up, stretched so tight across the moment that she could not think her own thoughts' (FM: p. 165). Despite herself, Lianne remains there fascinated and begins to experience uncanny flashbacks and disorienting visions of Keith 'in a high window with smoke flowing out' (FM: p. 167). 'Falling Man' jumps and Lianne watches, in a simulacrum of the crowds who watched from the streets and on TV as the towers were crashed into and of the people who hopelessly attempted to escape the fire and smoke:

> But the fall was not the worst of it. The jolting end of the fall left him upside-down, secured to the harness, twenty feet above the pavement. The jolt, the sort of midair impact and bounce, the recoil, and now the stillness, arms at his sides, one leg bent at the knee. There was something awful about the stylized pose, body and limbs, his signature stroke. (FM: p. 168)

The confluence of art and trauma causes Lianne to flee from the scene, her proximity to the act a deciding factor in her emotional and visual disturbance. She encounters a man who is frozen, staring up at the dangling figure and realises that he too is seeing 'something elaborately different' from ordinary reality and that he too was trying to 'learn how to see it correctly, [and] find a crack in the world where it might fit' (FM: p. 168).

The performance of the 'Falling Man' causes Lianne and the other witnesses to relive the trauma of the attacks. His 'art' re-enacts the cognitive and ontological shock of seeing real events that cannot successfully be recalibrated back into language. The 'unbelievability' of the hijacked planes and the falling bodies and the towers' eventual collapse is matched by the shock of an artwork that demands new aesthetic criteria for it to be judged and understood. In another sense the art of 'Falling Man' offers something of a meta-commentary on the novelist's (or artist's) position vis-à-vis 9/11: what can be said, or rather added, to the vast array of 9/11 imagery that isn't already being, as it were, 'said' by the attacks themselves? 'Falling Man's' spectacle has no conventional artistic context, as 9/11 seemed to have no historical or representational context to understand it. Thus, DeLillo implies, both radically challenge interpretation and potentially upset previous held notions of aesthetic form and historical reality. The artist, figuratively, hangs perilously from a position of hindsight, able to look back and comment on events but uncertain as to what that comment might add up to and how an audience might comprehend it. Lianne is likewise unable fully to assimilate the provocative re-enactment of 'Falling Man' into her fragile psyche and cannot fix its intended meaning, seeing only a 'blankness' in his face, a 'kind of lost gaze' (*FM*: p. 167). Keith immerses himself in professional poker in order to find some semblance of control and order after his survival and here, exacerbated by her own sense of mortality and the powerful symbolism of 'Falling Man', Lianne gradually moves towards religion with the hope that it might provide solace from her paranoia and loss.

Another layer of this trope of the uncertainty of meaning occurs later when the identity of 'Falling Man' is revealed.[10] Lianne reads his obituary in the newspaper and then goes on-line to find out more about him. His name was David Janiak and he apparently died from natural causes because of a heart ailment. His 'falls were headfirst, none announced in advance' and they were 'not designed to be recorded by a photographer' (*FM*: p. 220). Lianne reads that his 'final fall' was planned not to include a safety harness' (*FM*: p. 221). There remains uncertainty about the position that 'Falling Man' assumed when in his performance pieces but she wonders whether he was deliberately paying homage to Richard Drew's famous photograph:[11]

> The man falling, the towers contiguous, she thought, behind him. The enormous soaring lines, the vertical column stripes. The man with blood on his shirt, she thought, or burn marks, and the effect of the columns behind him, the composition, she thought, darker stripes for the nearer tower, the north, lighter for the other, and the mass, the immensity of it, and the man set almost precisely between the rows of darker and lighter stripes. Headlong, free fall, she though, and this picture burned a hole in her mind and heart, dear God, he was a falling angel and his beauty was horrific. (*FM*: pp. 221–2)

Both Janiak's 'art' and Drew's photograph are representations and Lianne tries to make sense of them in relation to each other. The uncanny simulacrum of 'Falling Man/Janiak' appears directly to quote from the photograph that was published in a number of newspapers across the world but was then, in a large part due to readers' protests, withdrawn by editors.[12] The image was seen to be too disturbing and there were accusations of exploitation and bad taste. Thus, Janiak's provocative reliving of the photograph breaks the taboo that arose surrounding the photograph.

Lianne's appreciation of the photograph's composition is especially telling, as is her rather mawkish assertion that the falling individual is 'a falling angel'. As Junod's article and the subsequent TV documentary attest, there remains uncertainty as to the identity of the man Drew photographed. His anonymity – matched by the mystery of Janiak's identity, at first, and then his intentions – allows him to be read within symbolic terms. Lianne, who has also been drawn to the paintings of Giorgio Morandi,[13] tries to understand the photograph aesthetically, noticing, as she does, the symmetry of the body's visual and spatial relationship with the sides of the towers. But her reading of it – inspired by her increasingly religious outlook- is entirely misplaced and misinformed. She sees 'horrific beauty' in the photograph but equates this with some kind of vague quasi-mystical martyrdom. Drew's image, taken from a series of frames showing the body in various positions as it hurtles to the ground, is itself merely a representation and as such has the potential to distort the reality of a falling body. Junod points this out in his article:

> Photographs lie. Even great photographs. Especially great photographs. The Falling Man in Richard Drew's picture fell in the manner suggested by the photograph for only a fraction of a second, and then kept falling. The photograph functioned as a study of doomed verticality, a fantasia of straight lines, with a human being slivered at the center, like a spike. In truth, however, the Falling Man fell with neither the precision of an arrow nor the grace of an Olympic diver. He fell like everyone else, like all the other jumpers – trying to hold on to the life he was leaving, which is to say that he fell desperately, inelegantly. In Drew's famous photograph, his humanity is in accord with the lines of the buildings. In the rest of the sequence – the eleven outtakes – his humanity stands apart. He is not augmented by aesthetics; he is merely human, and his humanity, startled and in some cases horizontal, obliterates everything else in the frame.[14]

Junod's phrase 'augmented by aesthetics' is particularly apposite in light of *Falling Man* in that it emphasises the fact that the photograph, in a sense, distorts the reality of the individual's descent. The image 'speaks', as Lianne suggests, of symmetry, beauty, pathos, even a kind of stoicism perhaps. Janiak's performance pieces evoke similar responses. Thus, Lianne tries to make sense of 9/11 – filtered through her own personal issues surrounding her marriage – through the realm of the symbolic and in this respect the novel wrestles with a central question of the Literature of Terror: namely, that if the artist has only the realm of the symbolic to respond to and then re-present, what can an added layer of symbolism add to the already existing image? DeLillo uses the figure of Janiak to explore this question – and arguably suggests something of his own dilemma as a novelist. Lianne discovers in her research that the jumps caused Janiak severe pain 'due to the rudimentary equipment he used' (*FM*: p. 222) and that his last jump would amount to a suicide. It is tempting to suggest that language might indeed be thought of as 'rudimentary equipment' when used to articulate the trauma of 9/11. Janiak's intentions remain opaque and therefore his performances also can only be understood as a simulacrum of a photograph that itself is inscrutable and open to endless interpretation.

Lianne, in her efforts to make meanings from all the signs and symbols that she encounters, recalls the moment that she witnessed his jump from the railway:

> She tried to connect this man to the moment when she'd stood beneath the elevated tracks, nearly three years ago, watching someone prepare to fall from a maintenance platform as the train went past. There were no photographs of that fall. She was the photograph, the photosensitive surface. That nameless body coming down, this was hers to record and absorb. (*FM*: p. 223)

Thus, in another example of 'ontological insecurity', Lianne momentarily loses her identity and 'becomes' a 'photosensitive surface', passively recording an image that defies a definitive interpretation. In the end, Lianne concedes that the 'man eluded her' (*FM*: p. 224) – mirroring the continued anonymity of the man captured in Drew's photograph – and all she has left is the memory, the image preserved on the 'negative' of her psyche. He is 'detailed and looming' (*FM*: p. 224) and cannot be successfully accommodated into Lianne's grasp of reality. Her rather bewildering and disturbing allusion to the falling man in the iconic (and largely taboo) photograph as an 'angel' is further proof of her detachment from the realm of the real. As Junod points out, there was nothing 'angelic' about the people who jumped or were forced from the towers and the reality of their traumatising predicament is potentially too shocking for art to include within its necessarily aestheticising forms.

So it becomes clear that this trope of 'ontological insecurity' is articulated through various crises surrounding identity, nomenclature and semiotics. Aside from the issues explored through the figure of the

'Falling Man', the novel includes interconnected characters that represent other sites of ambiguity. Martin Ridnour, the art-dealer lover of Lianne's mother, Nina, is revealed to have had a previous incarnation as a radical terrorist in 1960s' Germany. His real name is Ernst Hechinger and he was a member of 'Kommune One'[15] (FM: p. 146), a Situationist inspired movement made up of activists demonstrating against the 'fascist state' (FM: p. 146). Nina reveals that she is uncertain as to what precisely he did: 'First they threw eggs. Then they set off bombs. After that I'm not sure what he did' (FM: p. 146). In conversations with Lianne and her mother – and after Nina's death with Lianne alone – Martin/Ernst articulates a European attitude towards the attack and America's place and role in the world. As Nina states, his attitude towards 9/11 is radically different from her's and her daughter's:

> He thinks these people, these jihadists, he thinks they have something in common with the radicals of the sixties and seventies. He thinks they're all part of the same classical pattern. They have their theorists. They have their visions of world brotherhood. (FM: p. 147)

Martin/Ernst thus correlates with 'Falling Man'/Janiak as an ambiguous, ultimately unknowable enigma that Lianne tries to unravel. But as with the performance artist, Martin/Ernst resists clear definition.

Despite having known him for twenty years, Nina has only a very sketchy idea as to what Martin/Ernst did as a radical in Germany (and Italy with the Red Brigades). Lianne is initially outraged at her mother's ignorance but later she relents: 'Maybe he was a terrorist but he was one of ours, she thought, and the thought chilled her, shamed her – one of ours, which meant godless, Western, white' (FM: p. 195). This conclusion is part of Lianne's own racist confusions surrounding the attacks: she is disturbed by the 'Islamic' (FM: p. 67) music that she hears from downstairs and she subsequently confronts and physically attacks her neighbour, accusing her of being deliberately insensitive 'under these circumstances' (FM: p. 119). There is also an obvious parallel between the terrorism of the 1960s and 1970s and that of the 9/11 hijackers. Nina recalls a wanted poster in Martin/Ernst's Berlin apartment of 'nineteen names and faces' (FM: p. 147), the same number as made up the 9/11 hijackers. And Martin/Ernst, like Keith in his poker games and Hammad in his religious fervour, appears to value discipline and order, emphasised by his decision to have unadorned walls: 'Is this part of the old longing? [Lianne asks] Days and nights in seclusion, hiding out somewhere, renouncing every trace of material comfort' (FM: p. 147). Nina defends him against Lianne's charges: 'He's not in hiding anymore, if he ever was. He's here, there and everywhere' (FM: p. 147). Again, identity is shown to be an endlessly mutable and fluctuating state – biographical details remain opaque and names and commitments are always open to (or vulnerable to) change.

Martin and Nina debate the motivations behind the attacks and Martin's interpretation unsettles both women. Whilst Nina speaks of the hijackers' focus on 'God' (*FM*: p. 112) and describes their 'misplaced grievance' as a 'viral infection' that remains 'outside history' (*FM*: pp. 112–13), Martin prefers to see the attacks in the context of a history of 'people in conflict' (*FM*: p. 112) who 'want their place in the world, their own global union, not ours' (*FM*: p. 116). DeLillo effectively uses Martin as a mouthpiece for certain philosophical and political ideas – the novel is at times essayistic and arguably rather pretentious in its scenes where characters speak in often stilted non-sequiturs and gnomic pronouncements.[16] It is a moot point whether this is merely a stylistic tic, so to speak, or a deliberate attempt to emphasise how detached and isolated each individual is within her/his existence. If we can accept that it might well be a combination of the two we can see how Martin performs a crucial role in the narrative as another complex male figure that embodies 'ontological insecurity'. The ways in which the characters correspond with each other – whilst often undeniably contrived and over-determined – capture *Falling Man*'s overall mood of deracinated individuals further atomised in the ruptured aftermath of 9/11.

Conclusion: 'I am a Lover of America'

As we have seen throughout this study, 9/11 has provided writers (and filmmakers) with profound problems of representation. In the ten years since the attacks there have been a huge number of novels, poems, plays and films that, in various different ways have responded to the attacks. It is, of course, comparatively early to begin establishing a poetics of 9/11 representation and this study is merely a contribution to this growing area of research. Nevertheless there is a sense that such representations are moving away from the 'sacralising', 'mythologising' and 'commemorative' discourses that have dominated how 9/11 has been written and spoken about. Hence, as we shall see with Pankaj Mishra's valuable essay, critics are gradually discerning a shift towards less 'respectful' responses, thus suggesting that the attacks will continue to figure in fiction but in more problematic and certainly more politicised ways. This conclusion will provide possible forms with which this will take place.

Pankaj Mishra's article 'The End of Innocence' appeared in *The Guardian* on 19 May 2007, in part as a review of DeLillo's then recently published *Falling Man* but also as a valuable over-view of 9/11 fiction up to that point. It is a sustained analysis of mostly American 9/11 fiction and it offers a perceptive critique of how the majority of these novels have failed to understand 9/11. This lack of understanding, he writes, mirrors a lack of historical consciousness in American writing as a whole:

In comparison [with other, non-American representations of the post 9/11 world], most of the literary fiction that self-consciously addresses 9/11 still seems underpinned by out-dated assumptions of national isolation and self-sufficiency. The 'reconsiderations' DeLillo promised after 9/11 don't seem to have led to a renewed historical consciousness. Composed within the narcissistic heart of the west, most 9/11 fictions seem unable to acknowledge political and ideological belief as a social and emotional realty in the world – the kind of fact that cannot be reduced to the individual experience of rage, envy, sexual frustration and constipation. (EI: p. 6)

Indeed, the title of Mishra's article is intended to be largely ironic: he accuses American authors of colluding with the myth of pre-9/11 innocence that was destroyed by the September 11 attacks. He argues that DeLillo, Messud, McInerney, Amis, McEwan et al. are guilty of a retreat to the concerns of the domestic and the individual (as if terrified by the implications of writing 'beyond' such local concerns) and of misreading the motives behind the attacks.

Mishra suggests that the 'dominant mood of American 9/11 commemoration' (EI: p. 6) has stopped writers from fully confronting the political and economic realities that fundamentally informed the motivations of the hijackers and that many people around the world share these feelings. These writers, particularly American novelists in the post-Cold War years, were caught up in 'the extraordinarily complacent mood of the decade' (EI: p. 4) in which economic boom and narcissism dominated the culture. In this reading, Mishra argues, 9/11 acts as a symbolic 'wake up call' for those Americans who had become isolated and pampered. But this discourse – which as has been seen dominates a large proportion of the American (and British) responses to the attacks – mirrors a much larger and more problematic ignorance of the rest of the world and the relationship between national and international concerns. As Mishra argues in light of DeLillo's description of the 'reconsiderations' that have arisen since 9/11, many of these novels articulate a false (and politically insidious) regression which clings to the culturally dominant sense of 9/11 as a 'unique' historical event.

Mishra writes that 'the western vision of endless prosperity and well-being had proved a deception for the billions of people living outside the west' (EI: p. 4). Despite the promises being made on behalf of the dotcom boom, the 'democracy' of the Net and the growing discourses of interdependency and globalisation, there were huge parts of the world that were not sharing in this economic revolution. Although some writers evidently did recognise this dichotomy – Jonathan Franzen, Richard Powers and of course DeLillo – subsequent 9/11 novels have retreated to 'the domestic life' (EI: p. 6) rather than engage with the wider political and economic realities and how America has been deeply involved largely thanks to its foreign policy. Indeed, when writers have attempted to confront these forces – *Falling Man*, *Terrorist* and 'The Last Days of Muhammad Atta' – they have failed, in part because of this cultural and political myopia. Mishra writes: 'Struggling to define cultural otherness, DeLillo, Updike and Amis fail to recognise that belief and ideology remain the unseen and overwhelming forces behind gaudy fantasies about virgins' (EI: p. 6).

Mishra makes a number of provocative points and it is useful to identify each one and respond to them in turn:

1. In comparison with the mostly European novelists who lived and wrote in the aftermath of the First World War, American writers responding to 9/11 have retreated towards the subjective, the domestic and the local.
2. Furthermore, the American novel in general (apart from writers in the Vietnam era, although this remains a moot point in the article) has shied away from 'the machinery of social and political power' (EI: p. 4).
3. A number of 9/11 novels – mainly written by white men – are dominated by masculine anxiety, stereotypes of the 'other' and tropes familiar from the American canon. These novels are 'underpinned by outdated assumptions of national isolation and self-sufficiency' (EI: p. 6).
4. Writers from different backgrounds and nationalities, from different ethnicities and from women have more fully described the 'fundamental instability' (EI: p. 6) of identity in the postmodern world. And this recognition of 'a new existential incoherence' (EI: p. 6) was an ongoing phenomenon before September 11th, a fact that Western writers have been extremely slow to recognise.[1]

Mishra's comparison between contemporary writers and the novelists who wrote before, during and after the First World War is illuminating and useful as a way of contextualising 9/11 fictions. The war 'forced European artists into self-appraisals even more severe than those undertaken by British and American writers after 9/11' (EI: p. 4). The rapidity and power of the rise and spread of 'commercial, military and diplomatic networks' meant that economies were 'internationalised to an unprecedented degree' (EI: p. 4). Evidently there are apt comparisons to be made between these tumultuous years and the decade following the end of the Cold War. But Mishra suggests that although writers could 'still appeal to 19th-century notions about the absolute autonomy of art ... they could not remain unaware of the challenges posed to them by the dramatic transformations around them'. These were 'new, impersonal forces' (EI: p. 4) that were 'simmering' (EI: p. 6) beneath the surface of mainstream, bourgeois society.

The First World War changed these last vestiges of belief in an 'old order' and instigated a 'sense of a severe rupture and crisis in civilisation'

(EI: p. 4). This in turn forced artists 'to try to describe how and why human relations had altered in the new conditions of modern life' (EI: p. 4). Even though writers such as James and Conrad wrote much of their work before this profound rupture, their work still recognised and engaged with the 'new, impersonal forces'. By comparison, contemporary American writers have been too preoccupied with purely national, local and domestic concerns and in doing so have ignored the importance of their relationship with global forces. Despite the comparative, but lesser, 'rupture' of 9/11, the majority of novelists have continued to perpetuate certain ideas about America, the foreign 'other' and the growing interdependence of both. These were the 'previously invisible conflicts and traumas' (EI: p. 4) that also 'simmered' beneath the surface of prosperous mainstream America.

Mishra's argument here is cogent, intelligent and helpful in identifying new ways to write about the growing poetics and politics of 9/11 writing. It is arguable though that at times Mishra, as it were, 'sweeps' through decades of American and European history to make this point and that there are certain reservations and caveats that one might raise. Mishra establishes a clear opposition between the European modernists and their American counterparts but modernism flourished in the USA and had an enormous impact on the arts following the First World War. Novels such as John Dos Passos' *Manhattan Transfer* (1925), F. Scott Fitzgerald's *The Great Gatsby* (1926),Thomas Wolfe's *Look Homeward, Angel* (1929) and William Faulkner's *The Sound and the Fury* (1929) all display modernist tropes and motifs.[2] In these texts there is a concern with form that mirrors European modernism and a growing ambition to forge new ways of writing about the self and its construction.

Certainly, though, as Mishra suggests, these novels are all intimately focused on America or rather 'America' and as such do not perhaps have the scope and scale of their European counterparts. But added to this is the unquestionable centrality of America in the twentieth century – culturally, politically and economically – and the profound sense that American writers work within this discourse of exceptionalism and global dominance. Many writers, Mishra argues, have been highly critical of such discourses (Mailer, Vidal, Vonnegut, Roth etc.) but their novels, even in light of 'the tragedy in Vietnam' 'proved too remote to inspire a sustained literary examination of national values and ideals' (*EI*: p. 4). This is a highly debatable point and one that ignores such hugely significant texts as Ellison's *Invisible Man* (1952), Bellow's *The Adventures of Augie March* (1953), Heller's *Catch 22* (1961), Capote's *In Cold Blood* (1968) and Pynchon's *Gravity's Rainbow* (1973), amongst many others. Whilst over-privileging the status of European and its former colonies' writers, Mishra misjudges the enormous impact of American novelists in this post-war period and although he does evoke many of these writers he remains unconvinced as to their lasting power.

Mishra quotes Philip Rahv from a symposium in 1953 who spoke of American hegemony making native writers believe the ' "illusion that our society is in its very nature immune to tragic social conflicts and collisions" and that "the more acute problems of the modern epoch are unreal as far as we are concerned" ' (EI: p. 4). Again, this argument fails to convince (and perhaps one should be mindful of the date of the quotation) due to the intensely critical, sceptical and challenging nature of so many American novels. Indeed, there is simply no sense at all that, say post-war American writing was in any way 'immune to tragic social conflicts and collisions'. Mishra's overall point – that the failure of the majority of American 9/11 fiction fully to grasp the attacks' signifi-cance mirrors a historical failure of American writers generally to write outside of merely local concerns – is directly tied to what seems to be a rather too convenient critique of modern and contemporary US writing. If anything, one might argue that the very notion of the 'Great American Novel' is predicated on a 'literary examination of national values and ideals'.

One might then suggest a reworking of Mishra's theory. Rather than American writing being parochial and uninterested in the politics and economics of the rest of the globe, it might be argued that 9/11 has signalled, in fact, another kind of 'retreat'. If Mishra is broadly correct about the relative failure of 9/11 fiction so far then this may have more to do with the impact that the attacks and the subsequent dominance of discourses of commemoration and remembrance have had upon America as a whole. Generally, as has been seen in the case of *Loose Change*, dissent from these hegemonic views has come largely on the Internet and, as Mishra goes on to argue, from non-American writers. The 'rupture' of 9/11 may well have, as it were, 'set back' American writing, trapping authors in tropes of melancholy, trauma, respectful-ness and bewilderment that have hindered, so far, representations of the attacks. Certainly, for example, DeLillo's *Falling Man* can be seen as a disappointing novel in comparison with his earlier *Underworld*. And it is disappointing for precisely the reasons that Mishra delineates. But this arguably stems from a pronounced timidity in DeLillo's approach to the subject given his previous writing on the threat of terrorism.

Added to this reservation about Mishra's reading of American fiction is the essay's charge that generally, with a few exceptions, the fiction of the 1990s simply reflected the nation's 'self-indulgent' mood (EI: p. 4). It would be reductive merely to list the novels that contradict Mishra's accusation (he does mention Franzen, Powers, Easton-Ellis and Bruce Wagner) but a glance at three writers' work emphasises the diversity and scope of American fiction from this period. Philip Roth's *Operation Shylock* (1993), *Sabbath's Theater* (1995), *American Pastoral* (1997) and *The Human Stain* (2000) represent a sustained investigation into the American psyche and also engage with the repercussions of the 1960s Vietnam protests, the Clinton administration and the Israel–Palestine conflict. Toni Morrison's *Jazz* (1993) and *Paradise* (1997) are the last two books in a trilogy begun with the Pulitzer Prize winning *Beloved* (1987) that attempt to retell major aspects of African-American history. The work of Chuck Palahniuk (*Fight Club* (1996), *Invisible Monsters* (1999), *Survivor* (1999)) is defined by a transgressive and subversive cynicism that attacks mainstream American culture.

Mishra's reading of McInerney, DeLillo, Safran Foer and Updike, in contrast, is perceptive and illuminating. As the previous chapters have shown, these writers have generally either ignored or failed to understand the terrorist 'character' and thus their novels have, perhaps unconsciously, re-enacted certain prevailing stereotypes. He writes that *Falling Man* is 'strangely incurious' about Hammad's past and cultural influences and that it 'ends up relying on received notions about Muslim "rage"' (EI: p. 6). Amis and Updike 'reach for some widely circulated clichés' and are keen to 'optimise [their] research'. Hence the authors' 'sympathy often breaks down' and their writing 'reduces individuals as well as movements to stereotypical motivations' (EI: p. 6). McInerney and Safran Foer 'are remarkable in that they strenuously avoid anything too intellectually alien and bewildering'. Mishra continues:

> They seem content to enlist the devastation in their city as a backdrop, and both use actual photographs of the event, either on the cover or within the text. But, for all that 9/11 stands for in their sentimental and nostalgic novels about New Yorkers coping with loss, it could be a natural disaster, like the tsunami. (EI: p. 6)

Throughout the study this insight has informed readings of American and European 9/11 fiction. This chapter will conclude with some thoughts on what a more fully engaged 9/11 representation might look like.

These criticisms feed directly into Mishra's point about the predominance of white, male writers and the implications of this bias. Mishra argues that it is only male writers who have lapsed 'into overexplicitness' (EI: p. 6) when describing the attacks themselves. This preoccupation with the violence and destruction of 9/11 is 'fuelled by masculine anxiety' that is defined by a 'voyeuristic urge' (EI: p. 6). As was seen in Amis' 9/11 writing the portrayal of Islamist followers was directly and explicitly informed by his presiding interest in male preoccupations. Likewise, DeLillo's novel replays many of the familiar tropes and motifs found in earlier male characters, thus revealing more about the novelist's oeuvre than the terrorist psyche. But more than this, Mishra implies a concern surrounding the 'emasculation' of America – in Freudian terms, 9/11 interpreted unconsciously as a castration complex. Although Mishra does not go into much further detail on this insight – indeed, there is something slightly glib about the way in which it is inserted into the essay – there is much to be considered in light of America's response to the attacks.

A final novel that deals with 9/11 and its aftermath is Mohsin Hamid's *The Reluctant Fundamentalist* (2007) that fulfils something of what Mishra has seen as a discernibly 'non-commemorative' perspective on the attacks. Hamid's novel is one of the first attempts to reconfigure the attacks through the eyes of a non-Westerner whose thoughts and feelings about 9/11 are strikingly ambiguous and finally ambivalent. The novel takes the form of a monologue spoken by Changez to an un-named American in a market café in Lahore.[3] The American may be a tourist or, more likely, a member of the armed or secret services – it appears as though he has a gun but it could also be a container for business cards. Likewise, Changez may simply be, as he attests, a radical university lecturer or he may in fact have more sinister motives for wanting to detain his American 'guest'. Changez proceeds to share his memories of America, occasionally interrupted by conversational asides (that become increasingly nervous and paranoid) in the present tense of the café in Lahore. These memories begin to coalesce into Changez's confession of disgust and anger with an America he once admired and revelled in: 'I made it my mission on campus to advocate a disengagement from your country by mine' (*RF*: p. 179). Finally, after Changez has finished his memoir, he escorts the American back to his hotel only to discover that there is a group of men beginning to surround them with the apparent intentions of kidnapping or assassination.

Thus Hamid's novel seems initially to be about Changez's radicalisation following the September attacks. He is, in effect, the 'fundamentalist' of the novel's title, however 'reluctant'[4] or otherwise he might be. But a further connotation of the title is suggested by a short story Hamid published in *The Paris Review* (2006) and took from *The Reluctant Fundamentalist*. This story is entitled 'Focus on the Fundamentals'[5] and anticipates Changez's initiation into the New York financial culture. Wainwright, Changez's closest friend at the company, reminds him that he is 'working for the *man*' and that all he needs to do is 'focus on the fundamentals' (*RF*: p. 98). These 'fundamentals', Changez points out, signified 'a single-minded attention to financial detail, [and] teasing out the true nature of those drivers that determine an asset's value' (*RF*: p. 98). Increasingly, Changez comes to see these economic 'fundamentals' as being crucial components of merciless American capitalism. In effect, Changez adopts the persona, reluctantly, of the American fundamentalist.

Changez speaks of his trainee days at Underwood Samson and Company after having been top of his class at Princeton University. He and a select group of fellow graduates were educated in 'soft skills training' and *'professionalism'* (*RF*: pp. 36 and 37) and they 'learned to prioritize – to determine the axis on which advancement would be most beneficial – and then to apply ourselves single-mindedly to the achievement of that objective' (*RF*: p. 37). He describes his own 'controlled aggression' and admits to 'subsisting on only a few hours of sleep a night' and still being able to study 'with utter concentration' (*RF*: p. 41). These comments deliberately evoke the language familiar from Islamist fundamentalists and increasingly Changez sees that aggressive American capitalism is a direct ideological corollary with the religious and political movements in the Middle East. And although he proves himself highly successful in this world, Changez remains troubled by the more acquisitive and interventionist aspects of his chosen career. He is reminded that although he has been rewarded for his dedication (partly thanks, he believes, to his 'foreignness' (*RF*: p. 42)) he will always remain an outsider. This status is exacerbated after the 9/11 attacks.

The 'pursuit of fundamentals' (*RF*: p. 116) that defines these market forces Changez grows to see as being a 'creed' that 'valued above all else maximum productivity' (*RF*: p. 116). Despite the rupture of the attacks this ideology 'remained utterly convinced of the possibility of progress' (*RF*: pp. 116–17) and, thanks to Changez's regular trips abroad, he witnesses the consequences of this fundamentalism. Thus Hamid attempts, with no small degree of irony, to turn the meaning of 'fundamentalist' around. And furthermore, in an echo of Naomi Klein's *The Shock Doctrine: The Rise of Disaster Capitalism* (2007), the fundamentals of market forces economics are intimately linked both with the myth of American superiority and its foreign policy. The initial stirrings of Changez's awakening begin when he holidays in Greece with his fellow Princeton students – and it is here that he first meets Erica. He is proud to be a member of 'this wealthy young fellowship' but also sees their arrogance: 'I ... found myself wondering by what quirk of human history my companions – many of whom I would have regarded as upstarts in my own country, so devoid of refinement were they – were in a position to conduct themselves in the world as though they were its ruling class' (*RF*: p. 221).

Changez visits the Philippines and revels in his newly found privileged status. He flies first-class and realises that he is acting and speaking 'more like an *American*' (*RF*: p. 65). He tells people he is from New York and jumps to the front of queues. He feels 'enormously powerful' (*RF*: p. 66) as he observes the factory floor of the record-music business he is helping to value and is aware that he is assisting in deciding the future of the company and its work-force (*RF*: p. 66). But, as throughout the novel, Changez also wrestles with an opposing set of thoughts (that he keeps hidden from his colleagues) in which he feels empathy and solidarity with the locals of Manila. This ambivalence reaches a breaking point when Changez sees the driver of a jeepney[6] from the limousine. The driver looks at him with 'undisguised hostility' (*RF*: p. 66) and this act angers Changez who returns the driver's stare. Later he speculates as to the reasons for the driver's evident distaste and identifies that in fact he and the driver 'shared a sort of Third World sensibility' (*RF*: p. 67).

Changez has something of an epiphany. He feels that his colleagues now seem '*foreign*' and that he was 'in that moment much closer to the Filipino driver'. Changez effectively sees through his own 'play-acting' (*RF*: p. 67) and thus begins his gradual disillusionment with America. Indeed, by the time he journeys to Santiago – following the September attacks and the deterioration of Erica's mental health – Changez has all but discarded his old 'self' and is profoundly troubled by his collaboration with economics and politics that are directly affecting Pakistan and other nearby countries. He acknowledges that his 'blinders were coming off' (*RF*: p. 145) and he becomes ever more sullen and withdrawn and resentful of his collusion. The chief of the publishing company Changez has been elected to value, Juan-Bautista,[7] confronts him with the implications of his career: ' "Does it trouble you," he enquired, "to make your living by disrupting the lives of others?" ' (*RF*: p. 151).

Juan-Batista refers to the janissaries, a word Changez is unfamiliar with:

'They were Christian boys,' he explained, 'captured by the Ottomans and trained to be soldiers in a Muslim army, at that time the greatest army in the world. They were ferocious and utterly loyal: they had fought to erase their own civilizations, so they had nothing else to turn to.' (*RF*: p. 151)

This reference to the sixteenth-century Islamic recruits represents another epiphany in Changez's perception of himself:

> I was a modern-day janissary, a servant of the American empire at a time when it was invading a country with a kinship to mine and was perhaps even colluding to ensure that my own country faced the threat of war. Of course I was struggling! Of course I felt torn! I had thrown in my lot with the men of Underwood Samson, with the officers of the empire, when all along I was predisposed to feel compassion for those, like Juan-Batista, whose lives the empire thought nothing of overturning for its own gain. (*RF*: p. 152)

Consequently, Changez is fired from his job. He makes some last efforts to resurrect his relationship with Erica who has been admitted to a health clinic and who eventually disappears, presumed to have killed herself, and then returns to Pakistan (in 2002) where he becomes a university lecturer. This position affords him an opportunity to 'advocate a disengagement from your country [America] by mine' (*RF*: p. 179). Changez's struggle – his 'reluctance' – with his embrace of American values reflects a shift in his political outlook: in essence he moves out from the personal to the public sphere.

This sense of developing disillusionment is also embodied in the character of Erica and in the scenes where Changez directly reflects on the significance and meaning of 9/11. As has been noted, Changez first encounters Erica on holiday in Greece and he is immediately attracted to her. She is an aspiring writer whose boyfriend, Chris, to whom she was devoted, died from lung cancer after an arduous three-year battle. Erica's continuing and debilitating obsession with him dominates her relationship with Changez who himself remains loyal to her. In what is perhaps an allusion to Gatsby's love for Daisy in Fitzgerald's *The Great Gatsby*, Changez develops a semi-mythological love that represents his unrequited dreams of America itself. Similarly, Eric's collapse into depression and even madness connotes Changez's view of the United States following the attacks. In this sense, Erica is another 'reluctant fundamentalist': she narrows her life down to living only in the past (a deeply romanticised past) that mirrors America's cultural and political retreat into the nation's cherished myths and legends. Both Erica and America withdraw into what Changez calls a 'chronic nostalgia' (*RF*: p. 148).

Even when Changez consummates his relationship with Erica it is refracted through memories of Chris. After an unsuccessful first attempt to seduce her Erica tells of her 'unusual love' for Chris and Changez concludes that she and Chris had experienced 'such a degree of commingling of identities' that Erica had 'lost herself' (*RF*: p. 91). Later

Changez experiences much the same disillusion of self when he suggests that when they make love Erica should think he is Chris:

> 'Then pretend,' I said, 'pretend I am him.' I do not know why I said it; I felt overcome and it seemed, suddenly, a possible way forward. 'What?' she said, but she did not open her eyes. 'Pretend I am him,' I said again. And slowly, in darkness and in silence, we did. (*RF*: p. 105)

This is another example of Changez's malleability and ability to 'be' whomsoever people desire him to be. He mimics the financial high-flyers he works with at Underwood and Sampson and then – after cultivating a thick beard – deliberately assumes what many Americans consider to be the look of a terrorist. Here he 'becomes' the embodiment of Erica's lost love and in the process again questions his real self.

Erica previously described the sensation of being 'haunted' (*RF*: p. 80) by Chris and Changez feels 'possessed' (*RF*: p. 105) after they have made love. The act itself is evoked in strikingly morbid language:

> The entrance between her legs was wet and dilated, but was at the same time oddly rigid; it reminded me – unwillingly – of a wound, giving our sex a violent undertone despite the gentleness with which I attempted to move. More than once I smelled what I thought to be blood, but when I reached down to ascertain with my fingers whether it was her time of month, I found them unstained. She shuddered towards the end – grievously, almost mortally; her shuddering called forth my own. (*RF*: pp. 105–6)

This is Changez's *petite mort* but also signals the last descent into disorientating depression of Erica. Changez senses his 'shame' and 'humiliation' in this act and fears that he 'had done Erica some terrible harm' (*RF*: p. 106) by inviting her to imagine him as Chris. On increasing medication, frail and withdrawn (and uninterested in writing or the future of her novella), Erica's 'powerful nostalgia' (*RF*: p. 113) makes Changez wonder whether it was 'the trauma of the attack on her city' that 'triggered her decline' (*RF*: p. 113). Thus, again, the reader is encouraged to equate Erica's predicament with the nation's response to 9/11.

Indeed the narrator insists more forcefully that there is a correlation between Erica's 'nostalgia' and post-9/11 American foreign policy. He sees that Chris' death made Erica aware of 'impermanence and mortality' (*RF*: p. 113) and that 'theirs was a past all the more potent for its being imaginary' (*RF*: p. 114). It amounted to 'a religion that would not accept me as a convert' (*RF*: p. 114). Hamid again evokes language familiar from 9/11 discourse – the 'impermanence' of the towers and how the attacks forced people to consider theirs and others' 'mortality', the myths of the American past being potently 'imaginary' and the

American Dream likened to a 'religion' that would not accept him (as an Asian immigrant) into its fold. Changez's final meeting with Erica, in the grounds of the clinic, consolidates this reading when he describes her as glowing 'with something not unlike the fervour of the *devout*' (*RF*: p. 133; author's italics). She is now living, or rather hiding, completely in the past. By extension, America has retreated into myths of heroism and national solidarity that helped to fuel the invasions of Afghanistan and Iraq. September 11 is the 'shock to the system' that is used to revitalise such language and imagery and helps to define the reassertion of American global power and its sense of 'hurt' and 'trauma' after the attacks.

After her 'death' – suicide seems likely, perhaps suggesting a similar fate for American hegemony – Changez concludes that 'she had chosen not to be part of my story; her own had proved too compelling, and she was – at that moment and in her own way – following it to its conclusion, passing through places I could not reach' (*RF*: p. 167). And by recognising this Changez is able both physically and figuratively to leave America behind him. Erica's fatal nostalgia initially made Changez feel 'treacherous' for even thinking that the reborn American confidence in its own dominance was 'fictitious' (*RF*: p. 115). But after her disappearance/suicide he is finally certain, fundamentally, as it were, of America's corruption:

> As a society, you were unwilling to reflect upon the shared pain that united you with those who attacked you. You retreated into myths of your own difference, assumptions of your own superiority. And you acted out these beliefs on the stage of the world, so that the entire planet was rocked by the repercussions of your tantrums, not least my family, now facing war thousands of miles away. Such an America had to be stopped in the interests not only of the rest of humanity, but also in your own. (*RF*: p. 168)

Changez thus rejects America at the moment when he has realised that he was never fully accepted in the same way that he realises that he was never fully accepted by Erica. His hitherto confused and hidden feelings about aspects of American society are more aggressively articulated now that its myths and pernicious ideologies have been exposed to him. He leaves (Am)erica behind him once and for all.

As Changez has already speculated, Erica's decline may have been precipitated by the 9/11 attacks. Changez's own stirrings of unease about his adopted nation are also deepened when the attacks occur. These scenes are what mark Hamid's novel out most distinctly from the vast majority of 9/11 fiction. As has been already noted there are other examples where writers have sought to 'step outside' the dominant discourses of 9/11 representation, but Hamid goes further in exploring what has almost become a taboo in culture and society: namely, of describing the attacks in a non-'sacred' or non-commemorative way. This is what Trevor Lewis refers to as Changez's 'dark epiphany'[8] when he understands that, despite all his best efforts, he is a 'foreigner' in America. September 11 'wakes' Changez from his dream of America. Changez is in Manila – significantly he is outside of New York – packing his things in a hotel room when he turns on the television:

> I . . . saw what at first I took to be a film. But as I continued to watch, I realized that it was not fiction but news. I stared as one – and then the other – of the twin towers of New York's World Trade Center collapsed. And then I *smiled*. Yes, despicable as it may sound, my initial reaction was to be remarkably pleased. (*RF*: p. 72)

Changez is aware that his comments are eliciting disgust in his American interlocutor and reassures him that he is 'not indifferent to the suffering of others' (*RF*: p. 72) and that he 'was pleased at the slaughter of thousands of innocents' with a 'profound sense of perplexity' (*RF*: p. 73). Changez is instead concerned with the '*symbolism*' (*RF*: p. 73) of the attacks that signified that 9/11 'had so visibly brought America to her knees' (*RF*: p. 73). This gendering of the nation is a common figure of speech but it is also tempting to read 'her' as signifying Erica whose defences Changez cannot break down; this would represent another blurring of the private and public spheres.

Changez asks his interlocutor if he has not felt 'joy at the video clips – so prevalent these days – of American munitions laying waste the structure of your enemies?' (*RF*: p. 73). And thus Hamid exposes what has hitherto been largely absent from other 9/11 fiction: namely that 9/11 was not an isolated, irrational act aimed at an 'innocent' nation but rather a direct result of American colonial, economic and military power. As has been seen throughout the study, many American and British writers have largely failed to reimagine the mind-set of the 'other' in relation to 9/11. Updike's Ahmad, DeLillo's Hammad and Amis' Atta each suffer from the familiar preoccupations of the respective authors overshadowing any insights into the terrorist mindset. But for now Mishra's description of many non-American (even non-Western) post-9/11 fictions as expressing a new 'existential incoherence' is useful when reading *The Reluctant Fundamentalist* because it articulates something of Changez's crisis.

For if Erica embodies the United States and all its seductive allures (and its propensity towards myth-making, nostalgia and finally madness),

Changez represents the position of the 'other'. Initially drawn to the nation and its wealth, opportunity and resources (its confidence in its own destiny), Changez is also uniquely situated to see how there has been an enormous price paid for this privilege. His collusion with the American Dream is predicated on precariously ambivalent feelings of arousal and disgust. This ambivalence is then played back at Changez when he returns to New York after the attacks. He is suddenly a suspicious individual because of his racial appearance. He is strip-searched in Manila and when he arrives in America he feels 'uncomfortable in [his] own face'. Inexplicably he feels 'under suspicion' and 'guilty' (*RF*: p. 74). This tension in New York immediately after the attacks is alluded to in DeLillo's *Falling Man* when Lianne confronts her neighbour Elena about her playing 'Arabic' or 'Islamic' music. Elena remains very much the 'other' in this novel – an impenetrable, inscrutable 'foreigner' whose very presence is an affront.

Previously, Changez had been 'armoured' with the appearance of a businessman but in the aftermath of the attacks he is instantly reconfigured as a potential threat. Whilst his colleagues join one queue for 'American citizens; I joined the one for foreigners' (*RF*: p. 75). He is questioned about the '*purpose*'[9] of his visit to the United States and is left to travel back to the city 'very much alone' (*RF*: p. 75). It is this profound deconstruction of his previously respectable self that breaks Changez from an ambivalent yet passionate commitment to American values to a position of barely concealed contempt for its hidden injustices. Changez describes the atmosphere in New York at this time as being defined by a 'self-righteous rage' (*RF*: p. 94) and it is this recognition of a barely concealed racism and resentment towards those considered 'suspicious' following the attacks that points towards possible ways in which the 'Literature of Terror' may well develop in the ensuing years. As the ten year anniversary provides us with an opportunity to survey how 9/11 has been represented in fiction, poetry, theatre, art and cinema, Changez's highly ambiguous response to the attacks and his subsequent existential crisis suggest that the impact of the event continues to be felt, in often disturbing and challenging ways, and will inevitably encourage more artists to reflect on its meaning.

Notes

Introduction

1. The American composer John Adams was commissioned by the New York Philharmonic and Lincoln Center's Great Performers to write an orchestral piece to commemorate 9/11. *On the Transmigration of Souls* utilises a chorus and pre-recorded sections inspired by real-life testimonies from victims, survivors and witnesses and premiered in 2002.
2. Craig A. Warren, ' "It Reads Like a Novel": The *9/11 Commission Report* and the American Reading Public', *Journal of American Studies* 41.3 (2007), pp. 533–56 (p. 534).
3. Ibid., p. 544.
4. In particular the collapse of WTC Building Seven that occurred later on September 11 at 5.25 pm. There are some who believe that the building collapsed in a 'controlled demolition'. See, in particular, Jim Marrs' *The Terror Conspiracy: Deception, 9/11, and the Loss of Liberty* (2006), pp. 60–2.
5. It is possible to do this at www.archive.org/details/sept_11_tv_archive (accessed 10 July 2010).
6. Martin Amis, *The Second Plane: September 11: 2001–2007* (London: Jonathan Cape, 2008), p. 3.
7. Paul Virilio, *Ground Zero* (London: Verso, 2002), p. 68.
8. Amis (2008), p. 11.
9. Ibid., pp. 12–13.
10. Ibid., p. 3.
11. Ibid., p. 13.
12. Ibid., p. 16.
13. Ibid., p. 16.
14. Ibid., p. 19.
15. Ibid., p. 18.
16. Ibid., p. 18.
17. See www.villagevoice.com/2006–02–14/news/the-seekers/2/ (accessed 17 July 2010).
18. See www.monbiot.com/archives/2007/02/12/short-changed/ (accessed 7 August 2010. (2002) at www.ubishops.ca/baudrillardstudies/spiegel.htm (accessed 12 Dec. 2009).

19. 'This is the Fourth World War: The *Der Spiegel* Interview with Jean Baudrillard'.
20. Ibid.

Chapter 1

1. Ian McEwan, 'Beyond Belief', *The Guardian*, 12 September, 2001, at www.ianmcewan.com/bib/articles/9–11
2. Ibid.
3. Ibid.
4. McEwan, *Saturday* (London: Jonathan Cape, 2005; repr. Vintage, 2006), p. 14.
5. Ibid., p. 14.
6. Ibid., p. 15.
7. Ibid., p. 15.
8. Ibid., p. 16.
9. Ibid., p. 16.
10. Don DeLillo, 'In the Ruins of the Future', *The Guardian*, 22 December 2001, at www.guardian.co.uk/Archive/Article/0,4273,4324579,00
11. Ibid.
12. Ibid.
13. Ibid.
14. Alvin H. Rosenfeld, 'The Problematics of Holocaust Literature' in H. Bloom (ed.), *Literature of the Holocaust* (Broomall: Chelsea House, 2004), p. 2115 Ibid., p. 22.

Chapter 2

1. David Aaronovitch, '*The Second Plane* by Martin Amis', *The Times*, 11 Jan. 2008 at www.entertainment.timesonline.co.uk/tol/arts_and_entertainment/books/non-fiction/article3170915.ece
2. An extensive selection of interviews and articles concerned with the disagreements between Amis and Terry Eagleton can be found at www.martinamisweb.com
3. For an example of this criticism see, in particular, Tim Gebhart's article at www.blogcritics.org/archives/2006/08/10/1220102.php (accessed 15 July 2008). Gebhart writes: 'Yet most damning is the lack of believability. Despite Updike's attention to detail, Ahmad never really comes off as real. Although he is a somewhat likeable character, he neither speaks nor acts like a teenager born and raised in New Jersey. Instead, he comes off as a caricature of a jihadist plunked down in a modern American urban area, spouting phrases like "Western culture is Godless", "the American way is the way of infidels", and movies are "sinful" and "foretastes of hell". Yet other than a general feeling of an impressionable youth being affected by an imam, we get virtually no insight into or understanding of how or why a teenager living with an Irish-American mother became so enthralled with Islam that God is now, as Ahmad puts it, "closer than the vein in my neck." '

4. Lionel Barber, 'A Crisis of Testosterone', at www.martinamisweb.com/reviews_files/Barber_secondplane.pdf (accessed 15 July 2008).

5. Sameer Rahim, 'Review: *The Second Plane* by Martin Amis', at www.martinamisweb.com/reviews_files/rahim_secondplane.pdf (accessed 15 July 2008).

6. A term first coined by John Middleton Murray in his *Jonathan Swift: A Hypocrite Reversed – A Critical Study* (1954) and alluded to frequently by Norman O. Brown: 'The Excremental Vision', in D. Lodge (ed.), *20th Century Literary Criticism: A Reader* (Harlow: Pearson Education, 1972), pp. 509–26.

7. Martin Amis, *House of Meetings* (London: Jonathan Cape, 2006), p. 22.

8. This lacuna in Atta's movements before 9/11 comes directly from the *9/11 Commission Report*: 'The next day, Atta picked up Omari at another hotel, and the two drove to Portland, Maine, for reasons that remain unknown' (p. 253).

9. Leon Wieseltier, 'The Catastrophist', at www.martinamisweb.com/reviews_files/wieseltier_secondplane.pdf (accessed 15 July 2008).

10. Most notably in *Money: A Suicide Note* (1984) in which 'Amis' has conversations with the novel's narrator John Self and tries to warn him what will ultimately happen to him.

11. This appears to be a fictional phone call before the actual phone conversation between Atta and Marwan al Shehhi, the pilot for the Flight 175 hijacking. See *The 9/11 Commission Report*, pp. 1 and 451 n3. Amis adds another call after this to Hani Hanjour, the pilot on the Flight 77 hijacking.

12. Medina is considered to be the second holiest city in Saudi Arabia. See www.religionfacts.com/islam/places/medina.htm (accessed 17 July 2008).

13. There may be further word play and punning in the choice of Volvic water. The spring from which this product hails is in a volcanic area of southern-central France. Immediately after drinking the water and boarding the plane, Atta's bowels, as it were, 'erupt'.

14. The *9/11 Commission Report* (pp. 160–1) states that Atta, in Hamburg, became more 'fundamentalist' during the 90s.

15. Adam Mars-Jones, 'Looking on the Blight Side', in N. Tredell (ed.), *The Fiction of Martin Amis: A Reader's Guide to Essential Criticism* (Cambridge: Icon Books, 2000), pp. 156 and 157.

16. James Diedrick, *Understanding Martin Amis* (Columbia: University of Columbia Press, 1995), p. 1.

17. Leon Wielseltier, 'The Catastrophist', at www.nytimes.com/2008/04/27/books/review/Wieseltier-t.html (accessed 21 July 2008).

18. From 'The Last Days of Muhammad Atta': 'Whatever else terrorism had achieved in the past few decades, it had certainly brought about a net increase in world boredom ... If the Planes Operation went ahead as planned, Muhammad Atta would bequeath more, perhaps much more, dead time, planet-wide. It was appropriate, perhaps, and not paradoxical, that terror should also sharply promote its most obvious opposite. Boredom' (*SP*: p. 108). From 'Terror and Boredom: The Dependent Mind': 'The age of terror, I suspect, will also be remembered as the age of boredom. Not the kind of boredom that afflicts the blasé and the effete, but a superboredom, rounding out and complementing the superterror of suicide-mass murder

... When I refer to the age of boredom, I am not thinking of airport queues and subway searches. I mean the global confrontation with the dependent mind' (*SP*: p. 78).

19. Throughout the collection one of Amis' central criticisms of Islamist culture is its treatment of women. Amis, of course, has been accused of misogyny before, most notably in the aftermath of the publication of *London Fields*. Its subsequent absence from that year's Booker prize list was generally considered to be because of the novel's treatment of women. Hence, perhaps, it might seem surprising that Amis frames one of his most persistent reservations about Islamism through a feminist discourse.

20. As Amis points out this location has great significance for the rise of radical Islam. It was here that Sayyid Qutb, a teacher and writer, lived and worked and wrote about America in the 1940s and 50s. His letters, essays, editorials and manifestos had a huge impact on Egyptian politics and subsequently on Islamist and Jihadist movements. For a detailed description of Qutb and of his vital role in radicalising parts of Islam, see Lawrence Wright, *The Looming Tower: Al-Qaeda's Road to 9/11* (London: Penguin, 2007), pp. 7–31.

21. Martin Amis, 'The Unknown Known', at www.granta.com/Magazine/100/The-Unknown-Known?view=articleAllPages (accessed 24 July 2008).

22. Amis is nothing if not fastidious in his research. *Time's Arrow* relies upon close readings of non-fictional books about the Holocaust, as does *House of Meetings* and *Koba the Dread* about the Stalinist regime.

23. *The Concise Oxford English Dictionary*, 11th edn (Oxford: Oxford University Press, 2006), p. 689.

24. Canadian playwright Judith Thompson's recent play *Palace of the End* (2008) contains a monologue spoken by a wife whose family was killed in the 'palace', the notorious place of torture where Uday Hussein worked. See www.theater2.nytimes.com/2008/06/24/theater/reviews/24pala.html?ref=theater (accessed 25 July 2008).

25. There is evidence that Uday Hussein may have employed 'doubles' or 'look-a-likes'. See www.news.bbc.co.uk/1/hi/world/middle_east/430006.stm; www.ynetnews.com/articles/0,7340,L-3224205,00.html; www.iraqi-mojo.blogspot.com/2007/12/i-was-uday-hussein.html (all accessed 26 July 2008).

26. Amis does not state where the story is set but it seems sensible to assume that this is, as it were, an allegorical Iraq.

27. See www.guardian.co.uk/world/2003/jul/23/iraq.suzannegoldenberg and www.mafhoum.com/press5/147P57.htm (both accessed 25 July 2008).

28. The article was originally titled 'The Palace of the End' (*The Guardian*, 3 March 2003): at www.martinamisweb.com/documents/palace_of_end.pdf (accessed 25 July 2008). In the Author's Note to *The Second Plane* Amis writes: '[But] I admit that I silently revised my remarks on Israel . . .' (p. ix). This is the first version of these 'remarks', from 'The Palace of the End': 'It also revealed the longstanding but increasingly dynamic loathing of this power in the Islamic world, where anti-Zionism and anti-semitism [sic] are exacerbated by America's relationship with Israel - a relationship that many in the west, this writer included, find unnatural.' The revised version, from 'The Wrong War', reads: 'It also revealed the longstanding but increasingly

dynamic loathing of *the West* in the *Islamic Nations, a loathing much* exacerbated by America's relationship with *their chief source of humiliation,* Israel; *this is* a relationship that many *non-Muslims consider* unnatural, *the* present writer included *(but for rather different reasons)*' (*SP*: p. 21; my italics, showing what Amis has altered). The main difference between the two passages is essentially the phrase 'their chief source of humiliation'. In the original passage Amis emphasises 'anti-Zionism and anti-semitism' as a reason for Arabic antipathy towards Israel. This is argued with more force in the second passage by using 'humiliation' as a reason and arguably reflects a deeper and perhaps more reactionary response to Islam.

29. *The Concise Oxford English Dictionary*, p. 1425: 'a form of punishment or torture in which the victim was secured to a rope and made to fall from a height almost to the ground before being stopped with an abrupt jerk'.
30. Ibid., p. 113: 'a form of punishment or torture that involves caning the soles of a person's feet'.
31. Ibid., p. 948.
32. Martin Amis, *Time's Arrow* (London: Jonathan Cape, 1991: repr. Penguin, 1992), p. 132).
33. Ibid., p. 143.
34. See http://www.southerncrossreview.org/35/sontag.htm (accessed 10 August 2010).
35. Ibid.
36. Ibid.

Chapter 3

1. Marina Thwaite, Murray's daughter, is also writing a book titled *The Emperor's Children Have No Clothes* concerning the cultural and social significance of children's fashions.
2. This trope of characters callously using their assumed death in the attacks is familiar from *The Mercy Seat*.
3. A French composer (1879–1957) renowned for adapting folk songs.
4. *The Concise Oxford English Dictionary* (Oxford: Oxford University Press, 2006), p. 75.
5. Danielle, tellingly, returns to her bed after Murray has left and after she has witnessed the footage of the attacks.
6. Kasia Boddy, 'Sense and the City', at www.telegraph.co.uk/culture/books/3655357/Sense-and-the-city.html (accessed 30 Mar. 2009).
7. Alfred Heckling, 'Point of Collapse', at www.guardian.co.uk/books/2006/sep/09/featuresreviews.guardianreview18 (accessed 30 Mar. 2009).
8. 'Bootie' has only just started *Infinite Jest*: 'Bits of it made him laugh, but he couldn't seem to keep track of the broader premise, or plot (was there a premise, or plot?). He often found this, in one way or another, with novels, but with this one more than with many' (*EC*: p. 51). Later, when he leaves home to travel to New York he pointedly leaves behind Foster Wallace's novel, along with Pynchon's *Gravity's Rainbow* (1973) (*EC*: p. 90).
9. Jean Baudrillard writes: 'The end of the spectacle brings with it the collapse of reality into hyperrealism, the meticulous reduplication of the real,

preferably through another reproductive medium such as advertising or photography. Through reproduction from one medium into another the real becomes volatile, it becomes the allegory of death, but it also draws strength from its own destruction, becoming the real for its own sake, a fetishism of the lost object which is no longer the object of representation, but the ecstasy of denegation and its own ritual extermination: the hyper-real': 'Symbolic Exchange and Death', in J. Rivkin, J and M. Ryan (eds), *Literary Theory: An Anthology* (Oxford: Blackwell, 1998), pp. 496–7 (pp. 488–508).

10. Josh Lacey, 'Minute by Minute', at www.guardian.co.uk/books/2004/sep/11/featuresreviews.guardianreview17 (accessed 30 Mar. 2009).

11. Beigbeder has been influenced here by the initial article '120 Minutes: Last Words at the Trade Center', published in the *New York Times* and written by Jim Dwyer, Eric Lipton, Kevin Flynn, James Glanz and Fred Fessenden, that grew into *102 Minutes: The Untold Story of the Fight to Survive Inside the Twin Towers* (2005) by Jim Dwyer and Kevin Flynn. This technique was also used in the documentary *102 Minutes That Changed America* (2008) produced by the History Channel and shown on Monday, 23 March 2009. This film is constructed exclusively with footage of the attacks taken from a vast number of amateur and professional sources.

12. Beigbeder is a media/literary celebrity in France whose most notable novel before *Windows on the World* is *99 Francs* (2000), a critique of advertising and the consumerist society that, like *WOTW*, was both controversial and a bestseller. He has appeared extensively on French television hosting the 'Hyper Show' (2002) amongst many others.

13. Beigbeder meets Alain Robbe-Grillet, the French novelist, and his wife in New York, visits an exhibition staged by the cultural theorist Paul Virilio (who has also written *Ground Zero* (2002)) and meets Troy Davis, a social activist who is the president of the World Citizen Foundation.

14. Stephen Metcalf, 'French Twist' at www.query.nytimes.com/gst/fullpage.html?res=9D05E1DF173EF934A25757C0A9639C8B63&sec=&spon=&pagewanted=1 (accessed 30 Mar. 2009).

15. There are a vast number of societies and groups formed around survivor and witness testimony. These include: www.survivorsnet.org/programs/bearing_witness.htm; www.11–sept.org/survivors.html; www.sep11mem ories.org/wiki/In_Memoriam; www.voicesofsept11.org/dev/index.php

16. See www.vaed.uscourts.gov/notablecases/moussaoui/exhibits/

17. Revelations surrounding the fabricated testimony of Tania Head, who claimed to have survived 9/11 by escaping from the 78th floor of the South Tower. For more on this story see www.nytimes.com/2007/09/27/nyregion/27survivor.html?ref=todayspaper. There is also a Channel 4 documentary about Tania Head's life entitled *The 9/11 Faker* shown on 11 September 2008.

18. At '9:49' Beigbeder writes: 'In the Windows, the few remaining survivors intone Irving Berlin's "God Bless America" (1939)' (*WW*: p. 239). Firstly, it is unclear whether this is attributed to Carthew or Beigbeder. Secondly, thus far, I have been unable to find a reference to this event. If it is accurate one might assume that the news would have had greater impact than

appears. If it is a product of Beigbeder's slightly sentimental imagination one must take issue.

19. Lacey, at www.guardian.co.uk/books/2004/sep/11/featuresreviews.guardianreview17 (accessed 30 Mar. 2009).

20. Translated as *Night and Fog* (1955), directed by Alain Resnais. A 32–minute documentary made up of footage from several concentration camps in Poland. Beigbeder follows this Holocaust reference by alluding to the director of the definitive *Shoah* (1985): 'Claude Lanzmann says that the Shoah is a mystery: September 11 is too' (*WW*: pp. 267–8).

21. Akin to the blacked-out screen with only the soundtrack of the attacks playing that Michael Moore choose to use in *Fahrenheit 9/11* (2004).

22. Frank Furedi, *Invitation to Terror: The Expanding Empire of the Unknown* (London: Continuum, 2007), p. 78.

23. Ibid.

24. Ibid.

25. Ernst Van Alphen, 'Caught by Images: Visual Imprints in Holocaust Testimonies', in S. Hornstein and F. Jacobowitz (eds), *Image and Remembrance: Representation and the Holocaust* (Indiana: Indiana University Press, 2003), p. 110 (pp. 97–113).

26. This is certainly not meant to imply any kind of moral equivalence between Auschwitz and 9/11: one is genocide, the other a terrorist attack. It is perhaps useful though to see both as traumatic moments in history that have had enormous impact upon the world.

27. Van Alphen (2003), p. 110.

28. Art Spiegelman's graphic novel *In the Shadow of No Towers* (London: Viking, 2004) similarly mixes the intensely personal with the historical/political in similar ways to his earlier *Maus* (1991).

29. For discussion on this sequence, see Michael Rothberg, *Traumatic Realism: The Demands of Holocaust Representation* (Minneapolis: University of Minnesota Press, 2000), pp. 222–47, in particular pp. 237–8. See also Daniel R. Schwarz, *Imagining the Holocaust* (Basingstoke: Macmillan Press, 1999), pp. 209–35.

30. There is, perhaps predictably, much comment on the Internet concerning the largely anecdotal 'evidence' of people who jumped from the towers either injuring or killing people on the ground. Much of this remains, equably predictably, on the level of hearsay and gossip. Beigbeder may, though, have been influenced by the story of the openly gay NYPD chaplain, Mychal F. Judge, who died on the ground when the South Tower collapsed. There are a handful of Internet rumours surrounding his death but it appears that falling debris, not a falling body, killed him (Dwyer and Flynn (2005), pp. 215 and 242).

31. Rothberg (2000), p. 237.

32. Ibid., pp. 37–8.

Chapter 4

1. *Out of the Blue*. Dir. Ned Williams. Silver River/Channel 5, 2006.

2. Simon Armitage, *Out of the Blue* (London: Enitharmon Press, 2008).

The poem was originally published in the *Sunday Times*, 6 September 2006.

3. Wendy Cope also wrote a poem concerning 9/11 for an Oxfam CD, entitled *Spared*:

> 'That Love is all there is,
> Is all we know of Love . . .'
> Emily Dickinson
>
> It wasn't you, it wasn't me,
> Up there, two thousand feet above
> A New York street. We're safe and free,
> A little while, to live and love,
>
> Imagining what might have been -
> The phone-call from the blazing tower,
> A last farewell on the machine,
> While someone sleeps another hour,
>
> Or worse, perhaps, to say goodbye
> And listen to each other's pain,
> Send helpless love across the sky,
> Knowing we'll never meet again,
>
> Or jump together, hand in hand,
> To certain death. Spared all of this
> For now, how well I understand
> That love is all, is all there is.

At www.news.bbc.co.uk/1/hi/entertainment/5052786.stm (accessed 17 April 2009). The poem's rather mawkish banality is reminiscent of the opening prologue in Richard Curtis' *Love Actually* (2003): 'When the planes hit the Twin Towers, as far as I know, none of the phone calls from the people on board were messages of hate or revenge. They were all messages of love.' At www.telegraph.co.uk/news/uknews/1451389/BA-under-fire-for-cutting-911–speech-from-Love-Actually.html (accessed 14 April 2009).

4. These include titles such as Dennis Loy and Valerie Merians (eds), *Poetry after 9/11: An Anthology of New York Poets* (New York: ebrandedbooks.com, 2002) and Allen Cohen and Clive Matson (eds), *An Eye for an Eye makes the Whole World go Blind: Poets on 9/11* (Oakland, CA: Regent Press, 2002).

5. See http://living.scotsman.com/books/The-poet-laureate-in-waiting. 25054 04.jp (accessed 12 May 2009). This was before the appointment of Carol Ann Duffy to the post on 1 May 2009.

6. See www.teachit.co.uk/armoore/anthology/simonarmitage.htm (accessed 12 May 2009).

7. *The Oxford Dictionary of Idioms* (Oxford: Oxford University Press, 2004), p. 314.

8. See also www.phrases.org.uk/meanings/on-a-wing-and-a-prayer.html (accessed 12 May 2009).

9. Later, in '11', Armitage continues this motif when he writes: 'The enormity

falls. / Then all sense fails. / The strings are cut / and the world goes slack' (*OB*: p. 27).

10. E. Cobham Brewer, *The Dictionary of Phrase and Fable* (Leicester: Galley Press, 1988), p. 514.

11. See Ian Sansom, 'Cliché!: The Poetry of Simon Armitage', at www.poetry magazines.org.uk/magazine/record.asp (accessed 5 April 2009).

12. Ibid. (accessed 5 April 2009).

13. Ibid. (accessed 5 April 2009).

14. The narrator's profession has a level of irony in that when he is revelling in his 'lofty' position at the 'top' of America he talks of '[t]he elation of trading in futures and risk' (*OB*: p. 11). Of course, at this point, he has no idea of quite how risky his own future will be – although readers do, putting them in a privileged position. This kind of negative ironic foreshadowing is a familiar trope from 9/11 texts.

15. See www.poetrymagazines.org.uk/magazine/record.asp (accessed 5 April 2009).

16. See Dan Chiasson, 'John Ashbery: "Look, Gesture, Hearsay"', at www.nybooks.com/articles/22576 (accessed 7 April 2009).

17. At www.timesonline.co.uk/tol/news/uk/article626664.ece (accessed 9 April 2009).

18. His solitude in these sequences effectively suggests his posthumous perspective.

Chapter 5

1. Although Petit's memoir *To Reach the Clouds* (New York: North Point Press, 2002; repr. London: Faber and Faber, 2008), on which the film is based, does explicitly refer to the terrorist attacks: 'My towers became our towers. I saw them collapse – hurling, crushing thousands of lives. Disbelief preceded sorrow for the obliteration of the buildings, perplexity descended before rage at the unbearable loss of life. Eyes close, I remember and pay my respects to the victims and their families' (*RC*: p. 221). He evokes the collapse of the Campanille in 1902, a tower in Venice that was rebuilt '*com'era, dov'era*: as it was, where it was' (*RC*: p. 22). Petit argues that the WTC should be similarly rebuilt and that he will walk between them when they are finished. He also provides a sketch of his own architectural design for these new buildings (*RC*: p. 224).

2. Bryan Appleyard, 'Is Man on Wire the Most Poignant 9/11 Film?' at www.entertainment.timesonline.co.uk/tol/arts_and_entertainment/film/article4353624.ece (accessed 7 August 2008).

3. Ibid.

4. Ibid.

5. Ibid.

6. Ibid.

7. Ibid.

8. See www.greatbuildings.com/buildings/World_Trade_Center.html (accessed 6 April 2009.

9. The day before President Richard Nixon's resignation.

10. There are a number of images that seem to be eerily prescient of the attacks. Of course these are entirely coincidental but one can see how, as Petit instinctively knew perhaps, the towers, from early on, quickly became iconic structures whose distinctive design and symbolic power inspired advertisers, the business world, the tourist industry and artists. For some of these pictures see www.weird-tube.blogspot.com/ (accessed 6 April 2009). Other examples include John Guillermin's version of *King Kong* (1976) that culminates with Kong standing astride the Twin Towers (used in one of the film's original posters); Californian rap group The Coup planned to release their album *Party Music* with a cover depicting two members of the band standing in front of the burning towers of the WTC in September 2001 but this was held back until another cover was designed; an early trailer for Sam Raimi's *Spider-Man* (2002) depicted a gang of bank robbers fleeing the scene of the crime in a helicopter only to be caught in a huge web suspended between the towers – the trailer was quickly taken out of circulation.

11. This air of nostalgia is further augmented by the use of Erik Satie's 'Gnossienne No. 1' and 'Gymnopédie No. 1'.

12. *Concise Oxford English Dictionary* (2006), p. 654.

13. An excellent account of the plan is contained within Lawrence Wright's *The Looming Tower: Al-Qaeda's Road to 9/11* (New York: Alfred A. Kopf, 2006).

14. There is also a literature of conspiracy that includes: David Ray Griffin's *The New Pearl Harbour; Disturbing Questions about the Bush Administration and 9/11* (Addlestrop: Arris, 2004), Jim Marrs' *The Terror Conspiracy: Deception, 9/11 and the Loss of Liberty* (New York: Disinformation, 2006), Ian Henshall's *9/11: The New Evidence* (London: Robinson, 2007) and Roland Morgan's *Flight 93 Revealed: What Really Happened on the 9/11 'Let's Roll' Flight?* (London: Robinson, 2006).

15. See www.nytimes.com/2001/09/30/arts/music-the-devil-made-him-do-it.html (accessed 9 April 2009).

16. See www.guardian.co.uk/uk/2002/sep/11/arts.september11 (accessed 9 April 2009).

17. Ibid.

18. Peter Bradshaw, 'World Trade Center', at www.guardian.co.uk/film/2006/sep/29/actionandadventure (accessed 10 April 2009).

19. The film's portrayal of historical figures is perhaps most problematic in the case of Dave Karnes, a former marine, who made his way to New York and Ground Zero and helped rescue John McLoughlin and Will Jimeno. He subsequently served in Iraq. For more on this issue see Rebecca Liss, 'Oliver Stone's World Trade Center Fiction: How the Rescue Really Happened', at www.slate.com/id/2147350/ (accessed 10 April 2009).

20. Daniel Cottom (2002), 'To Love to Hate', in *Representations 80* (Fall), pp. 119–38.

21. See www.phillipsdepury.com/auctions/lotdetail.aspx?sn=NY010307&search=&p=&order=&lotnum=264 (accessed 17 April 2009).

22. See www.dreadscott.home.mindspring.com/enduring.html (accessed 17 April 2009).

23. It is valuable to remember that Burden's '747', and for that matter Petit's

walk, occurred in a climate of tension surrounding terrorist attacks instigated by members of the Black Panther Party, the Black Liberation Army,
the IRA, ETA and the Baader-Meinhoff Gang. The Munich Massacre of
Israeli athletes by the Black September Group happened on 5 September
1972.
24. There are further connections with Situationist Theory, in particular the
work of Guy Debord and Raoul Veneigem. For more on this topic see:
www.bopsecrets.org/PS/situationism.htm;www.nothingness.org/;   www.
situationist.cjb.net/. One particular essay by Debord, 'On Terrorism and
the State', is particularly illuminating and suggestive in light of 9/11. At
www.notbored.org/on-terrorism.html (accessed 17 April 2009).
25. At www.newyorker.com/archive/2001/09/24/010924ta_talk_wtc (accessed
14 February 2009).
26. Ibid.
27. Author of *All That's Solid Melts Into the Air* (1983), an analysis of modernism and its impact on the twentieth century.
28. Herbert Muschamp, 'The Commemorative Beauty of Tragic Wreckage',
at www.nytimes.com/2001/11/11/arts/design/11MUSC.html (accessed 14
April 2009).
29. Ibid.
30. Ibid.
31. Ibid.

Chapter 6

1. There are other plays that have dealt with 9/11. These include Charles
Evered, *Adopt a Sailor* (2002), Craig Wright, *Recent Tragic Events* (2003),
Robert Marese, *The Fallen 9/11* (2005), Larry Kirwin, *The Heart Has a
Mind of its Own* (2007).
2. Neil LaBute, *The Mercy Seat* (London: Faber & Faber, 2003).
3. Anne Nelson, *The Guys* (New York: Random House, 2001).
4. *Concise Oxford English Dictionary*, 11th edn (Oxford: Oxford University
Press, 2006): '**mercy seat 1** the golden covering placed on the Ark of the
Covenant. **2** the throne of God in heaven' (p. 893).
5. LaBute's work includes the films (as writer and director) *In the Company
of Men* (1997), *Your Friends and Neighbours* (1998) and a version of his
own play *The Shape of Things* (2003). Aside from *The Mercy Seat* his
plays include *Fat Pig* (2004), *Some Girl(s)* (2005) and *This is How it Goes*
(2005). He has also published a collection of short stories titled *Seconds of
Pleasure* (2004).
6. Jumana Farouky, 'It's So Good To Be Bad', at www.time.com/time/maga
zine/article/0,9171,1066876–1,00.html (accessed 6 July 2009).
7. David Edelstein, 'Boy Hates Girl', at www.slate.com/id/2082750/ (accessed
6 July 2009).
8. Neil LaBute, 'How American Theatre Lost It', at www.guardian.co.uk/
world/2008/jan/15/usa.theatre (accessed 8 July 2009).
9. Some of these cases include: Natarajan Venkataram, director of the New
York office of the Chief Medical Examiner who pleaded guilty to charges

of embezzlement, money laundering and conspiracy (see www.edition.cnn. com/2007/US/10/30/911.embezzlement/index.htm); Scott Shields who was involved in a scam to cheat money from the Red Cross, claiming falsely that he lived near the WTC (see www.scottshieldsfraud.com); Carlton McNish who lied about his wife dying in the attacks in order to receive money from various relief organisations (see www.abcnews.go.com/US/story?id=2183522&page=1); Fred Parisi who lied about his contribution to the operations at Ground Zero (see www.nydailynews.com/news/ny_crime/2008/03/30/2008–03–30_ground_zero_hero_arrested_at_fundraiser_.html); and perhaps most notoriously Tania Head who lied about surviving from above the crash site in the South Tower (see www.nytimes. com/2007/09/27/nyregion/27survivor.html).

10. See R.W. Rasband, 'Without Mercy? Neil LaBute as Mormon Artist: A Consideration of *Your Friends and Neighbours*, *Bash*, *The Mercy Seat* and *The Shape of Things*', at www.dialoguejournal.metapress.com/app/home/content.asp (accessed 14 July 2009).

11. The other two epigraphs shed more light on LaBute's intentions. The first is an extract from Edna St Vincent Millay's poem 'The Ballad of the Harp-Weaver' published in 1922: 'A wind with a wolf's head / Howled about our door, / And we burned up the chairs / And sat upon the floor' (*MS*: p. vii). The collection that this poem gave its title to earned Millay the Pulitzer Prize for Poetry the next year. The poem details a destitute widower and her son, who narrates, and their endurance of extreme poverty in the winter months leading up to Christmas. The boy has no clothes and hence is unable to go to school but his mother comforts him by playing a harp they have. As she sings and plays she magically weaves clothes for her son. See www.digital.library.upenn.edu/women/millay/ballad/ballad.html (accessed 15 July 2009). LaBute's other epigraph is from Nick Cave and the Bad Seeds' 'The Mercy Seat', a song from the album Tender Prey (1988): 'And the mercy seat is waiting / And I think my head is burning / And in a way I'm yearning / To be done with all this measuring of truth' (*MS*: p. vii). The song is written from the perspective of a condemned man whose punishment (for a crime the song does not specify) is to be executed in the electric chair – another kind of 'mercy seat'. The song is full of Christian allusions and symbolism and despite the narrator's protestations of innocence it becomes increasingly clear that he may well be guilty. See www.lyricsdepot.com/nick-cave-and-the-bad-seeds/the-mercy-seat.html (accessed 12 July 2009). Interestingly, Johnny Cash, a singer famous for his Christian convictions, has covered both Millay's poem and Cave's song.

12. See www.bible-history.com/tabernacle/TAB4The_Mercy_Seat.htm (accessed 14 July 2009).

13. See www.bible-history.com/tabernacle/TAB4The_Mercy_Seat.htm (accessed 14 July 2009).

14. See www.newadvent.org/cathen/01594b.htm (accessed 14 July 2009).

15. Rasband at www.dialoguejournal.metapress.com/app/home/content.asp (accessed 14 July 2009).

16. See www.bbc.co.uk/religion/religions/mormon/beliefs/salvation_1.shtml (accessed 14 July 2009).

17. Rasband at www.dialoguejournal.metapress.com/app/home/content.asp (accessed 14 July 2009).

18. Sex has been a trope in much of LaBute's work, especially in his films *In the Company of Men* and *Your Friends and Neighbours*. Both films include unrepentant misogynists, offering a highly critical view of the motivations and impulses of heterosexual men. *Your Friends and Neighbours* includes a scene in which Cary – a promiscuous and cynical doctor – describes his best sexual experience. As Peter Matthews writes: 'It's clear that LaBute means to stop one's breath by including the lengthy monologue where slime bucket Cary expostulates on the spiritual advantages to be gained from committing homosexual gang rape. But besides being psychologically ludicrous, the sequence is too conscious of its own clever malignancy to count as anything more than cheap titillation' ('Your Friends and Neighbours', *Sight and Sound* 8.10 (Oct. 1998), p. 61.

19. This is hinted at earlier in the play when one of Abby's neighbours stops by (she remains unseen) to ask to borrow some milk. Abby unhesitatingly provides her neighbour with some milk and tells Ben that 'her [the neighbour's] husband works down there . . . somewhere in the area' (*MS*: p. 51).

20. Although it is subsequently revealed that Chad's partner is still with him – implying that he was merely playing a 'game' with both Howard and Christine.

21. See Charles Taylor, 'Are Men Really This Evil?', at www.salon.com/aug97/entertainment/company970801.html (accessed 20 July 2009).

22. See Peter Matthews, 'Business as Usual', *Sight and Sound* 8.2 (Feb. 1998), pp. 36–7.

23. Throughout the play Ben inadvertently reveals a lack of cultural awareness: He doesn't know who Kreskin is (better known as 'The Amazing Kreskin'), a popular TV mystic in the 1970s; he is unaware of Audie Murphy, an American soldier and war hero who later found fame as an actor; he confuses the spy Guy Burgess with the novelist Anthony Burgess.

24. An American clothing company founded in 1926.

25. Nelson's other theatrical work includes *The Anglo-American Alliance* (2005) and *Savages* (2006). She also wrote the screenplay for the film version of *The Guys* (2002), directed by Jim Simpson and starring Sigourney Weaver and Anthony LaPaglia.

26. Bruce Weber, 'Standing in for New Yorkers: Expressions of Grief over Sept. 11', at www.nytimes.com/2002/01/28/theater/theater-review-standing-in-for-new-yorkers-expressions-of-grief-over-sept-11.html?pagewanted=2 (accessed 6 July 2009).

27. Susan Faludi, *The Terror Dream: What 9/11 Revealed about America* (New York: Metropolitan Books, 2007; repr. Atlantic, 2008), p. 14.

28. Ibid., p. 66.

29. Ibid.

30. Ibid., p. 70

31. Ibid., p. 72.

32. Ibid., p. 73.

33. Ibid., p. 74.

34. Ibid., p. 89.

35. Ibid., p. 66.

36. Faludi writes: 'The firefighters entered the World Trade Center armed with fifteen-year-old radios that were well known to malfunction in high-rise buildings; in particular, they had failed when the fire department last responded to a crisis at the twin towers, after the 1993 bombing. (Nor did the radios communicate with the police department. If they had, the fire-fighters would have heard the warning from the police helicopter pilot that the second tower was about to fall – more than twenty minutes before its collapse.) When the South Tower fell, the firefighters in the North Tower has no idea what had happened. And when the fire chief radioed a Mayday order to evacuate the North Tower, almost none of the firefighters heard it' (ibid., pp. 66–7).

37. Ibid., p. 81.

38. See www.potw.org/archive/potw162.html (accessed 4 July 2009).

39. Robert Preyer writes in ' "The Fine Delight that Fathers Thought": Gerard Manley Hopkins and the Romantic Survival', in *Victorian Poetry* (London: Edward Arnold, 1972): 'Hopkins concludes, not with the usual Victorian exhaustion and bafflement or show or bravado at the spectacle of incomprehensibility, but rather with a vigorous and orthodox assertion which runs counter to the relativistic currents of the age: God is the author of all this' (p. 181) (pp. 177–96).

40. *Concise Oxford English Dictionary*, praise.2, p. 1127.

41. Claire Fox, 'The Guys' at www.culturewars.org.uk/edinburgh2002/guys.htm (accessed 7 July 2009).

42. The original definition of hagiography is 'the writing of the lives of the saints' (*Concise Oxford English Dictionary*, p. 641), an appropriate allusion given Nelson's use of Manley Hopkins' poem.

Chapter 7

1. Don DeLillo, *Falling Man* (London: Picador, 2007).

2. DeLillo has included references to the WTC in his earlier fiction. In *Underworld* he writes: 'The World Trade Center was under construction, already towering, twin-towering, with cranes tilted at the summits and work elevators sliding up the flanks. She saw it almost everywhere she went. She ate a meal and drank a glass of wine and walked to the rail or ledge and there it usually was, bulked up at the funneled end of the island, and a man stood next to her one evening, early, drinks on the roof of a gallery building – about sixty, she thought, portly and jowled but also sleek in a way, assured and contained and hard-polished, a substantial sort, European.

   "I think of it as one, not two," she said. "Even though there are clearly two towers. It's a single entity, isn't it?"

   "Very terrible thing but you have to look at it, I think."

   "Yes, you have to look." (New York: Simon and Schuster, 1997; repr. Picador, 1998), p. 372.

   As Toby Litt points out, DeLillo also referenced the towers in *Mao II*. See 'The Trembling Air', *The Guardian*, 26 May 2007, p. 16. Coincidentally, the front cover for *Underworld* used a photograph of the towers taken by Andre Kertesz entitled *New York, 1972*. See www.exporevue.com/magazine/fr/biennale_liege.html (accessed 25 June 2009).

3. It would appear that Hammad is in fact a fictional construct based on the actual hijackers who were involved with Atta and the 'Hamburg Cell'. The hijackers on Flight 175 were Marwan Al Shehhi, Fayez Banihammad, Ahmed Al Ghamdi, Hamza Al Ghamdi and Mohand Al Shehri. Hammad shares elements of these hijackers' biographies and DeLillo uses much of what has been reported of their movements and actions in the years leading up to the attacks. Indeed, given some of the confusion that has arisen in some quarters surrounding the precise identities of some of the hijackers – in particular Waleed Al Shehri – DeLillo's decision to imagine a fictional composite rather than use an actual historical figure, such as Atta, might be redolent of the novel's use of pseudonyms and mistaken identities. The terrorists regularly used fake documents and false passports and ID cards. Likewise it might be argued that this is simply DeLillo, perhaps inadvertently or even unconsciously, re-enacting certain American, or more precisely Western, ignorance of the Asian 'other'. This lack of cultural understanding also informs Updike's *Terrorist* and perhaps Amis' fictional Atta.

4. In Hamburg Hammad's lustful voyeurism is underlined: 'They stood in silence for a time, waiting for the rain to stop, and he kept thinking that another woman would come by on a bike, someone to look at, hair wet, legs pumping' (*FM*: p. 78).

5. Laura Miller, 'Falling Man', at www.salon.com/books/review/2007/05/11/delillo (accessed 5 Nov.2007).

6. Toby Litt, 'The Trembling Air',p. 16.

7. Michael Johnstone, *Liberty or Death*, Commentary, unpublished PhD thesis, University of Gloucestershire, p. 42.

8. See the chapter on 'Man on Wire' for more on the relationship between 9/11 and art/spectacle.

9. For more on the photograph of the 'Falling Man' see Tom Junod, 'The Falling Man' in *Esquire* (Sept. 2003), at www.esquire.com/print-this/ESQ0903–SEP_FALLINGMAN (accessed 8 May 2007).

10. A Channel 4 documentary, *9/11: The Falling Man* (2006), directed by Henry Singer, explored the possible identity of the individual photographed by Drew.

11. Junod (2003).

12. Laura Miller writes: 'These appearances [by Janiak] are exactly the sort of cryptic, arty motif that seems quintessentially DeLillo and quintessentially '80s, an artifact of the pre-Internet days. Back when the mass media disseminated all images and information, maybe someone like the Falling Man would have been able to strike and then vanish like Zorro, leaving nothing behind but a big question mark. In the 2000s, everything you could ever want to know about the guy would be on the Web, with photos, within a couple of weeks. He'd have a Wikipedia entry. His intentions and their validity would be hashed and rehashed in blogs and cable new programs and Op-Ed columns, ad nauseum' ('Falling Man', at www.salon.com/books/review/2007/05/11/delillo (accessed 25 June 2009).

13. Lianne is first drawn to Morandi's work when she describes two still lifes

in her mother's apartment (*FM*: p. 12). Later she visits an exhibition of his work: 'She looked at the third painting for a long time. It was a variation on one of the paintings her mother had owned. She noted the nature and shape of each object, the placement of objects, the tall dark oblongs, the white bottle. She could not stop looking. There was something hidden in the painting' (*FM*: p. 210).

14. Junod (2003).
15. The members of this group indulged in various satirical public provocations including a simulated 'assassination' plot aimed at visiting US Vice President Hubert Humphrey involving bombs filled with blancmange. For more on the group and their relationship with the media see Kathrin Fahlenbrach's 'The Aesthetics of Protest in the Media of 1968 in Germany', at www.arts. ualberta.ca/igel/igel2004/Proceedings/Fahlenbrach.pdf (accessed 24 June 2009).
16. Laura Miller writes: 'The characters in *Falling Man* are typically sketchy and the dialogue improbable; everyone speaks in exactly the same stagy, portentous manner as the mouthpiece characters in an experimental play, at 'www.salon.com/books/review/2007/05/11/delillo (accessed 25 June 2009).

Conclusion

1. The exception here is, as Mishra acknowledges, Don DeLillo. Mishra argues, persuasively, that *Falling Man* disappoints because of its concern with the state of a marriage and that its depiction of the terrorist psyche relies on 'received notions about Muslim "rage"' (EI: p. 6).
2. There are other references to literature in *The Reluctant Fundamentalist*. These include Italo Calvino, *Mr Palomar* (1983), Washington Irving, 'The Legend of Sleepy Hollow' (1820) and Joseph Conrad, *Heart of Darkness* (1902). Changez also visits the home of Pablo Neruda when he is in Chile.
3. Changez is the Urdu version of 'Ghengiz'. It also suggests 'change': the narrator's sense of self shifts and alters throughout the novel.
4. An additional layer of meaning attached to this word comes from its origin. *The Concise Oxford English Dictionary* identifies this as (in the sense 'offering opposition'): from L. *reluctant -*, *reluctari* 'struggle against' (p. 1215). This emphasises Changez's own internal struggle with his protective loving feelings towards (Am)Erica and his growing disenchantment with the post-9/11 foreign policy of the Bush administration.
5. See www.theparisreview.org/viewmedia.php/prmMID/5645 (accessed 18 August 2008).
6. A popular mode of public transport in the Philippines. See www.stuart xchange.org/Jeepney.html (accessed 19 August 2008).
7. The narrator of Camus' *The Fall* is called Jean-Baptiste Clamence.
8. See www.mohsinhamid.com/trfsundaytimesreview.html (accessed 21 August 2008).
9. This word is used ironically only two pages later when Changez says: 'If you are not ready to reveal your *purpose* in travelling here . . .' (*RF*: p. 77).

Bibliography

Fiction

Amis, M., 'The Last Days of Mohammed Atta', *The Observer*, 3 Sept. 2006.

—— *The Second Plane: September 11, 2001–2007* (London: Jonathan Cape, 2008).

—— *Yellow Dog* (London: Jonathan Cape, 2003).

Archer, J., *False Impression* (London: Macmillan, 2005).

Armitage, Simon, *Out of the Blue* (London: Enitharmon Press, 2008).

Auster, P., *The Brooklyn Follies* (London: Faber and Faber, 2005).

Baer, U. (ed.), *110 Stories: New York Writes after September 11* (New York: New York University Press, 2002).

Ballard, J.G., *Millennium People* (London: Flamingo, 2003).

Banks, I., *Dead Air* (London: Little Brown, 2002).

Beard, P., *Dear Zoe* (New York: Plume, 2005).

Beigbeder, F., *Windows on the World*, trans. by Frank Wynne (London: Fourth Estate, 2004).

Chernozemsky, V., *Phase One After Zero* (Los Angeles: Triumvirate, 2005).

Conrad, J., *The Secret Agent* [1907] (London: Penguin, 1994).

DeLillo, D., *Falling Man* (London: Picador and New York: Scribner, 2007).

Easton Ellis, B., *Glamorama* (New York: Alfred A. Knopf, 1998).

Fernandez, R., *September 11 from the Inside: A Novel* (Lincoln: iUniverse, 2003).

Fitzgerald, F.S., *The Great Gatsby* (London: Penguin, 1990).

Forde, P., 'In Spirit', at http://www.analogsf.com/Hugos/spirit.shtml

Foster Wallace, D., *Oblivion: Stories* (London: Abacus, 2004).

Gibson, W., *Pattern Recognition* (New York: GP Putnam's Sons, 2003).

Hamid, M., *The Reluctant Fundamentalist* (London: Hamish Hamilton, 2007).

Hancock Rux, C., *Asphalt* (New York: Washington Square Press, 2004).

Kalfus, K., *A Disorder Peculiar to the Country* (New York: Ecco, 2006).

LaBute, N., *The Mercy Seat* (London: Faber and Faber, 2003).

Lana, V., *The Savage Quiet September Sun: A Collection of 9/11 Stories* (Lincoln: iUniverse, 2005).

Llewellyn, D., *Eleven* (Bridgend: Seren, 2006).

McCann, C., *Let the Great World Spin* (London: Bloomsbury, 2009).

McDonell, N., *The Third Brother* (New York: Grove Press, 2005).

McEwan, I., *Saturday* (London: Jonathan Cape, 2005).

McGrath, P., *Ghost Town: Tales of Manhattan Then and Now* (London: Bloomsbury, 2006).

McInerney, J., *Brightness Falls* (London: Bloomsbury, 1992).

——*The Good Life* (London: Bloomsbury, 2006).

McPhee, M., *L'America* (Orlando: Harcourt, 2003).

Maynard, J., *The Usual Rules* (New York: St Martin's Press, 2003).

Messud, C., *The Emperor's Children* (New York: Alfred A. Knopf, 2006).

Nelson, A., *The Guys* (New York: Random House, 2001).

Nissenson, H., *Days of Awe* (Naperville: Sourcebooks, 2005).

O'Neill, J., *Netherland* (London: Fourth Estate, 2008).

Price, R., *The Good Priest's Son* (New York: Scribner, 2005).

Rinaldi, N., *Between Two Rivers* (London: Bantam Press, 2004).

Robert Lennon, J., *The Light of Falling Stars* (London: Granta, 1997).

Safran Foer, J., *Extremely Loud and Incredibly Close* (New York: Houghton Mifflin, 2005).

Sharon Schwartz, L., *The Writing on the Wall* (New York: Counterpoint, 2005).

Spiegelman, A., *In the Shadow of No Towers* (London: Viking, 2004).

Turner Hospital, J., *Due Preparations for the Plague* (London: Fourth Estate, 2004).

Updike, J., *Terrorist* (New York: Alfred A. Knopf, 2006).

Walter, J., *The Zero* (New York: Harper Collins, 2006).

West, P., *The Immensity of the Here and Now: A Novel of 9.11* (Ringwood, NJ: Voyant, 2003).

Films

Collateral Damage. Dir. Andrew Davis. Warner Bros, 2002.

Cloverfield. Dir. Matt Reeves. Bad Robot, 2008.

11'9'01 September 11. Pr. Alain Brigand. CIH Shorts, 2002.

Executive Decision. Dir. Stuart Baird. Warner Bros, 1996.

Fahrenheit 911. Dir. Michael Moore. Lions Gate, 2004.

Fight Club. Dir. David Fincher. Art Linson Productions, 1999.

Flight 93. Dir. Peter Markle. Fox Television, 2006.

The Gangs of New York. Dir. Martin Scorsese. Miramax, 2002.

The Guys. Dir. Jim Simpson. Content Film, 2002.

The Hamburg Cell. Dir. Antonia Bird. Channel4/CBC, 2004.

Independence Day. Dir. Roland Emmerich. Centropolis Entertainment, 1996.

Infinite Justice. Dir. Jamil Dehlavi. Dehlavi Films, 2008.

Les Invasions Barbares. Dir. Denys Arcand. Astral Films, 2003.

Loose Change. Dir. Dylan Avery. Louder Than Words, 2005–7.

Man on Wire. Dir. James Marsh. Discovery Films, 2008.

The Man Who Predicted 9/11. Dir. Steve Humphries. Testimony, 2005.

Munich. Dir. Steven Spielberg. Dreamworks SKG, 2005.

9/11. Dirs Jules and Gedeon Naudet. CBS Television, 2002.

Out of the Blue. Dir. Ned Williams. Silver River/Channel 5, 2006.
The Path to 9/11. Dir. David L. Cunningham. Marc Blatt Pro, 2006.
Reign Over Me. Dir. Mike Binder. Greentree Films, 2007.
Schindler's List. Dir. Steven Spielberg. Universal, 1993.
Spider-Man. Dir. Sam Raimi. Columbia Pictures Production, 2002.
The Sum of all Fears. Dir. Phil Alden Robinson. Paramount, 2002.
25th Hour. Dir. Spike Lee. 25th Hour Productions, 2002.
United 93. Dir. Paul Greengrass. Universal, 2006.
The War of the Worlds. Dir. Steven Spielberg. Paramount, 2005.
World Trade Center. Dir. Oliver Stone. Paramount, 2006.

Websites

www.ctheory.com
www.9–11commission.gov
www.911revealed.co.uk
www.911digitalarchive.org
www.911Truth.org
www.september11news.com
www.ebsco.com
www.loosechange911.com
www.othervoices.org
www.ianmcewan.com
www.hitchensweb.com
www.journalof911studies.com
www.martinamisweb.com
www.emperors-clothes.com
www.perival.com/delillo
www.theatlantic.com
www.richmondreview.co.uk
www.tcs.sagepub.com
www.911visibility.org
www.archive.org
www.salon.com
www.mitworld.mit.edu
www.stj911.org
www.guardian.co.uk

Secondary Texts

Aaronovitch, David, *Voodoo Histories: How Conspiracy Theory has Shaped Modern History* (London: Vintage, 2010).
Annesley, J., *Blank Fictions: Consumerism, Culture and the Contemporary American Novel* (London: Palgrave, 1998).
Baravalle, G., *Rethink: Cause and Consequences of September 11* (New York: de.Mo, 2003).
Baudrillard, J., *The Spirit of Terrorism* (London: Verso, 2002).

Berman, M., *All That is Solid Melts into the Air: The Experience of Modernity* (New York: Simon and Schuster, 1982; repr. Verso, 1991).

Bernstein, M.A., *Foregone Conclusions: Against Apocalyptic History* (Berkeley: University of California Press, 1994).

Bilton, A., *An Introduction to Contemporary American Fiction* (Edinburgh: Edinburgh University Press, 2002).

Bourke, J., *Fear: A Cultural History* (London: Virago, 2005).

Brooker, P., *New York Fictions: Modernity, Postmodernism, the New Modern* (Harlow: Longman, 1996).

Burleigh, M., *Blood and Rage: A Cultural History of Terrorism* (London: Harper Press, 2008).

Caruth, C., *Unclaimed Experience: Trauma, Narrative, and History* (Baltimore: Johns Hopkins University Press, 1996).

Chase-Coale, S., *Paradigms of Paranoia: The Culture of Conspiracy in Contemporary American Fiction* (Tuscaloosa: University of Alabama Press, 2005).

Chomsky, N., *9/11* (New York: Seven Stories Press, 2001).

Chomsky, N., *Imperial Ambitions: Conversations with Noam Chomsky on the Post-9/11 World* (New York: Metropolitan Books, 2005).

Crockatt, R., *America Embattled: September 11, Anti-Americanism and the Global Order* (London: Routledge, 2003).

Currie, M., *Postmodern Narrative Theory* (Basingstoke: Macmillan Press, 1998).

De Zengotita, T., *Mediated: How the Media Shape Your World* (London: Bloomsbury, 2005).

Didion, J. and F. Rich, *Fixed Ideas: America since 9/11* (New York: New York Review of Books, 2006).

Diedrick, J., *Understanding Martin Amis* (Columbia: University of Columbia Press, 1995).

Dwyer, J. and K. Flynn, *102 Minutes: The Untold Story of the Fight to Survive inside the Twin Towers* (New York: Times Books, 2005).

El-Ayouty, Y., *Perspectives on 9/11* (Westport: Greenwood Press, 2004).

Elias, A.J., *Sublime Desire: History and Post-1960s Fiction* (Baltimore: Johns Hopkins University Press, 2001).

Faludi, Susan, *The Terror Dream: What 9/11 Revealed about America* (London: Atlantic, 2008).

Furedi, F., *Invitation to Terror: The Expanding Empire of the Unknown* (London: Continuum, 2007).

Gregson, I., *Postmodern Literature* (London: Arnold, 2004).

Griffin, D.R., *The New Pearl Harbour: Disturbing Questions about the Bush Administration and 9/11* (Moreton-in-Marsh: Arris, 2004).

Griffin, D.R. and P.D. Scott (eds), *9/11 and American Empire: Intellectuals Speak Out* (Moreton-in-Marsh: Arris, 2007).

Halberstam, D., *Firehouse* (New York: Hyperion, 2003).

Heller, D. (ed.), *The Selling of 9/11* (London: Palgrave Macmillan, 2005).

Henshall, I., *9/11: The New Evidence* (London: Robinson, 2007).

Hitchens, C., *Love, Poverty and War: Journeys and Essays* (New York: Nation, 2004).

Hustvedt, Siri, *A Plea for Eros* (London: Sceptre, 2006).

Huyssen, A., *Twilight Memories: Marking Time in a Culture of Amnesia* (London: Routledge, 1995).

Jacobson, S. and E. Colón, *9/11: The Illustrated 9/11 Commission Report* (New York: Hill and Wang, 2006).

King, G. (ed.), *The Spectacle of the Real: From Hollywood to Reality TV and Beyond* (Bristol: Intellect Books, 2005).

King, N., *Memory, Narrative, Identity: Remembering the Self* (Edinburgh: Edinburgh University Press, 2000).

Langewiesche, W., *American Ground: Unbuilding the World Trade Center* (New York: Farrar, Straus and Giroux, 2002).

Luckhurst, R. and P. Marks (eds), *Literature and the Contemporary: Fictions and Theories of the Present* (Harlow: Longman, 1999).

Marrs, J., *The Terror Conspiracy: Deception, 9/11, and the Loss of Liberty* (New York: Disinformation, 2006).

Meyerowitz, J., *Aftermath* (New York: Phaidon, 2006).

Millard, K., *Contemporary American Fiction: An Introduction to American Fiction since 1970* (Oxford: Oxford University Press, 2000).

Millard, K., *Coming of Age in Contemporary American Fiction* (Edinburgh: Edinburgh University Press, 2007).

Milner, A., *Literature, Culture and Society* (London: UCL Press, 1996).

Morgan, R., *Flight 93: What Really Happened on the 9/11 'Let's Roll' Flight?* (London: Robinson, 2006).

National Commission on Terrorist Attacks upon the United States, *The 9/11 Commission Report: The Final Report of the National Commission on Terrorist Attacks upon the United States* (New York: W.W Norton and Co., 2004).

Orbán, K., *Ethical Diversions: The Post-Holocaust Narratives of Pynchon, Abish, DeLillo, and Spiegelman* (Abingdon: Routledge, 2005).

Petit, P., *To Reach the Clouds* (New York: North Point Press, 2002; repr. Faber and Faber, 2008).

Ray, G., *Terror and the Sublime in Art and Critical Theory: From Auschwitz to Hiroshima to September 11* (London: Palgrave, 2005).

Ray Griffen, D., *The New Pearl Harbor: Disturbing Questions about the Bush Administration and 9/11* (Adlestrop: Arris, 2004).

Rockmore, T., J. Margolis and A. Marsoobian (eds), *The Philosophical Challenge of September 11* (Oxford: Blackwell, 2004).

Salon.com (eds), *Afterwords: Stories and Reports from 9/11 and Beyond* (New York: Washington Square Press, 2002).

Scraton, P. (ed.), *Beyond September 11: An Anthology of Dissent* (London: Pluto, 2002).

Simpson, D., *9/11: The Culture of Commemoration* (Chicago: University of Chicago Press, 2006).

Tredell, N. (ed.), *The Fiction of Martin Amis: A Reader's Guide to Essential Criticism* (Cambridge: Icon Books, 2000).

Virilio, P., *Ground Zero*, trans. Chris Turner (London: Verso, 2002).

Winston Dixon, W. (ed.), *Film and Television after 9/11* (Carbondale: Southern Illinois University Press, 2004).

Woodward, B., *Bush at War: Inside the Bush Whitehouse* (London: Simon and Schuster, 2002).

Zelizer, B. and S. Allan (eds), *Journalism after September 11* (London: Routledge, 2002).

Zizek, S., *Welcome to the Desert of the Real* (London: Verso, 2002).

Journal and Newspaper Articles

Abel, Marco, 'Don Delillo's "In the Ruins of the Future": Literature, Images, and the Rhetoric of *Seeing* 9/11', *DMLA* 118.5 (1 Oct. 2003), pp. 1236–50.

Alexander, Jeffrey C., 'From the Depths of Despair: Performance, Counterperformance, and "September 11"', *Sociological Theory* 22.1 (Mar. 2004), pp. 88–105.

Amis, Martin, 'Fear and Loathing', *The Guardian*, 18 September 2001, at http:www.guardian.co.uk/2001/sep/18/september11.politicsphilosophyand society (accessed 15 Sept. 2009).

Anker, Elisabeth, 'Villains, Victims and Heroes: Melodrama, Media, and September 11', *Journal of Communication* (Mar. 2005), pp. 22–37.

Behnke, Andreas, 'Terrorising the Political: 9/11 within the Context of the Globalisation of Violence', *Millennium: Journal of International Studies* 33.2 (Mar. 2004), pp. 279–312.

Bleiher, Roland, 'Aestheticising Terrorism: Alternative Approaches to 11 September', *Australian Journal of Politics and History* 49.3 (Sept. 2003), pp. 430–45.

Boggs, Carl and Tom Pollard, 'Hollywood and the Spectacle of Terrorism', *New Political Science* 28.3 (Sept. 2006), pp. 335–51.

Bourne, Richard, 'The Significance of 11 September 2001 and After', *The Round Table* 363 (1 Jan. 2002), pp. 77–90.

Bradley, Gerald V., 'E Pluribus Unum: The Aftermath of September 11', *The Journal of the Historical Society* 2.2 (Apr. 2002), p. 193.

Byerly, Carolyn M., 'After September 11: The Formation of an Oppositional Discourse', *Feminist Media Studies* 5.3 (2005), pp. 281–96.

Chouliaraki, Lilie, 'Watching 11 September: The Politics of Pity', *Discourse and Society* 15.2–3 (1 May 2004), pp. 185–98.

Cottom, Daniel, 'To Love to Hate', *Representations* 80 (Fall 2002), pp. 119–38.

Dallmayr, Fred, 'Lessons of September 11', *Theory, Culture and Society* 19.4 (2002), pp. 137–45.

DeLillo, Don, 'In the Ruins of the Future', *The Guardian*, 22 September 2001, at http://www.guardian.co.uk/books/2001/dec/22/fiction.dondelillo (accessed 7 Aug. 2008).

Dittmer, Jason, 'Captain America's Empire: Reflections on Identity, Popular Culture, and Post 9/11 Geopolitics', *Annals of the Association of American Geographers* 95.3 (Sept. 2005), pp. 626–43.

Edwards, John, 'After the Fall', *Discourse and Society* 15.2–3 (1 May 2004), pp. 155–84.

Farouky, Jumana, 'It's So Good To Be Bad at http://www.time.com/time/maga zine/article/0,9171,1066876,00.html.

Grayling, A.C., 'Aftershock and After Lives', *The Times* (12 May 2007), p. 5.

Green, Leila, '11 September', *Continuum: Journal of Media and Cultural Studies* 17.1 (2003), pp. 95–103.

Hammond, Philip, 'Do Mention the War: 9/11 and After', *Media, Culture and Society* 25.4 (1 July 2003), pp. 557–9.

Houchin Winfield, Betty, Barbara Friedman and Vivarn Trisnadi, 'History as the Metaphor through which the Current World is Viewed: British and American Newspapers' Uses of History following the 11 September 2001 Terrorist Attacks', *Journalism Studies* 3.2 (1 Apr. 2001), pp. 289–300.

Houen, Alex (2004), 'Novel Spaces and Taking Place(s) in the Wake of September 11', *Studies in the Novel* 36, pp. 419–37.

Junod, Tom, 'The Falling Man', at www.esquire.com/print-this/ESQ0903–SEP_FALLINGMAN (accessed 8 May 2007).

Kirshenblatt-Grimblett, Barbara, 'Kodak Moments, Flashbulbs Memories', *TDR: The Drama Review* 47.1 (1 Mar 2003), pp. 11–48.

Lloyd, Genevieve, 'Providence Lost: "September 11" and the History of Evil', *Critical Horizons* 6.1, pp. 22–43.

Lowenstein, Adam, 'Cinema, Benjamin, and the Allegorical Representation of September 11', in *Critical Quarterly* 45.1–2 (July 2003), pp. 73–84.

McEwan, Ian, 'Beyond Belief', *The Guardian*, 12 September 2001, at http:/// guardian.co.uk/world/2001/sep/12/september11.politicsphilosophyand society (accessed 20 June 2007).

Meyerowitz, Joe, 'History and September 11: An Introduction', *The Journal of American History* 89 (Sept. 2002), pp. 413–15.

Mishra, Pankaj, 'The End of Innocence', *The Guardian* (19 May 2007), pp. 4–6.

Purcell, Richard, 'The New State of Peace after 11 September 2001', *Critical Quarterly* 45. 1–2 (July 2003), pp. 132–47.

Rockmore, Tom, 'Hegel on History, 9/11, and the War on Terror, or Reason in History', *Cultural Politics: An International Journal* 2.3 (Nov. 2006), pp. 281–94.

Rutherford, Jonathan, 'At War', *Cultural Studies* 19.5 (Sept. 2005), pp. 622–42.

Ryan, David, 'Framing September 11: Rhetorical Device and Photographic Opinion', *European Journal of American Culture* 23.1 (2004), pp. 5–20.

Sawhney, Sabina and Simona Sawhney, 'Reading Rushdie after September 11, 2001', *Twentieth Century Literature* 47 (2001), pp. 431–43.

Serritslev Petersen, Per, '9/11 and the Problem of Imagination: *Fight Club* and *Glamorama* as Terrorist Pretexts', *Orbis Litteratum* 60.2 (Apr. 2005), pp. 133–44.

Spencer, Robert and Anastasia Valassopoulos, 'Literary Responses to the War on Terror', *Journal of Postcolonial Writing* 46.3–4 (July 2010), pp. 330–5.

Srinivasan, K., 'The 11 September 2001 and After', *The Round Table* 363 (1 Jan. 2002), pp. 5–10.

Weber, Cynthia, '*Fahrenheit 9/11*: The Temperature where Morality Burns', *Journal of American Studies* 40.1 (2006), pp. 113–31.

Zehfuss, Maja, 'Forget September 11', *Third World Quarterly* 24.3 (2002), pp. 513–28.

Index